63
64
65
70
71
73
74-5
78
80
82-3
109
148-9
157
108-9
162

THE GREEK GENIUS AND ITS INFLUENCE

THE GREEK GENIUS AND
ITS INFLUENCE

SELECT ESSAYS AND EXTRACTS

EDITED BY
LANE COOPER

PROFESSOR EMERITUS OF THE ENGLISH LANGUAGE
AND LITERATURE IN CORNELL UNIVERSITY

CORNELL UNIVERSITY PRESS

ITHACA, NEW YORK, 1952

CORNELL UNIVERSITY PRESS

LONDON: GEOFFREY CUMBERLEGE

OXFORD UNIVERSITY PRESS

First published, October, 1917

Reissued, 1952

PRINTED IN THE UNITED STATES OF AMERICA

GREECE, THE NURSE OF ALL GOOD ARTS.—*Spenser*

PREFACE

This volume appears in response to the needs of one of my classes, and is meant to supply a part of the necessary background for the study of Greek and Latin masterpieces in standard English translations, and to stimulate and rectify the comparison of ancient with modern literature. But I hope it will be useful also to classical students in the narrower sense, and trust it may in some fashion promote the study of Greek in America, if only by striking a blow at the provincial notion that we have nothing to learn from the past.

Doubtless there is an element of chance in the selection of materials for a volume like this. Indeed, I must admit at the outset my inability to secure from the publishers the right to reprint Butcher's first essay (What We Owe to Greece) in *Some Aspects of the Greek Genius,* and Livingstone's third chapter (The Note of Directness) in *The Greek Genius and its Meaning to Us,* both of which I would gladly have included. But aside from these I may affirm that the choice is probably less fortuitous than may appear on the surface, since I have been guided by conscious principles in selecting and rejecting materials, and for the most part in arranging the materials selected.

Of purposeful omissions, what shall I say? I seem to have read much (of course, not all) of what has latterly been written on the nature of the Greek genius and its legacy to modern times; and a great deal of what is said on the topic strikes me as misleading. Partly under the influence of Boeckh and Croiset, I have, in the course of a dozen years, formed a somewhat definite notion of the Greek spirit, and have come almost instinctively, and yet for definite reasons, to eliminate what have seemed to me perilous deviations from a true perspective. One could not very well proceed otherwise.

The selections have been taken from humbler and loftier, and from more or less erudite, sources. I have had to keep in mind the probable effect of the part and the whole upon a certain kind of student, and have not scrupled to use any legitimate means to this end, however remote and abstract, or however homespun the means (as, for example, in the Introduction) may be; it is better to risk the ridicule of the unsympathetic than to fail in attaining one's object. The most important of all the selections, the keystone of my arch, is my translation from Boeckh's *Encyclopädie und Methodologie der Philologischen Wissenschaften*. No apology need be made for the length of this extract from a book of extraordinary significance in modern classical scholarship, but one that is sadly neglected by our day and generation. The selection may not offer easy reading, for Boeckh makes heavy demands upon the translator, yet to the judicious student it will serve as a touchstone for the worth of other characterizations of antiquity.

There may, in point of fact, be slight differences of opinion in the various authors represented. But when allowance is made for the diversity of sources, and the variety of special purposes entertained by the several writers, I trust that one selection will not often contradict another in any serious way, but that all will in the long run reinforce one another in such fashion that casual error will make no lasting impression, and substantial truth, constantly reappearing, will disengage itself from what is accidental, and take firm possession of the memory.

As for the order, an attempt has been made, where possible, to let one selection lead up to another, sometimes by a more superficial, sometimes by a deeper, association of ideas. In general, the sequence is this. We pass from the external environment of the Greeks to a characterization of the race, and of Athens at the zenith of its power. Then come three intermediate selections (from Professor von Wilamowitz-Moellendorff, Professor Murray, and Professor Rand), representing the links between the ancient and the modern world. And finally, beginning with Dr. Osgood's remarks on Milton's use of classical mythology, we have a series of essays and extracts more directly concerned with modern times and the surviving element of antiquity. It will be found, however, that virtually every writer here included has dwelt with some force upon the relation of Greece to the modern era or our own day. An occasional reference to Rome and Latin literature, as intermediary between Hellenism and modern times, could not be avoided—nor has there been any desire to avoid it, in the Bibliography or elsewhere. Even so, the title of the book does not improperly indicate the contents.

Apart from any special interest they may have for students of literature, I could wish that the characterizations of the Greek race might meet the eye of the geographer and anthropologist. Having rather in mind the modern European nations and America, Friedrich Ratzel used to deplore the scarcity of such characterizations from the hands of competent writers. And indeed, such appraisals as that of the American character in Bryce's *American Commonwealth,* or that of the French in Lanson's *Histoire de la Littérature Française,* or even the suggested characterization of the English in Jespersen's *Growth and Structure of the English Language,* are rare. Whether any considerable number exists for the Hebrew race I cannot say; one thinks, of course, of Matthew Arnold's 'Hebraism and Hellenism,' and the like, which would hardly content the scholar and the scientist. If the number is large, it would be well to collect them and publish certain excellent specimens. Meanwhile, is it not worth noting that for the Greek race, which would commonly be chosen as typical of humanity, we have very many of these characterizations? So far as I am aware, the present volume, designed in the main for other purposes, constitutes the first attempt to present a body of such material.

Finally, I have the pleasant duty of thanking several of my friends and pupils for direct assistance and helpful suggestions, of which I availed myself particularly in the translations; and of expressing my obligations to the authors and publishers who have kindly allowed me to reprint copyright material. These obligations, as I hope, are all fully recorded in the proper places.

LANE COOPER.

Ithaca, New York,
   June 15, 1917.

CONTENTS

INTRODUCTION

THE SIGNIFICANCE OF THE CLASSICS [1]

By Lane Cooper

The literature of Greece and Rome is a fountain of life, yet the languages are often called 'dead.' What is a 'dead' language? Once it is uttered, all language is dead. The language of Shakespeare, of Milton, and of Tennyson, is dead. The language you uttered half an hour ago is dead, and these words of mine, if spoken, would be dying as fast as they were born. My opening sentence would already have passed away—and my closing one you could not know, since for you it would not yet have come into being. Your language of half an hour ago can easily be revived, and these syllables which I pronounced some two years since, should you read them aloud, would be breathing again this very moment. Thanks to an alphabet which England and America owe to Greece and Rome, the language of Tennyson and Milton likewise can be brought to life again. So, too, with the language of Shakespeare—though here the vitalizing process demands a conscious expenditure of energy. But Chaucer, that well-spring of English undefiled, is 'dead' (which at this point means *difficult*) to many. And so is Virgil, that fount which for the living Dante spread so broad a stream of speech. 'Why then,' asks Saint Augustine, after mentioning his love of the *Aeneid*, 'Why then did I hate the Greek language in which like songs are sung?—for Homer also was skilful in weaving the like fables, and is most sweetly-vain; yet was he bitter to my boyish taste. And so I suppose would Virgil be to Grecian children, when forced to learn him as I was the other. Difficulty, in truth, the difficulty of learning a foreign tongue, sprinkled as it were with gall all the sweetness of Grecian fables.' Thus Augustine, in the fourth century of what we call 'our era.' Were he at school to-day, and free to pick

[1] For an Introduction to the volume I have adapted an address of mine, delivered before the English Club of Bryn Mawr College, December 13, 1914.—Editor.

his studies, what courses would he cunningly avoid? Courses in the 'dead languages'! A dead language, then, is one that some persons are too indolent to learn—or, when they attempt to learn it, they find their spirits running bankrupt. To tell the truth, the written language remains just what it was and is, a fountain of life if it be Greek, and something less if it be Choctaw; but the discovery is made that certain persons, who seemed to be alive, are dead to the language. Lacking some measure of vitality or sensitiveness, they desire, as they say, to study the things of the present.

What is the present? Is it this minute, or day, or year? Is it 'our era'? And what is our era? Not the past ten years certainly. Strictly speaking, the present can hardly be anything that is past, the very form of words precludes this. We may describe the present as an advancing line, and only a line, between the future, of which we know nothing (save through a study of the past), and the past, from which, if we choose our methods wisely, we may learn much. Paradoxically enough, we can only know the present when it has ceased to be such, and has become history. The past is the field of human experience; if recorded, it is the field of human knowledge. Accordingly, for the individual, speaking more generally, the present is so much of human experience as he may at any moment revive within himself. For the artisan it may include his memory of the last strike; for the statesman it may embrace the political and economic history of Europe and America from the age of Pericles in Athens to this very day. It is one thing for Milton, who first relived the life of antiquity as a scholar, then served his country as an officer of state, and finally bequeathed the best he knew in human life to succeeding ages in his immortal poetry. It is another thing for the modern youth who hears the word 'Czar' or 'Kaiser,' and does not recognize in it a Latin word which for twenty centuries has issued daily from the lips of living men; and who does not know that 'Christ' is a Greek word that will never die.

There are, then, no dead languages, though there be men and women who have a name that they live, and are dead. And the present is either a line without breadth, or it is a tract as extensive and as full of life and meaning as the insight of the student can make it. The only real limit is the measure of his sympathy. He fills the present with life and meaning by a study of the past.

By a study of all the past? No, that is impossible; no one could examine all the records of the past, or even all the main ones. By a study of the past ten years, then? No, ordinarily that will not be wise. Every decade in its time has been a past ten years, and a decade or a century must have something to recommend it beyond the fact that it preceded a certain date. We will permit the historian to say that to him one period is as instructive as another, since he must add that, in order to know one as a historian should, he must know many others. But for the ends of a preliminary education, we must allow that some periods have shown a more abundant life than others. And the farther back our rich and vital period happens to be, within recorded history, the longer will it have been studied and elucidated by the gifted in succeeding ages, and hence the clearer and fuller will its message be to us. Witness the great age of creative activity in Greece: for an interpretation of this we of to-day are indebted first to the poems and other works of art themselves, then to the critics of Alexandria, then to the literary men of Rome, then, in some sort, to the Middle Ages, then to the scholars of the Renaissance—Italian, Dutch, and English—then to the universities of France and Germany, and finally to the last generation of learned men in every civilized nation.

One patent aim in these reflections has been to suggest the idea of a continuity in human life. To sever our connection with the past means cutting ourselves off from humanity; it means spiritual atrophy; it means death. Another aim has been to emphasize our need of selecting parts or periods of civilization for intensive study as especially deserving it. What are such periods?

It will be conceded that the epoch which has most vitally influenced the subsequent culture of Europe, and of peoples like our own that derive from Europe, is what we call the beginning of our era, the years that furnished the world with a Christian civilization. If it is the function of humane study to provide mankind with a self-perpetuating and ever more exalted ideal of human life, and thus to make life more and more abundant, there can be little doubt as to the century that first demands the attention of serious students. It is the century embracing the life of Christ and the lives of his immediate followers; and the chief document by virtue of which one may include it in one's experience is a little book in Greek, containing four biographies, with a sequel to one of them, twenty-one letters, and a vision—all commonly misunderstood by those who read about the work more than they read the work itself. Here we have the living and life-giving record of a human ideal so ennobled that we term it, no longer human, but divine. In

spite of constant misinterpretation, it is ever present among us.
May I add that a so-called higher education which does not enable
the student to read the highest things as they ought to be read is
not worthy of the name? Yet a good teacher of Greek can put
any intelligent undergraduate in America into vital contact with
the New Testament within the space of three or four months.

Next in importance we may set the thirteenth century, 'the age
which of all whose memory remains to us [except the one just
mentioned] produced the greatest number of great men. This was
the age of Frederick the Second, Lewis the Ninth, Simon of Mont-
fort, Thomas Aquinas, Roger Bacon; the age which saw the revival
of painting in Cimabue and Giotto, of sculpture in Nicholas; while
Amiens and Westminster, the Old Palace of Florence and the Holy
Field of Pisa, are living evidence of what it could do in the noblest
of all the arts.'[2] It was the representative century of the Middle
Ages, which have given us the modern nations of Europe, modern
as distinct from Roman law, government through elected deputies,
modern languages and modern poetry in the vernacular, the *Divine
Comedy*, and the French cathedrals. Here again the contribution
of the epoch may be summarily described as the establishment of
an ideal pattern for the life of posterity. How clearly we may
behold this exalted ideal of humanity as it forms, reforms, and
transcends itself in the poem of Dante—in the poet himself as he
travels from Hell through Purgatory to Heaven, in his Virgil,
type of the wisdom of classical antiquity, in Matilda, in Beatrice,
in Bernard, rising ever higher until, suffused with the light of the
eternal, the human is merged in the divine! Nor am I aware of
any substitute from the rest of secular literature that will perform in the education of our youth just the service that this poem
will render if properly studied, that is, in connection with its age.
Assuredly, in more than one respect the classics will not take its
place.

Then what of the value of the classics? The representative age
of classic literature, and this must mean of Greece, the hundred
years or so from Pericles to Alexander, we shall not rate too high
if we put it third in importance among the epochs that have served
to form and fashion modern life. That the influence of Greece
has been exerted upon Europe mainly through the instrumentality
of Rome does not at the moment concern us. And that modern
Europe has learned grammar through Latin (which is a better way
than trying to learn it from modern English) rather than from

[2] Arthur John Butler, *The Purgatory of Dante*, Preface, p. xii.

Greek (which is better still)—this need not detain us, either; though no one could wish more ardently than the writer that the present generation might take this now neglected discipline more seriously. How indeed are we to study economics, or pedagogy, or domestic science (the latest fads, yet all with names betraying the vitality of Greek and Latin), when our pupils cannot keep the peace between two nouns and a verb, much less appreciate the meaning of scientific terms?—for our scientific terminology is still supplied by persons who know the ancient tongues. The value, disciplinary or otherwise, of linguistic study, however, great as it is in the case of the classics, is not my topic. My topic is the significance of the human ideal, considered in outline, which classic Greece transmitted to imperial Rome, and hence to modern times.

I have already tried to define this ideal in a negative way, for it has its limitations. The Magnanimous Man of the *Nicomachean Ethics* falls short, far short, of the Christian ideal; and, wise though she be, that reverend dame, Diotima, who unlocks the final truth for Socrates, has not the depth of knowledge, and has none of the tenderness, of Dante's Beatrice. The dialogues on love of Plato, his *Phaedrus* and *Symposium,* show what could be done by the Greek who was nearest in soul to the Christian, in representing the highest aspirations of the human heart; but they are pale and cold beside Dante's *Vita Nuova,* not to speak of the Thirteenth Chapter of First Corinthians. The mediaeval doctrine of 'the gentle heart,' which created a literature of its own with the sweet new style of modern poetry, and which underlies our present-day notions of a lady and a gentleman, we shall hardly look for in the writings of pagan Greece and pagan Rome; occasionally, not often, we may find a something of the sort; the thing itself is lacking, unless perhaps in Virgil, in a few passages where he seems to be scarcely pagan.

For all that, when we have made allowance for his lack of Christian humility, and of 'the gentle heart,' the Magnanimous Man of Aristotle continues to be illuminating as a standard by which to judge the aims and deserts of our Roosevelts, Tafts, and Wilsons; the goddess Athena still typifies the utmost exaltation of pure intellect; and the myths of Plato still serve to disengage our higher from our lower impulses, and to put the higher in command. Above all, the *Republic* of Plato will never fail to attain its end as often as it is studied. The unthinking may complain of it as an impractical dream, incapable of being realized in actual life. It is realized whenever it is read, for the purpose of its author is accomplished in the reader's mind. There a new ideal of human justice is always evoked, and an image of right action so distinct that no subsequent experience can wholly efface it.

Accordingly, we may pass from the negative to the positive value of the Greek ideal. In discussing this, I must say something of the Greeks as a race, taken at their best, and must illustrate a few of their characteristics from translations of their masterpieces; for it is the men themselves that are mirrored in their literature.

The Greeks were the most versatile and evenly developed race that nature has yet brought forth, our American stock not excepted. They had seemingly the most diverse powers, both intellectual and artistic, which were held in equipoise by a most unusual capacity for checking wayward impulse. 'The Hellene,' says Maurice Croiset, 'always possessed judgment in imagination, intellect in sentiment, and reflection in passion. We never see him entirely carried away in one direction. He has, so to speak, a number of faculties ready for every undertaking, and it is by a combination of these that he gives to his creations their true character.'[3] Others have reduced the essential qualities of the Greek to a single habit, variously displayed—that of constant unbiased observation. Thus Matthew Arnold says of Sophocles, 'He saw life steadily, and saw it whole.' And so George Herbert Palmer writes: 'After puzzling long about the charm of Homer, I once applied to a learned friend, and said to him, "Can you tell me why Homer is so interesting? Why can't you and I write as he wrote? Why is it that his art was lost with him, and that to-day it is impossible for us to quicken such interest as he?" "Well," said my friend, "I have meditated on that a great deal, but it seems to me it comes to about this: Homer looked long at a thing. Why," said he, "do you know that if you should hold up your thumb and look at it long enough, you would find it immensely interesting?" Homer looks long at his thumb; he sees precisely the thing he is dealing with. He does not confuse it with anything else. It is sharp to him; and because it is sharp to him it stands out sharply for us over all these thousands of years.'[4] I also, in a humble way, have reflected upon this very question; and it seems to me that the fundamental Hellenic traits are neither many nor one, but three: direct vision, a high degree of sensitiveness, and an extraordinary power of inhibition. Homer and Sophocles saw clearly, felt keenly, and refrained from much. Their power of inhibition enabled the

[3] Croiset, *Histoire de la Littérature Grecque* 1. 4; see below, p. 87.
[4] Palmer, *The Glory of the Imperfect*, pp. 23-24.

Greeks to look long and steadily at every object, great and small, from the structural features of the landscape, the mountains and the clouds, to man both as an individual and in combination with others of his kind, and from man to the wasp and the frog or the meanest flower that blows; and their sensitiveness made the impression distinct and permanent. As a result, they learned to see parts as parts, and the relation between them, and wholes as wholes, with the relation between part and whole. This accounts for their discovery of order and organization in the world about them—in what they termed the cosmos; it accounts also (if genius can be explained) for their own constructiveness—for the perfection of their architecture, and for the architectonic qualities of their prose and poetry. What they conceived was distinct and orderly, like the cosmos itself; hence what they executed, whether temple or epic poem, had the finished structure of a living organism: every detail was subordinate to the function of the whole. Thus the deed of horror, the slaying of Aegisthus at the hand of Orestes, was subordinate to the total effect of the tragic story; the frieze of the horsemen was contributory to the general but distinct effect of the Parthenon; and the worth of the individual was measured by his service to the State. But the State itself was a being, so to speak, like an animal of a higher sort, whose function was to live the life of reason, contemplating and realizing justice and truth, which were divine. Wherever they looked, these sensitive men saw life, divine, distinct, and orderly.

Accordingly, the Greeks were religious. Saint Paul, in fact, speaking to the Athenians in their decline, remarked that they were excessively religious. We are not prone to think of them as such. We think of them as a joyous race, loving the sunlight, adorning themselves on every occasion with garlands of flowers, worshipers of human youth and beauty; inquisitive, too, and loquacious: 'For all the Athenians, and strangers which were there, spent their time in nothing else, but either to tell or to hear some new thing.' But, after all, there is such a thing as a religion of joy; nor does a delight in youth and beauty preclude a serious view of human life. Moreover, the practice of discussion need not interfere with the habit of severe thought about the highest things. The Socratic method of arriving at truth through question and answer is proverbial. Yet we recall the story told of Socrates in the *Symposium:* 'One morning he was thinking about something which he could not resolve; he would not give it up, but continued thinking from early dawn until noon—there he stood, fixed in thought;

and at noon attention was drawn to him, and the rumor ran through the wondering crowd that Socrates had been standing and thinking about something ever since the break of day. At last, in the evening after supper, some Ionians out of curiosity (I should explain that this occurred not in winter but in summer) brought out their mats and slept in the open air that they might watch him and see whether he would stand all night. There he stood until the following morning; and with the return of light he offered up a prayer to the sun, and went his way.' And so the Greeks thought out the nature of Deity. The beauty of their loftiest religious conceptions is obscured by a gross indelicacy in some of their traditional observances; and the monotheism in which their philosophy culminated is often lost to us through the bewildering fecundity of their artistic imagination, which beheld a separate deity, or nymph, or demon, in every manifestation of nature. Our idea of Greek religion has been distorted also by Matthew Arnold's insistence upon the religious genius of the Hebrew as contrasted with the intellectual genius of the Greek.

Because of Arnold and his misleading emphasis, this point may need some reinforcement. I shall reinforce it with a quotation from Mr. Haigh on Aeschylus.

'In his hands the religion of the Greeks has been raised to a higher level of moral dignity than it ever attained either before or since.

'The first point to be noticed, in regard to his religious views, is the sublime conception of Zeus as the supreme ruler of the universe. The other deities are represented as merely the ministers of his will, and though still possessing their usual characteristics, stand in a subordinate rank. The language applied to Zeus is monotheistic in tone, and his praises are chanted in strains of the loftiest exaltation. He is "king of kings, most blessed of the blessed, most mighty of rulers." His power "knows no superior, nor is any one enthroned above him; swifter than speech is the accomplishment of his purpose." He "holds for ever the balance of the scales: nothing comes to mortal man but by the will of Zeus." "Zeus is sky, and earth, and heaven; Zeus is all things, yea, greater than all things." His power, though invisible, is omnipotent and omnipresent. "Dark and shadowy," it is said, "are the pathways of his counsels, and difficult to see. From their high-towering hopes he hurleth down to destruction the race of men. Yet setteth he no forces in array, all his works are effortless.

Seated on holiest throne, from thence, unknown to us, he bringeth
his will to pass.'' . . .

'Such being the scheme of divine government, as conceived by
Aeschylus, in which the laws of eternal justice are administered by
an all-powerful deity, it follows that injustice can never prosper,
and that the punishment of sin is certain and inevitable.'[5]

As for the intellectual faculty of the Greeks, their habit of
making fine yet clear and true distinctions, of inserting the edge
of the mind at the joint between ideas, this went hand in hand
with their clear and sharp discrimination of objects in the world
about them, and has led to their superiority in the mental, moral,
and political sciences. Their excellence here has so often been
emphasized that every one is aware of our debt to the Greeks for
the foundations of logic, mathematics, ethics, psychology, and the
science of government.

Something, too, is generally known of the attention they paid
to the human body, their study of which was interfered with only
by their reverence for it. There are those who think that in many
respects Greek civilization attained a stage of development much
higher than that which any other Aryan stock has reached; that
in the general progress of the Indo-Germanic races the Greeks in
some respects anticipated our own future; and that herein lies
much of the value their example has for us. Since our infancy
came later, they, like an elder brother, point out the course that
we must run. However this may be, it cannot be gainsaid that in
the one article of disciplining the human body, and perfecting the
human form, they set a standard which no nation since, nor any
part of it, has equaled, or is likely soon to equal. The indubitable
sign of this excellence is their sculpture. We may think if we like
that Shakespeare is not inferior to Sophocles in moving the heart
through the tragic drama, though I for one would hesitate to say
so; and we may agree that the southwest tower of Chartres Cathe-
dral shows the art of man engaged in the service of God as no
structural feature of the Parthenon can show it, to which I would
readily assent; but where is the English or Italian sculptor who
can rival the Hermes of Praxiteles at Olympia? Encomiums of
Greek sculpture are superfluous. On the other hand, it may occasion some astonishment when we learn, upon the authority of Dr.
Osler, that the establishments of the ancients for the care of bodily

[5] A. E. Haigh, *The Tragic Drama of the Greeks*, pp. 87, 88, 91.

health far surpassed in extent and magnificence our twentieth-century institutions of a comparable sort. One thinks of the group of buildings sacred to Asclepius at Epidaurus, which included a theatre that would seat twelve thousand persons. Or one thinks of the extravagant Baths of Caracalla at Rome. Here, perhaps, we might learn from the mistakes of the ancients, since we seem in this country to be on the point of letting the care of the body run away with our institutions of learning. At their best, however, the Greeks preserved a just balance in the training of their youth between gymnastic for the body and a thorough literary and artistic, or, as they would call it, 'musical,' education for the soul. They wished the motions of both mind and body to be harmonious and direct. They were saved from excess by their sense of proportion, which arose from their clearness of vision.

But their powers of observation were directed also to the world around them. Thus 'Phidias, like most of the other great artists of Greece, was as much distinguished for accuracy in the minutest details as for the majesty of his colossal figures; and, like Lysippus, he amused himself, and gave proofs of his skill, by making images of minute objects, such as cicadas, bees, and flies.'[6] And thus the modern ornithologist has something to learn even from the poet Aristophanes in his comedy of the *Birds,* as the entomologist has something to learn from the *Wasps,* and the Weather Bureau from the *Clouds.* Much more has the natural scientist to learn from the actual researches of the Greeks in several branches, above all in zoölogy; mainly in respect to method, of course, though the results which we find in Aristotle's work on animals, for instance, are not negligible. Yet it is to be feared that most of our zoölogists are ignorant of the very existence of his *Animalia.* The experimental psychologists, however, the newest of the new in modern science, have not been slow to recognize the importance of his work on the soul. One could wish that those who nowadays are prating in such wretched taste about 'eugenics,' which they think has just been discovered, were equally well acquainted with the *Republic* of Plato. It may be accidental, but I have heard very few American botanists mention the fifteen surviving books of Theophrastus on the *Natural History and Physiology of Plants.*

In general, what the modern scientist may learn from Aristotle, taking him as the representative of scientific investigation among the ancients, is, first of all, the habit of exact personal observation, which, as Agassiz knew, is the corner-stone of science. Secondly, it

6 Smith's *Dictionary of Greek and Roman Biography and Mythology* 3. 254.

is the method of research : to collect as many examples of a given form as possible—that is, without expending all one's time in mere collection ; and to select from these the typical cases, for the purpose of comparison and inference. Finally, it is a sense of the relation of every part of science to the whole, and a recognition of the fact that, while any science may at any time be subservient to any other, even the higher to the lower, still some sciences in the long run are subordinate. A knowledge of the habits of birds and fishes, for example, is less important than a knowledge of the characteristic actions of men.

This brings us to the last trait of the Greeks that needs remark, their scientific interest in human conduct, which, with their profound belief in a First Cause, determined their attitude to human life. To begin with, we must not forget that they found no such opposition as we seem to make between theory and practice, or between knowledge and its application. The distinction between theory and practice we owe, indeed, like many another distinction, to the Greeks, but the divorce is our own contrivance. Accordingly, a theoretical knowledge of human, as of animal, behavior would mean to them the sort of knowledge that corresponds to the facts, arising from exact observation and comparison of the facts, and enabling one to deal with the facts in a practical way. They would not, for example, condemn a candidate for the presidency of the United States on the ground that he was 'too theoretical'; but if his knowledge was one-sided and unfit for use, they would say he was not theoretical enough, and hence was ill-prepared to govern. If he knew books, that is, history in some narrow sense, but not the motives of men, or if he knew Tom, Dick, and Harry, but not the vital truths of history, he could have no true theory of government, and so he would be likely to fail as a leader. With their habitual thoroughness, then, the Greeks observed and classified the various types of men, and the ways in which men act, individually as well as in combination, and in the different periods of life. The powers of men, resulting in right action and happiness, they called virtues, and the characteristic lapses from the normal, resulting in imperfect action and absurdity or ruin, they called vices. They thus built up, as we find in the *Ethics, Rhetoric,* and *Politics* of Aristotle, and in the *Characters* of Theophrastus, a thoroughgoing science of the types and ages of men, of their virtues and vices, and of the several species of organization that arise when families combine to form states. They described youth, or the magnanimous man, or the coward, or a democracy, with the same precision we use, and they too used, in describing the natural history and physiology of a plant. The thing is defined, and its mode of action explained. So in the *Rhetoric,* Aristotle analyzes the qualities of youth, old age, and middle life, because the public orator will have men of each sort in his audience, and must know what kind of argument will gain or lose their votes. So in the *Ethics,* with scientific objectivity, he represents the man of perfect virtue, the norm or standard by which other men are to be judged. So in the *Characters,* Theophrastus exhibits the nature and activity of The Flatterer, The Surly Man, The Boor, and so on, some thirty types in all, who depart from the standard set in the *Ethics,* treating them as dispassionately as if they were flowers. From what I can learn, there has been no comparable body of systematic knowledge produced upon this subject since the Middle Ages, and none on any part of it that is not either copied from Greece, or, if to some extent original, inferior to the work of Aristotle and Theophrastus as a guide to the individual in studying himself, or to the leader in studying his fellows.

Let us turn to a few passages from Greek literature which may serve to illustrate at least a part of what has been said, and to build up, perhaps in the rough, the conception I have thus far been trying to take to pieces. They represent to me, either directly or by contrast, the Greek ideal of humanity—that human ideal which, in spite of its limitations, still makes the classics worth our study.

The Greeks conceived of the ideal man as one possessing insight enough to distinguish between the sorrows which every one must undergo, such as the pains attendant upon age and death, and the sorrows which men bring upon themselves through folly and hardness of heart. Thus, near the opening of the *Odyssey,* Homer puts into the mouth of Zeus the following speech upon the relations of fate and free will:

'Lo you now, how vainly mortal men do blame the gods! For of us they say comes evil, whereas they even of themselves, through the blindness of their own hearts, have sorrows beyond that which is ordained. Even as of late Aegisthus, beyond that which was ordained, took to him the wedded wife of the son of Atreus and killed her lord on his return, and that with sheer doom before his eyes, since we had warned him by the embassy of Hermes the keen-sighted, the slayer of Argos, that he should neither kill the man, nor woo his wife. For the son of Atreus shall be avenged at the hand of Orestes, so soon as he shall come to man's estate and long for his own country. So spake Hermes, yet he prevailed not on the heart of Aegisthus, for all his good will; but now hath he paid one price for all.'[7]

On the evidence of this passage at least, it would be unsafe to accuse the Greeks of fatalism. But such evidence is not uncommon in the Greek poets, if we are careful to watch when their dramatic characters are not misled or purposely deceiving, but are telling the ultimate truth. In Sophocles' *Antigone,* for example, there is a similar utterance, made by the tyrant Creon, when his eyes are opened, and he finds himself, through his own misguided action, bereft of his wife, and of Haemon, his son, and hated of gods and men:

'*Enter* CREON, *on the spectators' left, with attendants, carrying the shrouded body of* HAEMON *on a bier.*
'CHORUS. Lo, yonder the king himself draws near, bearing that which tells too clear a tale—the work of no stranger's madness— if we may say it—but of his own misdeeds.
'CREON. Woe for the sins of a darkened soul, stubborn sins, fraught with death! Ah, ye behold us, the sire who hath slain, the son who hath perished! Woe is me, for the wretched blindness of my counsels! Alas, my son, thou hast died in thy youth, by a timeless doom, woe is me!—thy spirit hath fled—not by thy folly, but by mine own!'[8]

Creon is a king, of noble blood. He does not lean to the worse, but, as we should say, is a person of good intentions. Yet in him there had been blindness of heart, an infatuate self-will, which recoiled upon himself in sorrows beyond those which are ordained for the man of insight. The poet is clear on this point. Death, the supreme evil, death, which to the Greek is not swallowed up in victory, is a thing that no one can avoid; but life can be ordered aright, and man, if he cleaves to divine justice, man the versatile, the courageous, is for life the master of circumstance.

'Wonders are many,' [sings the Chorus in *Antigone,*] 'and none is more wonderful than man; the power that crosses the white sea, driven by the stormy south-wind, making a path under surges that threaten to engulf him; and Earth, the eldest of the gods, the

[7] Translation by Butcher and Lang, p. 2.
[8] Jebb, *The Tragedies of Sophocles, translated into English prose,* p. 169.

immortal, the unwearied, doth he wear, turning the soil with the offspring of horses, as the plows go to and fro from year to year.

'And the light-hearted race of birds, and the tribes of savage beasts, and the sea-brood of the deep, he snares in the meshes of his woven toils, he leads captive, man excellent in wit. And he masters by his arts the beast whose lair is in the wilds, who roams the hills; he tames the horse of shaggy mane, he puts the yoke upon its neck, he tames the tireless mountain bull.

'And speech, and wind-swift thought, and all the moods that mould a state, hath he taught himself; and how to flee the arrows of the frost, when 'tis hard lodging under the clear sky, and the arrows of the rushing rain; yea, he hath resource for all; without resource he meets nothing that must come: only against Death shall he call for aid in vain; but from baffling maladies he hath devised escapes.

'Cunning beyond fancy's dream is the fertile skill which brings him, now to evil, now to good. When he honors the laws of the land, and that justice which he hath sworn by the gods to uphold, proudly stands his city: no city hath he who, for his rashness, dwells with sin. Never may he share my hearth, never think my thoughts, who doth these things!'[9]

The seamy side of human nature, we observe, did not escape the vision of the Greeks. As a further illustration, I may quote from the *Politics* of Aristotle, which often has a bearing upon the commonest problems of to-day. Does not the following recall the recent history of our laboring classes, with their successive strikes, and the constant growth of their demands?

'The avarice of mankind is insatiable; at one time two obols was pay enough, but now, when this sum has become customary, men always want more and more without end; for it is of the nature of desire not to be satisfied, and most men live only for the gratification of it. The beginning of reform is not so much to equalize property as to train the nobler sort of natures not to desire more, and to prevent the lower from getting more; that is to say, they must be kept down, but not ill-treated.'[10]

Does our higher education in America school the nobler sort of natures in the art of self-restraint? Will our college graduates

9 Jebb, *The Tragedies of Sophocles, translated into English prose*, pp. 138-139.

10 Aristotle, *Politics*, tr. Jowett, 2. 7.

appreciate the saw of Hesiod, whether in the outlay of words or in the acquisition of wealth, that the half is more than the whole? Can our emancipated ladies take to heart the thought of Nicias, which he uttered just before the dreadful termination of the siege at Syracuse? When they have done as men sometimes do, will they suffer what men can bear?

But Greek literature in general has an application to modern life. Let us take at random one of the Characters of Theophrastus, The Complaisant Man. Have we not met him in business, among traveling salesmen, in our college halls, and among professional politicians? He is perennial.

'THE COMPLAISANT MAN

'Complaisance may be defined as a mode of address calculated to give pleasure, but not with the best tendency.

'The Complaisant Man is very much the kind of person who will hail one afar off with "my dear fellow"; and, after a large display of respect, seize and hold one by both hands. He will attend you a little way, and ask *when* he is to see you, and will take his leave with a compliment upon his lips. Also, when he is called in to an arbitration, he will seek to please, not only his principal, but the adversary as well, in order that he may be deemed impartial. He will say, too, that foreigners speak more justly than his fellow-citizens. Then, when he is asked to dinner, he will request the host to send for the children; and will say of them, when they come in, that they are as like their father as figs, and will draw them towards him, and kiss them, and establish them at his side—playing with some of them, and himself saying "Wineskin," "Hatchet," and permitting others to go to sleep upon him, to his anguish.'[11]

But we must hasten to a close. Without further preliminary, I will quote from the description of the Magnanimous or High-minded Man in the *Nicomachean Ethics:*

'Highmindedness, as its very name suggests, seems to be occupied with high things. Let us begin, then, by ascertaining the character of those things. It makes no difference whether we consider the moral state or the person in whom the moral state is seen.

'A highminded person seems to be one who regards himself as

[11] *The Characters of Theophrastus,* ed. Jebb-Sandys (1909), pp. 43, 45.

worthy of high things, and who is worthy of them; for he who does so without being worthy is foolish, and no virtuous person is foolish or absurd.

'Such, then, is the highminded person. One who is worthy of small things, and who regards himself as worthy of them, is temperate *or sensible,* but he is not highminded; for highmindedness can only exist on a large scale, as beauty can only exist in a tall person. Small people may be elegant and well-proportioned, but not beautiful.

'He who regards himself as worthy of high things, and is unworthy of them, is conceited—although it is not every one who takes an exaggerated view of his own worth that is a conceited person.

'He who takes too low a view of his own worth is mean-minded, whether it be high things, or moderate, or even small things that he is worthy of, so long as he underrates his deserts. This would seem to be especially a fault in one who is worthy of high things; for what would he do, it may be asked, if his deserts were less than they are?

'The highminded man, while he holds an extreme position by the greatness of his deserts, holds an intermediate . . . position by the propriety of his conduct, as he estimates his own deserts aright, while others rate their deserts too high or too low.

'But if, then, he regards himself as worthy of high things, and is worthy of them, and especially if he is worthy of the highest things, there will be one particular object of his interest. Desert is a term used in reference to external goods, but we should naturally esteem that to be the greatest of external goods which we attribute to the gods, or which persons of high reputation most desire, or which is the prize awarded to the noblest actions. But honor answers to this description, as being the highest of external goods.

'The highminded man, then, bears himself in a right spirit towards honors and dishonors. It needs no proof that highminded people are concerned with honor; for it is honor more than anything else of which the great regard themselves, and deservedly regard themselves, as worthy. The mean-minded man underestimates himself both in respect of his own deserts and in comparison with the acknowledged deserts of the highminded man. The conceited man overestimates his own deserts, but he does not estimate his own deserts more highly than the highminded man.

'The highminded man, as being worthy of the highest things, will be in the highest degree good, for the better man is always worthy of the higher things, and the best man of the highest things. It follows, then, that the truly highminded man must be good.

'It would seem, too, that the highminded man possesses such greatness as belongs to every virtue. It would be wholly inconsistent with the character of the highminded man to run away in hot haste, or to commit a crime; for what should be his object in doing a disgraceful action, if nothing is great in his eyes? If one examines the several points of character, it will appear quite ridiculous to say that the highminded man need not be good. Were he vicious, he would not be worthy of honor at all; for honor is the prize of virtue, and is paid to none but the good.

'It seems, then, that highmindedness is, as it were, the crown of the virtues, as it enhances them, and cannot exist apart from them. Hence it is difficult to be truly highminded, as it is impossible without the perfection of good breeding.

'A highminded man, then, is especially concerned with honors and dishonors. He will be only moderately pleased at great honors conferred upon him by virtuous people, as feeling that he obtains what is naturally his due, or even less than his due; for it would be impossible to devise an honor that should be proportionate to perfect virtue. Nevertheless he will accept honors, as people have nothing greater to confer upon him. But such honor as is paid by ordinary people, and on trivial grounds, he will utterly despise, as he deserves something better than this. He will equally despise dishonor, feeling that it cannot justly attach to him. While the highminded man, then, as has been said, is principally concerned with honors, he will, at the same time, take a moderate view of wealth, political power, and good or ill fortune of all kinds, however it may occur. He will not be excessively elated by good, or excessively depressed by ill fortune. . . .

'The possessors of such goods [as power and wealth] belong to the class of people who are apt to become supercilious and insolent; for without virtue it is not easy to bear the gifts of fortune in good taste. Not being able to bear them, and imagining themselves to be superior to everybody else, such people treat others with contempt, and act according to their own sweet will; for they imitate the highminded man without being like him, but they imitate him only so far as they have the power; in other words, they do not perform virtuous actions, but they treat other people with contempt. The highminded man is justified in his contempt for others, as he forms a true estimate of them, but ordinary people have no such justification. Again, the highminded man is not fond of encountering small dangers, nor is he fond of encountering dangers at all, as there are few things which he values *enough to endanger himself for them*. But he is ready to encounter great dangers, and in the hour of danger is reckless of his life, because he feels that life is not worth living without honor. He is capable of conferring benefits, but ashamed of receiving them, as in the one case he feels his superiority, and in the other his inferiority. . . . It is characteristic, too, of the highminded man that he never, or hardly ever, asks a favor, that he is ready to do anybody a service, and that, although his bearing is stately towards persons of dignity and affluence, it is unassuming towards the middle class. . . . Such a person, too, will not be eager to win honors or to dispute the supremacy of other people. He will not bestir himself or be in a hurry to act, except where there is some great honor to be won, or some great result to be achieved. His performances will be rare, but they will be great, and will win him a great name. He will, of course, be open in his hatreds and his friendships, as secrecy is an indication of fear. He will care for reality more than for reputation; he will be open in word and deed, as his superciliousness will lead him to speak his mind boldly. Accordingly, he will tell the truth, too, except where he is ironical, although he will use irony in dealing with ordinary people. He will be incapable of ordering his life so as to please anybody else, unless it be a friend. . . . Nor again will he be given to admiration, as there is nothing which strikes him as great. Nor will he bear grudges; for no one who is highminded will dwell upon the past, least of all upon past injuries; he will prefer to overlook them. He will not be a gossip, he will not talk much about himself or about anybody else; for he does not care to be praised himself or to get other people censured. On the other hand, he will not be fond of praising other people. And not being a gossip, he will not speak evil of others, even of his enemies, except for the express purpose of insulting them. He will be the last person to set up a wailing, or cry out for help, when something happens which is inevitable or insignificant, as to do so is to attach great importance to it. He is the kind of person who would rather possess what is noble, although it does not bring in profit, than what is profitable but not noble, as such a preference argues self-sufficiency.

'It seems, too, that the highminded man will be slow in his movements, his voice will be deep and his manner of speaking sedate; for it is not likely that a man will be in a hurry, if there are not many things that he cares for, or that he will be emphatic, if he does not regard anything as important, and these are the causes which make people speak in shrill tones and use rapid movements.'[12]

Is the picture somewhat harsh? It nevertheless is not devoid of a sober inspiration. Here we behold an idealized portrait of the man who is fitted to live a noble life, as the Greeks thought of life; a man possessed of every virtue, and adorning them all with the perfection of good breeding; self-centered, of course, yet existing for the welfare of the State. It is not meant for an actual person, though it is based upon a lifelong observation of real men. It certainly represents no definite individual like Alexander, who was not a man of peace and did not live the life of contemplation, or, on the other hand, like the philosopher Sócrates, whose humility, though at times affected, was for the most part ingrained. Probably it is not intended as a pattern of complete humanity; for us at least this Magnanimous Man has the irritating, inhuman trick of never being astonished at anything. Possibly it was not the highest single type of which its author could conceive; yet, when all is said, it stands as a masterpiece of delineation by the subtlest student of mankind to be found outside the Christian tradition. Greek poets now and then may elevate a tragic character above the level of the Magnanimous Man, through the force of an imaginative insight that transcends philosophy; but even in those poets we should not search for the loftiest embodiments of faith, or of hope, or of charity, since these are Christian virtues. This picture is the very incarnation of temperance, prudence, fortitude, and justice. And ideals of temperance, prudence, fortitude, and justice being the special gift of the classic to the modern world, we shall do well to seek them at their inexhaustible sources.

One would hardly care to leave this subject without bestowing a glance on the relation which the study of the classics bears to the interpretation of modern literature. The simplest way to obtain a glimpse of this important topic is to read a few lines from a modern poet who, in the directness of his vision, in his sensitiveness, and in the quality of self-restraint, is very close to the Greek spirit. But the lines of Wordsworth's *Character of the Happy Warrior* have another quality in addition, and betray a gentleness of heart which is not ancient, but modern:

[12] The *Nicomachean Ethics*, J. E. C. Welldon's translation, pp. 111 ff.

Who is the Happy Warrior? Who is he
That every man in arms should wish to be?
—It is the generous spirit, who, when brought
Among the tasks of real life, hath wrought
Upon the plan that pleased his boyish thought:
Whose high endeavors are an inward light
That makes the path before him always bright:
Who, with a natural instinct to discern
What knowledge can perform, is diligent to learn;
Abides by this resolve, and stops not there,
But makes his moral being his prime care;
Who, doomed to go in company with Pain,
And Fear, and Bloodshed, miserable train!
Turns his necessity to glorious gain;
In face of these doth exercise a power
Which is our human nature's highest dower;
Controls them and subdues, transmutes, bereaves
Of their bad influence, and their good receives:
By objects which might force the soul to abate
Her feeling, rendered more compassionate;
Is placable—because occasions rise
So often that demand such sacrifice;
More skilful in self-knowledge, even more pure,
As tempted more; more able to endure,
As more exposed to suffering and distress;
Thence, also, more alive to tenderness.
—'Tis he whose law is reason; who depends
Upon that law as on the best of friends;
Whence, in a state where men are tempted still
To evil for a guard against worse ill,
And what in quality or act is best
Doth seldom on a right foundation rest,
He labors good on good to fix, and owes
To virtue every triumph that he knows:
—Who, if he rise to station of command,
Rises by open means; and there will stand
On honorable terms, or else retire,
And in himself possess his own desire;
Who comprehends his trust, and to the same
Keeps faithful with a singleness of aim;

And therefore does not stoop, nor lie in wait
For wealth or honors, or for worldly state;
Whom they must follow; on whose head must fall
Like showers of manna, if they come at all:
Whose powers shed round him in the common strife,
Or mild concerns of ordinary life,
A constant influence, a peculiar grace;
But who, if he be called upon to face
Some awful moment to which Heaven has joined
Great issues, good or bad for human kind,
Is happy as a lover; and attired
With sudden brightness, like a man inspired;
And, through the heat of conflict, keeps the law
In calmness made, and sees what he foresaw;
Or if an unexpected call succeed,
Come when it will, is equal to the need:
—He who, though thus endued as with a sense
And faculty for storm and turbulence,
Is yet a soul whose master-bias leans
To homefelt pleasures and to gentle scenes;
Sweet images! which, wheresoe'er he be,
Are at his heart; and such fidelity
It is his darling passion to approve;
More brave for this, that he hath much to love:—
'Tis, finally, the man, who, lifted high,
Conspicuous object in a nation's eye,
Or left unthought-of in obscurity,—
Who, with a toward or untoward lot,
Prosperous or adverse, to his wish or not—
Plays, in the many games of life, that one
Where what he most doth value must be won:
Whom neither shape of danger can dismay,
Nor thought of tender happiness betray;
Who, not content that former worth stand fast,
Looks forward, persevering to the last,
From well to better, daily self-surpast:
Who—whether praise of him must walk the earth
For ever, and to noble deeds give birth,
Or he must fall, to sleep without his fame,
And leave a dead unprofitable name—

Finds comfort in himself and in his cause;
And, while the mortal mist is gathering, draws
His breath in confidence of Heaven's applause:
This is the Happy Warrior; this is he
That every man in arms should wish to be.

'Remember,' said Wordsworth to his nephew, 'first read the ancient classical authors; *then* come to *us;* and you will be able to judge for yourself which of us is worth reading.'

I

FROM *HELLAS* [1]

By Percy Bysshe Shelley

The apathy of the rulers of the civilized world to the astonishing circumstance of the descendants of that nation to which they owe their civilization, rising as it were from the ashes of their ruin [1822], is something perfectly inexplicable to a mere spectator of the shows of this mortal scene. We are all Greeks. Our laws, our literature, our religion, our arts, have their root in Greece. But for Greece, Rome—the instructor, the conqueror, or the metropolis of our ancestors—would have spread no illumination with her arms, and we might still have been savages and idolaters; or, what is worse, might have arrived at such a stagnant and miserable state of social institution[s] as China and Japan possess.

The human form and the human mind attained to a perfection in Greece which has impressed its image on those faultless productions, whose very fragments are the despair of modern art, and has propagated impulses which cannot cease, through a thousand channels of manifest or imperceptible operation, to ennoble and delight mankind until the extinction of the race. . . .

> Herald of Eternity. . . .
>
> Within the circuit of this pendent orb
> There lies an antique region, on which fell
> The dews of thought in the world's golden dawn
> Earliest and most benign, and from it sprung
> Temples and cities and immortal forms
> And harmonies of wisdom and of song,
> And thoughts, and deeds worthy of thoughts so fair.
> And when the sun of its dominion failed,
> And when the winter of its glory came,
> The winds that stripped it bare blew on and swept

[1 The first of these four extracts is from the Preface to *Hellas*, Shelley's *Poetical Works*, Oxford Edition, ed. Hutchinson, p. 442.—Editor.]

That dew into the utmost wildernesses
In wandering clouds of rain that thawed
The unmaternal bosom of the North.[2]

SEMICHORUS 1

Let there be light! said Liberty,
And, like sunrise from the sea,
Athens arose!—Around her born,
Shone like mountains in the morn
Glorious states;—and are they now
Ashes, wrecks, oblivion? . . .
. . . Temples and towers,
Citadels and marts, and they
Who live and die there, have been ours,
And may be thine, and must decay;
But Greece and her foundations are
Built below the tide of war,
Based on the crystàlline sea
Of thought and its eternity;
Her citizens, imperial spirits,
Rule the present from the past;
On all this world of men inherits
Their seal is set.[3]

Through exile, persecution, and despair,
Rome was, and young Atlantis shall become
The wonder, or the terror, or the tomb
Of all whose step wakes Power lulled in her savage lair.
But Greece was as a hermit-child,
Whose fairest thoughts and limbs were built
To woman's growth, by dreams so mild,
She knew not pain or guilt.
And now, O Victory, blush! and Empire, tremble
When ye desert the free.—
If Greece must be
A wreck, yet shall its fragments reassemble,
And build themselves again impregnably
In a diviner clime,
To Amphionic music on some Cape sublime,
Which frowns above the idle foam of Time.[4]

[2 From the Prologue to *Hellas* 31-43, *ibid.*, p. 444.—EDITOR.]
[3 *Hellas* 682-687, 692-703, *ibid.*, pp. 463-464.—EDITOR.]
[4 *Hellas* 992-1007, *ibid.*, pp. 470-471.—EDITOR.]

II

THE LEGACY OF GREECE: THE LAND AND ITS PEOPLE [1]

BY JOHN CLARKE STOBART

'Greece' and 'Greek' mean different things to different people. To the man in the street, if he exists, they stand for something proverbially remote and obscure, as dead as Queen Anne, as heavy as the British Museum. To the average finished product of 'higher education' in England they recall those dog-eared text-books and grammars which he put away with much relief when he left school; they waft back to him the strangely close atmosphere of the classical form-room. The historian, of course, will inform us that all Western civilization has Greece for its mother and nurse, and that unless we know something about her our knowledge of the past must be built upon sand. That is true—only nobody cares very much what historians say, for they deal with the past, and the past is dead and disgusting. To some cultured folk who have read Swinburne (but not Plato) the notion of the Greeks presents a world of happy pagans, children of nature, without any tiresome ideas of morality or self-control, sometimes making pretty poems and statues, but generally basking in the sun without much on. There are also countless earnest students of the Bible who remember what St. Paul said about those Greeks who thought the Cross foolishness and those Athenians who were always wanting to hear something new. St. Paul forgot that 'the Cross' was a typical Stoic paradox. Then there are a vast number of people who do not distinguish between 'Greek' and 'classical.' By 'classics' they understand certain tyrannous conventions and stilted affectations against which every free-minded soul longs to rebel. They distinguish the classical element in Milton and Keats as responsible for all that is dull and far-fetched and unnatural. Classicism repels many people of excel-

[1 From *The Glory that Was Greece* (pp. 1-11). London and New York, 1911. The selection is reprinted by permission of J. B. Lippincott, Publishers, Philadelphia.—EDITOR.]

lent taste, and Greek art is apt to fall under the same condemnation. It is only in the last generation that scholars have been able to distinguish between the true Greek and the false mist of classicism which surrounds it. Till then everybody had to look at the Greeks through Roman and Renaissance spectacles, confounding Pallas with Minerva and thinking of Greek art as represented by the Apollo Belvedere and the Laocoön. We are now able, thanks to the labors of scholars and archaeologists, to see the Greeks as they were, perfectly direct, simple, natural, and reasonable, quite as antagonistic to classicism as Manet and Debussy themselves.

Lastly, there are a few elderly people who have survived the atmosphere of 'the classics,' and yet cherish the idea of Greece as something almost holy in its tremendous power of inspiration. These are the people who are actually pleased when a fragment of Menander is unearthed in an Egyptian rubbish-heap, or a fisherman fishing for sponges off Cape Matapan finds entangled in his net three-quarters of a bronze idol. And they are not all schoolmasters, either. Some of them spend their time and money in digging the soil of Greece under a blazing Mediterranean sun. Some of them haunt the auction-rooms and run up a fragment of pottery, or a marble head without a nose, to figures that seem quite absurd when you look at the shabby clothes of the bidders. They talk of Greece as if it were in the same latitude as heaven, not Naples. The strange thing about them is that, though they evidently feel the love of old Greece burning like a flame in their hearts, they find their ideas on the subject quite incommunicable. Let us hope they end their days peacefully in retreats with classical façades, like the Bethlehem Hospital.

Admitting something of this weakness, it is my aim here to try and throw some fresh light upon the secret of that people's greatness, and to look at the Greeks, not as the defunct producers of antique curios, but, if I can, as Keats looked at them, believing what he said of Beauty, that

It will never
Pass into nothingness, but still will keep
A bower quiet for us, and a sleep
Full of sweet dreams, and health, and quiet breathing.

It cannot be done by studying their history only. Their history must be full of battles, in which they were only moderately great, and petty quarrels, to which they were immoderately prone. Their literature, which presents the greatest bulk of varied excellence of any literature in the world, must be considered. But as it can only reach us through the watery medium of translation, we must supplement it by studying also their statues and temples, their coins, vases, and pictures. Even that will not be sufficient for people who are not artists, because the sensible Philistine part of the world knows, as the Greeks knew, that a man may draw and fiddle and be a scoundrel. Therefore we must look also at their laws and governments, their ceremonies and amusements, their philosophy and religion, to see whether they knew how to live like gentlemen and freemen. If we can keep our eyes open to all these sides of their activity, and watch them in the germ and bud, we ought to get near to understanding their power as a living source of inspiration to artists and thinkers. Lovers of the classics are very apt to remind us of the Renaissance as testifying the power of Greek thought to awaken and inspire men's minds. Historically they are right, for it is a fact which ought to be emphasized. But when they go on to argue that if we forget the classics we ourselves shall need a fresh Renaissance, they are making a prophecy which seems to me to be very doubtful. I believe that our art and literature has by this time absorbed and assimilated what Greece had to teach, and that our roots are so entwined with the soil of Greek culture that we can never lose the taste of it as long as books are read and pictures painted. We are, in fact, living on the legacy of Greece, and we may, if we please, forget the testatrix.

My claim for the study of Hellenism would not be founded on history. I would urge the need of constant reference to some fixed canon in matters of taste, some standard of the beautiful which shall be beyond question or criticism; all the more because we are living in eager, restless times of constant experiment and veering fashions. Whatever may be the philosophical basis of aesthetics, it is undeniable that a large part of our idea of beauty rests upon habit. Hellas provides a thousand objects which seventy-five generations of people have agreed to call beautiful, and which no person outside a madhouse has ever thought ugly. The proper use of true classics is not to regard them as fetishes which must be slavishly worshiped, as the French dramatists worshiped the imaginary unities of Aristotle, but to keep them for a compass in the cross-currents of fashion. By them you may know what is permanent and essential from what is showy and exciting. That Greek work is peculiarly suited to this purpose is partly due, no doubt, to the winnowing of centuries of time, but partly also to its own intrinsic qualities. For one thing, all the best Greek work was done, not to please private tastes, but in a serious spirit of religion to honor the god of the city; that prevents it from being trivial or meretricious. Secondly, it is not romantic; and that renders it a very desirable antidote to modern extravagances. Thirdly, it is idealistic; that gives it a force and permanence which things designed only for the pleasure of the moment must generally lack. With all these high merits, it might remain very dull, if it had not the charm and grace of youth perfectly fearless, and serving a religion which largely consisted in health and beauty.

THE LAND AND ITS PEOPLE

A glance at the physical map of Greece shows you the sort of country which forms the setting of our picture. You see its long and complicated coast line, its intricate system of rugged hills, and the broken strings of islands which they fling off into the sea in every direction. On the map it recalls the features of Scotland or Norway. It hangs like a jewel on a pendant from the south of Europe into the Mediterranean Sea. Like its sister peninsulas of Italy and Spain, it has high mountains to the north of it; but the Balkans do not, as do the Alps and Pyrenees, present the form of a sheer rampart against northern invaders. On the contrary, the main axis of the hills lies in the same direction as the peninsula itself, with a northwest and southeast trend, so that on both coasts there are ancient trade routes into the country; but on both sides they have to traverse passes which offer a fair chance of easy defence.

The historian, wise after the event, deduces that the history of such a country must lie upon the sea. It is a sheltered, hospitable sea, with chains of islands like stepping-stones inviting the timid mariner of early times to venture across it. You can sail from Greece to Asia without ever losing sight of land. On the west it is not so. Greece and Italy turn their backs upon one another. Their neighboring coasts are the harborless ones. So Greece looks east and Italy west, in history as well as geography. The natural affinities of Greece are with Asia Minor and Egypt.

A sea-going people will be an adventurous people in thought as well as action. The Greeks themselves fully realized this. When Themistocles was urging his fellow-Athenians to build a great fleet and take to the sea in earnest, opposition came from the conservatives, who feared the political influence of a 'nautical mob' with radical and impious tendencies. The type of solid conservative

was the heavy-armed land soldier. So in Greek history the inland
city of Sparta stands for tradition, discipline, and stability, while
the mariners of Athens are progressive, turbulent, inquiring idealists.

This sea will also invite commerce if the Greeks have anything to
sell. It does not look as if they will have much. A few valleys and
small plains are fertile enough to feed their own proprietors, but as
regards corn and foodstuffs Greece will have to be an importer, not
an exporter. In history we find great issues hanging on the
sea routes by which corn came in from the Black Sea. Wine and
olive oil are the only things that nature allowed Greece to export.
As for minerals, Athens is rich in her silver mines, and gold is to
be found in Thrace under Mount Pangaeus. But if Greece is to
grow rich, it will have to be through the skill of her incomparable
craftsmen and the shield and spear of her hoplites.

The map will help to explain another feature of her history.
Although at first sight the peninsula looks as if it possessed a
geographical unity, yet a second glance shows that nature has split
it up into numberless small plains and valleys divided from one
another by sea and mountain. Such a country, as we see in Wales,
Switzerland, and Scotland, encourages a polity of clans and can-
tons, each jealous of its neighbor over the hill, and each cherishing
a fierce local patriotism. Nature, moreover, has provided each
plain with its natural citadel. Greece and Italy are both rich in
these self-made fortresses. The traveler in Italy is familiar with
the low hills or spurs of mountains, each crowned with the white
walls of some ancient city. If ever geography made history, it was
where those flat-topped hills with precipitous sides, such as the
Acropolis of Athens and Acrocorinthus, invited man to build his
fortress and his shrine upon their summit. Then, perched safely
on the hill-top and ringed with her wall, the city was able to develop
her peculiar civilization even in troubled times while the rest of
the world was still immersed in warfare and barbarism. The
farmer spends the summer in the plain below for sowing and
reaping, the mariner puts out from harbor, the soldier marches out
for a summer campaign, but the city is their home, their refuge,
and the centre of their patriotism. We must not overrate the
importance of this natural cause. Even the plains of Greece, such
as Thessaly and Boeotia, never developed a unity. There, too, the
citadel and the city-state prevailed. Geography is seldom more
than a contributory cause, shaping and assisting historical tendencies; but in this case it is impossible to resist the belief that in

Italy and Greece the hill-top invited the wall, and the wall enabled
the civilization of the city-state to rise and flourish long in advance
of the rest of Europe.

Greece enjoys a wonderful climate. The summer sun is hot,
but morning and evening bring refreshing breezes from the sea.
The rain average is low and regular; snow is almost unknown in
the valleys. Hence there is a peculiar dry brightness in the atmosphere which seems to annihilate distance. The traveler is struck
with the small scale of Greek geography. The Corinthian Gulf,
for instance, which he remembers to have been the scene of famous
sea battles in history, looks as if you could throw a stone across it.
From your hotel window in Athens you can see hill-tops in the
heart of the Peloponnese. Doubtless this clearness of the atmosphere encouraged the use of color and the plastic arts for outdoor
decoration. Even to-day the ruined buildings of the Athenian
citadel shine across to the eyes of the seafarers five miles away at
the Piraeus. Time has mellowed their marble columns to a rich
amber, but in old days they blazed with color and gilding. In
that radiant sea air the Greeks of old learned to see things clearly.
They could live, as the Greeks still live, a simple, temperate life.
Wine and bread, with a relish of olives or pickled fish, satisfied the
bodily needs of the richest. The climate invited an open-air life,
as it still does. To-day, as of old, the Greek loves to meet his
neighbors in the market square and talk eternally over all things
both in heaven and earth. Though the blood of Greece has suffered
many admixtures and though Greece has had to submit to centuries
of conquest by many masters and oppressors, her racial character is
little changed in some respects. The Greek is still restless, talka-
tive, subtle, and inquisitive, eager for liberty without the sense of
discipline which liberty requires, contemptuous of strangers and
jealous of his neighbor. In commerce, when he has the chance, his
quick and supple brain still makes him the prince of traders.
Honesty and stability have always been qualities which he is
quicker to admire than to practise. Courage, national pride, intellectual self-restraint, and creative genius have undoubtedly suffered under the Turkish domination. But the friends of modern
Greece believe that a few generations of liberty will restore these
qualities which were so eminent in her ancestors, and that her
future may rival her past. Not in the field of action, perhaps. We
must never forget, when we praise the artistic and intellectual
genius of Greece, that she alone rolled back the tide of Persian
conquest at Marathon and Salamis, or that Greek troops under

Alexander marched victoriously over half the known world. But it is not in the field of action that her greatness lies. She won battles by superior discipline, superior strategy, and superior armor. As soon as she had to meet a race of born soldiers, in the Romans, she easily succumbed. Her methods of fighting were always defensive in the main. Historians have often gone astray in devoting too much attention to her wars and battles.

The great defect of the climate of modern Greece is the malaria which haunts her plains and lowlands in early autumn. This is partly the effect and partly the cause of undrained and sparsely populated marsh-lands like those of Boeotia. It need not have been so in early Greek history. There must have been more agriculture and more trees in ancient than in modern Greece. An interesting and ingenious theory has lately been advanced which would trace the beginning of malaria in Greece to the fourth century. Its effect is seen in the loss of vigor which begins in that period and the rapid shrinkage of population which marks the beginning of the downfall in that and the succeeding century. In Italy the same theory has even better attestation, for the Roman Campagna, which to-day lies desolate and fever-stricken, was once the site of populous cities and the scene of agricultural activity.

The scenery of Greece is singularly impressive. Folded away among the hills there are, indeed, some lovely wooded valleys, like Tempe, but in general it is a treeless country, and the eye enjoys, in summer at least, a pure harmony of brown hills with deep blue sea and sky. The sea is indigo, almost purple, and the traveler quickly sees the justice of Homer's epithet of 'wine-dark.' Those brown hills make a lovely background for the play of light and shade. Dawn and sunset touch them with warmer colors, and the plain of Attica is seen 'violet-crowned' by the famous heights of Hymettus, Pentelicus, and Parnes. The ancient Greek talked little of scenery, but he saw a nereid in every pool, a dryad under every oak, and heard the pipe of Pan in the caves of his limestone hills. He placed the choir of Muses on Mount Helicon, and, looking up to the snowy summit of Olympus, he peopled it with calm, benignant deities.

In this beautiful land lived the happy and glorious people whose culture we are now to study. Some modernists, indeed, smitten with the megalomania of to-day, profess to despise a history written on so small a scale. Truly Athens was a small state at the largest. Her little empire had a yearly revenue of about £100,000. It is doubtful whether Sparta ever had much more than ten thousand free citizens. In military matters, it must be confessed, the importance attached by historians to miniature fleets and pygmy armies, with a ridiculously small casualty list, does strike the reader with a sense of disproportion. But for the politician it is especially instructive to see his problems worked out upon a small scale, with the issues comparatively simple and the results plainly visible. The task of combining liberty with order is in essentials the same for a state of ten thousand citizens as for one of forty millions. And in the realms of philosophy and art considerations of size do not affect us, except to make 'us marvel that these tiny states could do so much.

To a great extent we may find the key to the Greek character in her favorite proverb, 'No excess,' in which are expressed her favorite virtues of *aidōs* and *sōphrosuné*—reverence and self-restraint. 'Know thyself' was the motto inscribed over her principal shrine. Know and rely upon thine own powers, know and regard thine own limitations. It was such a maxim as this which enabled the Greeks to reach their goal of perfection even in the sphere of art, where perfection is proverbially impossible. They were bold in prospecting and experimenting, until they found what they deemed to be the right way, and when they had found it, they followed it through to its conclusion. Eccentricity they hated like poison. Though they were such great originators, they cared nothing for the modern fetish of originality.

In politics also they looked for a definite goal and traveled courageously along to find it. Herein they met with disastrous failures which are full of teaching for us. But they reached, it may be said, the utmost possibility of the city-state. The city-state was, as we have seen, probably evolved by natural survival from the physical conditions of the country. Being established, it entailed certain definite consequences. It involved a much closer bond of social union than any modern territorial state. Its citizens felt the unity and exclusiveness of a club or school. A much larger share of public rights and duties naturally fell upon them. They looked upon their city as a company of unlimited liability in which each individual citizen was a shareholder. They expected their city to feed and amuse them. They expected to divide the plunder when she made conquests, as they were certain to share the consequences if she was defeated. Every full citizen of proper age was naturally bound to fight personally in the ranks, and from that duty his rights as a citizen followed logically. He must naturally be consulted about peace and war, and must have a voice in foreign policy. Also, if he was to be a competent soldier he must undergo proper education and training for it. There will be little privacy inside the walls of a city-state; the arts and crafts will be under public patronage. Inequalities will become hatefully apparent.

But for us, an imperial people, who have inherited a vast and scattered dominion which somehow or other has got to be managed and governed, the chief interest will centre in the question of how these city-states acquired and administered their empires. Above all, it is to Athens and perhaps Rome alone that we can look for historical answers to the great riddle for which we cannot yet boast of having discovered a solution—whether democracy can govern an empire.

In Greek history alone we have at least three examples of empires. Athens and Sparta both proceeded to acquire empire by the road of alliance and hegemony, Athens being naval and democratic, Sparta aristocratic and military. Both were despotic, and both failed disastrously for different reasons. Then we have the career of Alexander the Great and his short-lived but important empire, a career providing a type for Caesar and Napoleon, an empire founded on mere conquest.

Lastly, on the same small canvas, we have a momentous phase of the eternal and still-continuing conflict between East and West and their respective habits of civilization.

III

EXTERNAL NATURE IN GREEK POETRY [1]

By Francis G. Allinson and Anne C. E. Allinson

It must not be assumed from the smallness of the land that the spurs to the imagination of the Greeks were few. On the contrary, within their narrow borders nature was prodigal of her inspiration. In the few miles from Thessaly to the Messenian Gulf are offered a variety of climate and an alternation of products well-nigh unparalleled for such a limited area. The warm air of the sea penetrating into sheltered valleys favors an almost tropical vegetation, while the lofty mountain ridges offer almost an Alpine climate. In Attica, in early spring, snow may occasionally be seen sprinkled on Hymettus, and glistening white on Mount Pentelicus, while oranges hang on the trees in Athens. Taygetus in the south may be a snow-covered mountain even as late as May, while in the Messenian plain below grows the palm and, more rarely, the edible date. In the Argolis are groves of lemons and oranges, and in Naxos, in the same latitude as Sparta, the tender lime ripens in the gardens. The gray-green olive is familiar throughout central and southern Greece. If we extend the survey farther north, the beeches of the Pindus range, west of Thessaly, are surrounded by the vegetation rather of northern Europe; in the interior of Thessaly the olive tree does not flourish; the northern shores of the Aegean have the climate of central Germany, while Mount Athos, whose marble walls jut far out into the Aegean and rise 6400 feet above the sea, offers on its slopes nearly all species of European trees in succession.

The different parts of Greece offer a varying development in literature. In this particular, some districts, like Acarnania, Aetolia, and Achaea, though possessed of great natural beauty, are negligible. Arcadia, though itself unproductive, inspired poetry; others, also, like Phocis, Locris, and Messenia, are inevitably drawn

[1 From *Greek Lands and Letters* (pp. 12-31). Boston and New York, 1909. The selection is reprinted by permission of the publishers, Houghton Mifflin Company.—EDITOR.]

into the associations of literature and history. In Epirus we find at Dodona the first known sanctuary of Zeus, the supreme god of the Greeks. In Thessaly the earliest Greeks, or Achaeans, may have first forged in the fire of their young imagination the tempered steel of the hexameter. Here was the home of Achilles, and here, perhaps, we must look for the kernel of the *Iliad*. Here most fitly, close to Olympus where dwelt the immortals, could the sons of men be 'near-gods.'

From the north and northwest successive waves of population descended into lower Greece to conquer, merge with, or become subject to, the previous comers. But prehistoric peoples, whether alien or Greek, like the Eteo-Cretans, the Pelasgi, the Minyae, the Leleges, the Hellenes, the Achaeans, and even great movements like the Dorian and Ionian migrations, are all foreshortened on a scenic background, as equidistant to the Greeks of the classic periods as is the vault of heaven to the eyes of children. One star, indeed, differed from another. The Dorian, for example, was of the first magnitude. But the relations of apparent magnitude and real distance were ignored or naïvely confused in the fanciful constellations of myth and saga, distant yet ever present, bending around them to their explored horizon. Heroic figures, impalpable but real as the gods themselves, intervened continually, controlling decisions, shaping policies, or determining disputed boundaries, among even the most intellectual of the Greeks. Royalty, oligarchy, democracy, and tyranny alike must reckon with personified tradition.

When we emerge into the light of more authentic records, it is well, in the confusing maze of inter-cantonal contentions, to focus the mind, for the purpose of appreciating the literature, upon certain broader relations and more clearly defined epochs in Greek history, like the so-called 'Age of the Despots' within the seventh and sixth centuries, the Persian wars, and the conflicts between Attica as a pivot and the Peloponnese, Thebes, and Macedon.

It might be expected from the variety of natural charm offered by Hellenic lands, from Ilium to Sicily, from Mount Olympus to Crete, that the Greeks would show in their literature a pervasive love of nature. This was, in fact, the case. The modern eye has not been the first to discover the beauty of form and color in the Greek flowers and birds, mountain, sky, and sea. Modern critics, ignoring all historical perspective, and assuming as a procrustean standard the one-sided and sophisticated attitude that has played a leading rôle in modern literature, announced as axiomatic that ancient Greek poets had no feeling for nature and found no pleasure in looking at the beauties of a landscape. This superficial idea still keeps cropping up, although thoughtful readers of Greek literature have long since pointed out the necessity both of a chronological analysis of the literature and of a more inclusive statement of the various forms in which a sentiment for the natural world is evinced.[2] It is a far cry from Homer to Theocritus, and, as might well be expected in a range of six centuries and more, new elements appear from time to time, due both to changing conditions of life and civilization and also to the personal equation.

A naïve feeling for nature is uppermost in the descriptive comparisons and similes of Homer and, generally speaking, in the myth-making of the Greeks. The concrete embodiment of natural phenomena and objects in some nature-divinity often obviated the necessity for elaborate description, and summarized their conceptions as if by an algebraic formula. The mystical element was not lacking, but by this myth-making process it became objective and real. The sympathetic feeling for nature becomes more and more apparent in lyric poetry and the drama until in Euripides there emerges, almost suddenly, the 'modern' romanticism. In the Hellenistic and imperial times, finally, the sentimental element is natural to men who turn to the country for relief from the stress of life in a city. One generalization for the classic periods may be safely made. Although the Greeks from Homer to Euripides thought of the world as the environment of man, yet they stopped short of a sentimental self-analysis. Charles Eliot Norton, more than thirty years ago, pointed out that the expression of a sentiment like Wordsworth's—

To me the meanest flower that blows can give
Thoughts that do often lie too deep for tears—

is foreign to the clear-eyed Hellene, reared amongst the distinct outlines of his mountains, and from the cradle to the grave at home upon the blue and wind-swept Aegean. Certainly this is true until the speculative questionings of the Ionic philosophers had time to react upon literature. As the Greeks accepted their pedigrees from the gods and heroes, so they accepted their environment of beauty. They were not unlike the child, content to betray by a stray word or caress his unanalyzed admiration for his mother's face.

Emphasis has often been laid, and rightly, upon the keen sensi-

[2] Cf. Fairclough, *The Attitude of the Greek Tragedians toward Nature.*

tiveness of the Greeks to beauty of form in sculpture, architecture, and literature. It is urged that they made this sense of form and proportion so paramount that they were blind to the beauty of coloring, and indifferent to the prodigal variety of nature's compositions. It may be readily admitted that this is a vital distinction between the ancient and modern attitudes. Both the craving for perfection of form and the preference given to man before nature come out in the pre-eminent development of sculpture by the Greeks. Their admiration of the beauty of the human form, unlike the sensitive shrinking of moderns, was extended even to the lifeless body. Aeschylus speaks of the warriors who have found graves before Troy as still 'fair of form.'

But a prevailing tendency does not necessarily exclude other elements. However meagre the vocabulary of the Greeks in sharp distinction of shades of color, their love for a bright color-scheme is shown not only by the brilliancy of their clothing and their use of coloring in statuary and architecture—for even in these mere form was not enough—but in unnumbered expressions like Alcman's 'sea-purple bird of the springtime.'

A few of the more obvious passages, illustrating the Greek attitude toward nature, are here given in general historic sequence. . . . Very often such references are casual and subordinate to some controlling idea, but they none the less reflect habitual observation. Even when we speak of Homeric 'tags,' like the 'saffron-robed' or 'rosy-fingered,' or of Sappho's 'golden-sandaled' Dawn, as 'standing epithets,' we are implying that these epithets made a general appeal. The naïve insertions in Homer of comparisons drawn from birds and beasts, from night and storm and other familiar elements of nature, would seem like an intrusive delay of the story, did they not carry with them the conviction that both poet and hearers alike were well content to linger by the way and observe the objects of daily life indoors and out. Thus in the *Odyssey:*

'The lion mountain-bred, with eyes agleam, fares onward in the rain and wind to fall upon the oxen or the sheep or wilding deer.'

Or, again:

'Hermes sped along the waves like sea-mew hunting fish in awesome hollows of the sea unharvested and wetting his thick plumage in the brine.'

One of the longer and best-known comparisons is the description in the *Iliad* of the Trojan encampment by night:

'Now they with hearts exultant through the livelong night sat by the space that bridged the moat of war, their watch-fires multitudinous alight. And just as in the sky the stars around the radiant moon shine clear; when windless is the air; when all the peaks stand out, the lofty forelands and the glades; when breaketh open from the sky the ether infinite, and all the stars are seen and make the shepherds glad at heart—so manifold appeared the watch-fires kindled by the Trojan men in front of Ilios betwixt the streams of Xanthus and the ships. So then a thousand fires burned upon the plain, and fifty warriors by the side of each were seated in the blazing fire's gleam, the while the horses by the chariots stood and champed white barley and the spelt and waited for the thronèd Dawn.'

Sappho's fragments are redolent of flowers; her woven verse, a 'rich-red chlamys' in the sunshine, has a silver sheen in the moonlight. We hear the full-throated passion of 'the herald of the spring, the nightingale'; the breeze moves the apple boughs, the wind shakes the oak trees. Her allusions to 'the hyacinths, darkening the ground, when trampled under foot of shepherds'; the 'fine, soft bloom of grass, trodden by the tender feet of Cretan women as they dance'; or the 'golden pulse growing on the shore'— all these seem inevitable to one who has seen the acres of bright flowers that carpet the islands or the near-by littoral of the Asian coast. Her comparison of a bridegroom to 'a supple sapling' recalls how Nausicaä, vigorous, tall, and straight as the modern athletic maiden, is likened by Odysseus to the 'young shaft of a palm tree' that he had once seen 'springing up in Delos by Apollo's altar.' In her Lesbian orchards the sweet quince-apple is still left hanging 'solitary on the topmost bough, upon its very end'; and there is heard 'cool murmuring through apple boughs while slumber floateth down from quivering leaves.' Nor need we attribute Sappho's love of natural beauty wholly to her passionate woman's nature. All the gentler emotions springing from an habitual observation of nature recur in poets of the sterner sex. 'The Graces,' she says, 'turn their faces from those who wear no garlands.' And at banquets wreaths were an essential also for masculine full dress. Pindar, in describing Elysian happiness, leads up to the climax of the companionship with the great and noble dead by telling how 'round the islands of the blest the ocean breezes blow, and flowers of gold are blooming; some from the land on trees of splendor, and some the water feedeth; with wreaths whereof they twine their heads and hands.'[3] Against the green background passes Evadne with her silver pitcher and her girdle of rich crimson woof, and her child is seen 'hidden in the rushes of the thicket unexplored, his tender flesh all steeped in golden and deep purple light from pansy flowers.'

To follow through the poetry of the Greeks the unfailing delight in the radiance of the moon would be to follow her diurnal course as she passes over Greek lands from east to west. The full moon looked down on all the Olympian festivals, and Pindar's pages are illuminated with her glittering argentry. The Lesbian nights inspire Sappho as did all things beautiful.

'The clustering stars about the radiant moon avert their faces bright and hide, what time her orb is rounded to the full and touches earth with silver.'

Wordsworth could take this thought from Sappho: 'The moon doth with delight look round her when the heavens are bare'; but the Lesbian certainly did not finish the fragment by lamenting that 'there hath past away a glory from the earth.'

The night and the day alike claimed the attention of the poets, and the interchange of dusk and dawn appealed to the sculptor also. In the east gable of the Parthenon the horses of the Sun and of the Moon were at either end. Nature's sleep is a favorite topic. Alcman's description is unusual only for its detail:

> Sleep the peaks and mountain clefts;
> Forelands and the torrent's rifts;
> All the creeping things are sleeping,
> Cherished in the black earth's keeping;
> Mountain-ranging beast and bee;
> Fish in depths of the purple sea;
> Wide-winged birds their pinions droop—
> Sleep now all the feathered troop.

Goethe, in his well-known paraphrase—

> Ueber allen Gipfeln
> Ist Ruh,—

[3] Translation by E. Myers (modified).

cannot refrain from adding the subjective conclusion of the whole matter:

> Die Vögelein schweigen im Walde.
> Warte nur, balde
> Ruhest du auch.

The great dramatists display an observation of the beauty of the external world not always sufficiently emphasized. In Aeschylus an intense feeling is evident; none the less because it is subordinated to his theme or used to point, by way of contrast, some awe-inspiring or pathetic situation or some scene of blood. Clytemnestra describes how she murdered her husband. His spattering blood, she says,

> Keeps striking me with dusky drops of murd'rous dew,
> Aye, me rejoicing none the less than God's sweet rain
> Makes glad the corn-land at the birth-pangs of the buds.

Comparisons, similes, and epithets drawn from the sea reappear continually in the warp and woof of Greek, and especially of Athenian, literature. Aeschylus, like the rest, knew the sea in all its moods, terrible in storm, deceitful in calm, beautiful at all times, and the pathway for commerce and for war. The returning herald in the *Agamemnon* rehearses the soldiers' hard bivouac in summer and in winter:

> And should one tell of winter, dealing death to birds,
> What storms unbearable swept down from Ida's snow,
> Or summer's heat when, ruffled by no rippling breeze,
> Ocean slept waveless, on his midday couch laid prone.

With the first lines of *Prometheus Bound* we are carried far from the haunts of men:

> Unto this far horizon of earth's plain we've come,
> This Scythian tract, this desert by man's foot untrod.

Hephaestus, reluctant, compelled by Zeus' order, rivets his kin-god, the Fire-bringer, to the desolate North Sea crag, and withdraws, leaving Prometheus in fetters to 'wrestle down the myriad years of time.' The night shuts off the warmth and light, drawing over him her 'star-embroidered robe,' and the fierce sun-god returns with blazing rays to 'deflower his fair skin' bared of the white counterpane of 'frost of early dawn.' Not until the emissaries of Zeus have departed does Prometheus deign to speak.

Then he 'communes with nature.' He has no hope of help from God, none from the 'helpless creatures of the day' whom he has helped. Alone with the forces of nature, he utters that outcry unsurpassed in sublimity and in pathos:

> O upper air divine and winds on swift wings borne;
> Ye river-springs; innumerous laughter of the waves
> Of Ocean; thou, Earth, the mother of us all;
> And thou, all-seeing orb of the Sun—to you I cry:
> Behold me what I'm suffering, a god from gods!

Sophocles, too, lets Philoctetes, in his misery and loneliness on the rocky Island of Lemnos, call out to the wild beasts and the landscape:

> Harbors and headlands, and ye mountain-ranging beasts,
> Companions mine, ye gnawed and hanging cliffs! Of this
> To you I cry aloud, for I have none save you—
> You ever present here—to whom to make my cry.

In his famous ode on the Attic Colonus he describes the natural beauty of his home with particularizing exactness. He has also a wealth of glittering epithet used for local coloring, for symbolism and personification. The contrast of day and night offers to him a welcome *mise en scène*. The sun's rays are Apollo's golden shafts, and the moon's light seems to filter through the trees as Artemis roams the uplands:

> O God of the light, from the woven gold
> Of the strings of thy bow, I am fain to behold
> Thy arrows invincible, showered around,
> As champions smiting our foes to the ground.
> And Artemis, too, with her torches flaring,
> Gleams onward through Lycian uplands faring.

Bacchus, also, the 'god of the golden snood,' 'lifts his pine-knot's sparkle,' and, roaming with his Maenads, seems to visualize for men the soul of nature.

Aristophanes with his common-sense objectivity was averse to the sentimental and romantic in Euripides, which seemed to him effeminate. His love for nature was clear-eyed and Hellenic. His lyrics shine like a bird's white wing in the sunlight. The self-invocation of the Clouds is alive with the radiance of the Attic atmosphere. A translation can only serve to illustrate the elements used in the description:

CHORUS OF CLOUDS

Come ever floating, O Clouds, anew,
Let us rise with the radiant dew
    Of our nature undefiled
From father Ocean's billows wild.
    The tree-fringed peak
Of hill upon lofty hill let us seek,
That we may look on the cliffs far-seen,
And the sacred land's water that lends its green
To the fruits, and the whispering rush of the rivers divine,
And the clamorous roar of the dashing brine;
    For Ether's eye is flashing his light,
    Untired by glare as of marble bright.

The 'meteor eyes' of the sun gaze 'sanguine' and unblinking upon the cloud-palisades, glaring bright as the marble of Mount Pentelicus. Readers of the Greek will recognize here and there how an Aristophanic epithet or thought has been precipitated and recombined by Shelley into new and radiant shapes that drift through his own cloud-land:

I change, but I cannot die.

Aristophanes' observation of nature is varied and exact. He had nothing but ridicule for the pale student within doors, and only a man who kept up an intimacy with 'the open road' could have made the naturalistic painting in the *Peace* of the serenity of country life:

'We miss the life of days gone by, the pressed fruit-cakes, the figs, the myrtles and the sweet new wine, the olive trees, the violet bed beside the well.'

Euripides in his attitude toward nature has all the qualities of the other tragedians except sublimity, to which he more rarely attains. Many qualities are much more conspicuous. His range of color is wider. His allusions to rivers and to the plant and animal world are more detailed. Picturesque scenes and setting delight him. Beyond all this, the reflection in nature of human emotion, occasional in his predecessors, plays in his verse almost a leading part. Modern romanticism, in short, is no longer exceptional.

Hippolytus, the acolyte of Artemis, and his attendants address the virgin goddess who ranges the woods and mountains, and who, as Aeschylus says, is 'kindly unto all the young things suckled at the breast of wild-wood roaming beasts.' The 'modern' element in the original loses nothing in this paraphrase by Mallock:

> Hail, O most pure, most perfect, loveliest one!
> 　Lo, in my hand I bear,
> Woven for the circling of thy long gold hair,
> Culled leaves and flowers, from places which the sun
> 　The spring long shines upon,
> Where never shepherd hath driven flock to graze,
> 　Nor any grass is mown;
> But there sound throughout the sunny, sweet warm days,
> 　'Mid the green holy place
> 　The wild bee's wings alone.

In one of the despairing chorals of the *Trojan Women* the personification of nature blends with the spirit of mythology. The name of Tithonus, easily supplied by a Greek hearer, is inserted for English readers in Gilbert Murray's beautiful paraphrase:

> For Zeus—O leave it unspoken:
> 　But alas for the love of the Morn;
> 　　Morn of the milk-white wing,
> 　　The gentle, the earth-loving,
> 　That shineth on battlements broken
> 　　In Troy, and a people forlorn!
> And, lo, in her bowers Tithonus,
> 　Our brother, yet sleeps as of old:
> O, she too hath loved us and known us,
> 　And the Steeds of her star, flashing gold,
> Stooped hither and bore him above us;
> 　Then blessed we the Gods in our joy.
> But all that made them to love us
> 　Hath perished from Troy.

When Dionysus addresses his Bacchantes, Euripides, in lines reminiscent of Alcman, imposes upon outward nature the solemn expectancy of the inward mind:

> Hushed was the ether; in hushed silence whispered not
> Leaves in the coppice nor the blades of meadow grass;
> No cry at all of any wild things had you heard.

The formal banns of the open wedlock of man and nature were declared in Euripides. Thereafter the treatment became more and more a matter of personal equation. In Plato's *Dialogues*, for example, the ethical element inevitably appears. In the famous scene beside the Ilissus, Socrates and young Phaedrus talk through the heated hours beneath the shade of the wide-spreading plane tree, where the agnus castus is in full bloom, where water cool to the unsandaled feet flows by, and in the branches the cicadae, 'prophets of the Muses,' contribute of their wisdom.

The Anthology, stretched through the centuries of Greek literature, links the old and the newer, the antique reserve and the fainness of modern romanticism. One of the epigrams attributed to Plato will serve to indicate the emergence of the latter:

> On the stars thou art gazing, my Star;
>   Would that the sky I might be,
>   For then from afar
> With my manifold eyes I would gaze upon thee.

Another seems like an artist's preliminary sketch for the picture by the Ilissus, the deeper motive not yet painted in:

> Sit thee down by this pine tree whose twigs without number
> Whisper aloft in the west wind aquiver.
> Lo! here by my stream as it chattereth ever
> The Pan-pipe enchanteth thine eyelids to slumber.

From this we pass without break to the piping shepherds and the country charms with which Theocritus filled his *Idyls* for city-jaded men:

>   There we lay,
>   Half-buried in a couch of fragrant reed
>   And fresh-cut vine-leaves, who so glad as we?
>   A wealth of elm and poplar shook o'erhead;
>   Hard by, a sacred spring flowed gurgling on
>   From the Nymphs' grot, and in the sombre boughs
>   The sweet cicada chirped laboriously.
>   Hid in the thick thorn-bushes far away,
>   The treefrog's note was heard; the crested lark
>   Sang with the goldfinch; turtles made their moan,
>   And o'er the fountain hung the gilded bee.[4]

[4] Translated by C. S. Calverley.

Notwithstanding the variety in landscape and the lack of unified nationality in the long centuries of Greek history, there is a unity in the impression of ancient life left upon the mind by a visit to Greece. This is in part due to the comparative meagreness of remains from periods subsequent to classic times. The long obliteration of mediaeval and modern constructive civilization leaves more clear the outlines of antiquity.

This is true even though the sum total of the remains of Byzantine and mediaeval life, on islands and on mainland, is large, and claims the attention from time to time. In Athens the traveler will come upon the small Metropolis church with its ancient Greek calendar of festivals, let in as a frieze above the entrance, and metamorphosed into Byzantine sanctity by the inscribing of Christian crosses. As he journeys to and fro in Greece he may see the venerable 'hundred-gated' church on the Island of Paros, recalling in certain details the proscenium of an ancient theatre; Monemvasia with its vast ruins, the home of Byzantine ecclesiasticism and a splendor of court life that vied with the pomp and magnificence of Western Europe; or the ivy-clad ruins of Mistra, an epitome of Graeco-Byzantine art from the thirteenth to the fifteenth century; the frowning hill and castle of Karytaena that guards the approach to the mountain fastnesses of Arcadia; or the ancient acropolis of Lindus on the Island of Rhodes with the impregnable fortress of the Knights of St. John.

Nor will the visitor ignore the reminders of the War of Independence and the renascence of life in modern Greece. Mesolonghi, Nauplia, and Arachova have contributed fresh chapters to human history. Aligned with ancient names are those of modern heroes in the nomenclature of the streets and of public squares, like the Karaiskakis Place that welcomes the traveler as he disembarks at Piraeus.

But all of these, whether mediaeval or modern, fail to blur the understanding of antiquity. They do not obtrude themselves. Often they even illustrate ancient life. The same wisdom that transferred allegiance from the Saturnalia to the Christmas festival has here also been careful to use for Byzantine churches the site of ancient shrines or temples: St. Elias is a familiar name on high mountains where once stood altars of the Olympians; the cult of Dionysus has been skilfully transformed, in vine-rearing Naxos, into that of St. Dionysius; SS. Cosmo and Damiano, patrons of medicine, and known as the 'feeless' saints, have established their free dispensary in place of an Asclepieion; the twelve Apostles have replaced the

'Twelve Gods'; and churches dedicated to St. Demetrius have been substituted for shrines of Demeter.

The thoughtful student of the literature of the Greeks, no matter how enthusiastic he may be, will not fail to draw warnings as well as inspiration from their history. But no defects of the Greeks nor achievements of posterity can dispossess Hellas of her peculiar lustre. 'No other nation,' as Mr. Ernest Myers has said with particular reference to the age of Pindar, 'has ever before or since known what it was to stand alone immeasurably advanced at the head of the civilization of the world.'

IV

FROM *PARADISE REGAINED* [1]

By John Milton

Behold
Where on the Aegean shore a city stands,
Built nobly—pure the air, and light the soil:
Athens, the eye of Greece, mother of arts
And eloquence, native to famous wits,
Or hospitable, in her sweet recess,
City or suburban, studious walks and shades.
See there the olive grove of Academe,
Plato's retirement, where the Attic bird
Trills her thick-warbled notes the summer long;
There flowery hill Hymettus with the sound
Of bees' industrious murmur oft invites
To studious musing; there Ilissus rolls
His whispering stream.   Within the walls then view
The schools of ancient sages—his who bred
Great Alexander to subdue the world;
Lyceum there, and painted Stoa next.
There thou shalt hear and learn the secret power
Of harmony in tones and numbers hit
By voice or hand, and various-measured verse,
Aeolian charms and Dorian lyric odes,
And his who gave them breath, but higher sung,
Blind Melesigenes, thence Homer called,
Whose poem Phoebus challenged for his own.
Thence what the lofty grave tragedians taught
In chorus or iambic, teachers best
Of moral prudence, with delight received,
In brief sententious precepts, while they treat

[1 *Paradise Regained* 4. 237-280. It should perhaps be remarked that the
sentiments are not precisely those of Milton, but such as he deems suitable to
a persuasive speech from Satan. In any case it is a notable piece of condensed
eloquence.—EDITOR.]

Of fate, and chance, and change in human life,
High actions and high passions best describing.
Thence to the famous orators repair,
Those ancient, whose resistless eloquence
Wielded at will that fierce democratie,
Shook the arsenal, and fulmined over Greece
To Macedon and Artaxerxes' throne.
To sage philosophy next lend thine ear,
From heaven descended to the low-roofed house
Of Socrates; see there his tenement,
Whom well-inspired the oracle pronounced
Wisest of men; from whose mouth issued forth
Mellifluous streams that watered all the schools
Of Academics old and new, with those
Surnamed Peripatetics, and the sect
Epicurean, and the Stoic severe.

V

ATTICA AND ATHENS [1]

By John Henry Newman

If we would know what a university is, considered in its elementary idea, we must betake ourselves to the first and most celebrated home of European literature and source of European civilization, to the bright and beautiful Athens—Athens, whose schools drew to her bosom, and then sent back again to the business of life, the youth of the Western World for a long thousand years. Seated on the verge of the Continent, the city seemed hardly suited for the duties of a central metropolis of knowledge; yet, what it lost in convenience of approach, it gained in its neighborhood to the traditions of the mysterious East, and in the loveliness of the region in which it lay. Hither, then, as to a sort of ideal land, where all archetypes of the great and the fair were found in substantial being, and all departments of truth explored, and all diversities of intellectual power exhibited, where taste and philosophy were majestically enthroned as in a royal court, where there was no sovereignty but that of mind, and no nobility but that of genius, where professors were rulers, and princes did homage— hither flocked continually from the very corners of the *orbis terrarum* the many-tongued generation, just rising, or just risen into manhood, in order to gain wisdom.

Pisistratus had in an early age discovered and nursed the infant genius of his people, and Cimon, after the Persian war, had given it a home. That war had established the naval supremacy of Athens; she had become an imperial state; and the Ionians, bound to her by the double chain of kindred and of subjection, were

[1 From Newman's *Historical Sketches* (pp. 18-23, 33-46), London, 1872. 'We need not,' says Newman, referring to his account of Athens, 'be very solicitous about anachronisms.' In point of fact, disregarding chronology, he has produced a composite picture of the city, putting in touches from different periods of its history, the general effect being to emphasize what is characteristic of later times somewhat more than the typical Hellenic civilization.— Editor.]

importing into her both their merchandise and their civilization. The arts and philosophy of the Asiatic coast were easily carried across the sea, and there was Cimon, as I have said, with his ample fortune, ready to receive them with due honors. Not content with patronizing their professors, he built the first of those noble porticoes, of which we hear so much in Athens, and he formed the groves, which in process of time became the celebrated Academy. Planting is one of the most graceful, as in Athens it was one of the most beneficent of employments. Cimon took in hand the wild wood, pruned and dressed it, and laid it out with handsome walks and welcome fountains. Nor, while hospitable to the authors of the city's civilization, was he ungrateful to the instruments of her prosperity. His trees extended their cool, umbrageous branches over the merchants, who assembled in the Agora, for many generations.

Those merchants certainly had deserved that act of bounty; for all the while their ships had been carrying forth the intellectual fame of Athens to the Western World. Then commenced what may be called her university existence. Pericles, who succeeded Cimon both in the government and in the patronage of art, is said by Plutarch to have entertained the idea of making Athens the capital of federated Greece; in this he failed, but his encouragement of such men as Phidias and Anaxagoras led the way to her acquiring a far more lasting sovereignty over a far wider empire. Little understanding the sources of her own greatness, Athens would go to war. Peace is the interest of a seat of commerce and the arts, but to war she went; yet to her, whether peace or war, it mattered not. The political power of Athens waned and disappeared; kingdoms rose and fell; centuries rolled away—they did but bring fresh triumphs to the city of the poet and the sage. There at length the swarthy Moor and Spaniard were seen to meet the blue-eyed Gaul; and the Cappadocian, late subject of Mithridates, gazed without alarm at the haughty conquering Roman. Revolution after revolution passed over the face of Europe, as well as of Greece, but still she was there—Athens, the city of mind—as radiant, as splendid, as delicate, as young, as ever she had been.

Many a more fruitful coast or isle is washed by the blue Aegean, many a spot is there more beautiful or sublime to see, many a territory more ample; but there was one charm in Attica, which in the same perfection was nowhere else. The deep pastures of Arcadia, the plain of Argos, the Thessalian vale, these had not the gift. Boeotia, which lay to its immediate north, was notorious for its very want of it. The heavy atmosphere of that Boeotia might be good for vegetation, but it was associated in popular belief with the dulness of the Boeotian intellect. On the contrary, the special purity, elasticity, clearness, and salubrity of the air of Attica, fit concomitant and emblem of its genius, did that for it which earth did not—it brought out every bright hue and tender shade of the landscape over which it was spread, and would have illuminated the face even of a more bare and rugged country.

A confined triangle, perhaps fifty miles its greatest length, and thirty its greatest breadth; two elevated rocky barriers, meeting at an angle; three prominent mountains, commanding the plain— Parnes, Pentelicus, and Hymettus; an unsatisfactory soil; some streams, not always full—such is about the report which the agent of a London company would have made of Attica. He would report that the climate was mild; the hills were limestone; there was plenty of good marble; more pasture land than at first survey might have been expected, sufficient certainly for sheep and goats; fisheries productive; silver mines once, but long since worked out; figs fair; oil first-rate; olives in profusion. But what he would not think of noting down was that that olive tree was so choice in nature, and so noble in shape, that it excited a religious venera- tion; and that it took so kindly to the light soil as to expand into woods upon the open plain, and to climb up and fringe the hills. He would not think of writing word to his employers how that clear air, of which I have spoken, brought out, yet blended and subdued, the colors on the marble till they had a softness and harmony, for all their richness, which in a picture looks exag- gerated, yet is after all within the truth. He would not tell how that same delicate and brilliant atmosphere freshened up the pale olive till the olive forgot its monotony, and its cheek glowed like the arbutus or beech of the Umbrian hills. He would say nothing of the thyme and thousand fragrant herbs which carpeted Hymet- tus; he would hear nothing of the hum of its bees; nor take much account of the rare flavor of its honey, since Gozo and Minorca were sufficient for the English demand. He would look over the Aegean from the height he had ascended; he would follow with his eye the chain of islands, which, starting from the Sunian headland, seemed to offer the fabled divinities of Attica, when they would visit their Ionian cousins, a sort of viaduct thereto across the sea. But that fancy would not occur to him, nor any admiration of the dark violet billows with their white edges, down below; nor of those graceful fan-like jets of silver upon the rocks, which slowly rise aloft like water spirits from the deep, then shiver, and break, and spread, and shroud themselves, and disappear, in a soft mist of foam; nor of the gentle, incessant heaving and panting of the whole liquid plain; nor of the long waves, keeping steady time, like a line of soldiery, as they resound upon the hollow shore—he would not deign to notice that restless living element at all, except to bless his stars that he was not upon it. Nor the distinct detail, nor the refined coloring, nor the graceful outline and roseate golden hue of the jutting crags, nor the bold shadows cast from Otus or Laurium by the declining sun—our agent of a mercantile firm would not value these matters even at a low figure. Rather we must turn for the sympathy we seek to yon pilgrim student, come from a semi-barbarous land to that small corner of the earth, as to a shrine where he might take his fill of gazing on those emblems and coruscations of invisible unoriginate perfection. It was the stranger from a remote province, from Britain or from Mauretania, who in a scene so different from that of his chilly, woody swamps, or of his fiery, choking sands, learned at once what a real university must be, by coming to understand the sort of country which was its suitable home.

Nor was this all that a university required, and found in Athens. No one, even there, could live on poetry. If the students at that famous place had nothing better than bright hues and soothing sounds, they would not have been able or disposed to turn their residence there to much account. Of course they must have the means of living, nay, in a certain sense, of enjoyment, if Athens was to be an Alma Mater at the time, or to remain afterwards a pleasant thought in their memory. And so they had. Be it recollected Athens was a port, and a mart of trade, perhaps the first in Greece; and this was very much to the point when a number of strangers were ever flocking to it whose combat was to be with intellectual, not physical, difficulties, and who claimed to have their bodily wants supplied that they might be at leisure to set about furnishing their minds. Now, barren as was the soil of Attica, and bare the face of the country, yet it had only too many resources for an elegant, nay, luxurious, abode there. So abundant were the imports of the place that it was a common saying that the productions which were found singly elsewhere were brought all together in Athens. Corn and wine, the staple of subsistence in such a climate, came from the isles of the Aegean; fine wool and carpeting from Asia Minor; slaves, as now, from the Euxine, and timber, too; and iron and brass from the coasts of the Mediter-

ranean. The Athenian did not condescend to manufactures himself, but encouraged them in others; and a population of foreigners
caught at the lucrative occupation both for home consumption and
for exportation. Their cloth, and other textures for dress and fur-
niture, and their hardware—for instance, armor—were in great
request. Labor was cheap; stone and marble in plenty; and the
taste and skill which at first were devoted to public buildings, as
temples and porticoes, were in course of time applied to the mansions of public men. If nature did much for Athens, it is undeniable that art did much more. . . .

It has been my desire, were I able, to bring before the reader
what Athens may have been, viewed as what we have since called
a university; and to do this, not with any purpose of writing a
panegyric on a heathen city, or of denying its many deformities,
or of concealing what was morally base in what was intellectually
great, but just the contrary, of representing things as they really
were; so far, that is, as to enable him to see what a university is,
in the very constitution of society and in its own idea, what is its
nature and object, and what it needs of aid and support external
to itself to complete that nature and to secure that object.

So now let us fancy our Scythian, or Armenian, or African, or
Italian, or Gallic student, after tossing on the Saronic waves, which
would be his more ordinary course to Athens, at last casting anchor
at Piraeus. He is of any condition or rank of life you please, and
may be made to order, from a prince to a peasant. Perhaps he is
some Cleanthes, who has been a boxer in the public games. How
did it ever cross his brain to betake himself to Athens in search of
wisdom? Or, if he came thither by accident, how did the love of it
ever touch his heart? But so it was, to Athens he came with three
drachms in his girdle, and he got his livelihood by drawing water,
carrying loads, and the like servile occupations. He attached himself, of all philosophers, to Zeno the Stoic—to Zeno, the most highminded, the most haughty of speculators; and out of his daily
earnings the poor scholar brought his master the daily sum of an
obolus, in payment for attending his lectures. Such progress did
he make, that on Zeno's death he actually was his successor in his
school; and, if my memory does not play me false, he is the author
of a hymn to the Supreme Being which is one of the noblest effu-
sions of the kind in classical poetry. Yet, even when he was the
head of a school, he continued in his illiberal toil as if he had been a
monk; and it is said that once when the wind took his pallium, and
blew it aside, he was discovered to have no other garment at all—

something like the German student who came up to Heidelberg with nothing upon him but a greatcoat and a pair of pistols.

Or it is another disciple of the Porch—Stoic by nature, earlier than by profession—who is entering the city; but in what different fashion he comes! It is no other than Marcus, Emperor of Rome and philosopher. Professors long since were summoned from Athens for his service when he was a youth, and now he comes after his victories on the battle-field, to make his acknowledgments at the end of life to the city of wisdom, and to submit himself to an initiation into the Eleusinian mysteries.

Or it is a young man of great promise as an orator, were it not for his weakness of chest, which renders it necessary that he should acquire the art of speaking without over-exertion, and should adopt a delivery sufficient for the display of his rhetorical talents on the one hand, yet merciful to his physical resources on the other. He is called Cicero; he will stop but a short time, and will pass over to Asia Minor and its cities, before he returns to continue a career which will render his name immortal; and he will like his short sojourn at Athens so well that he will take good care to send his son thither at an earlier age than he visited it himself.

But see where comes from Alexandria (for we need not be very solicitous about anachronisms) a young man from twenty to twenty-two, who has narrowly escaped drowning on his voyage, and is to remain at Athens as many as eight or ten years, yet in the course of that time will not learn a line of Latin, thinking it enough to become accomplished in Greek composition, and in that he will succeed. He is a grave person, and difficult to make out; some say he is a Christian—something or other in the Christian line his father is, for certain. His name is Gregory, he is by country a Cappadocian, and will in time become pre-eminently a theologian, and one of the principal Doctors of the Greek Church.

Or it is one Horace, a youth of low stature and black hair, whose father has given him an education at Rome above his rank in life, and now is sending him to finish it at Athens. He is said to have a turn for poetry. A hero he is not, and it were well if he knew it; but he is caught by the enthusiasm of the hour, and goes off campaigning with Brutus and Cassius—and will leave his shield behind him on the field of Philippi.

Or it is a mere boy of fifteen; his name Eunapius. Though the voyage was not long, seasickness, or confinement, or bad living on board the vessel, threw him into a fever, and when the passengers landed in the evening at Piraeus he could not stand. His countrymen who accompanied him took him up among them, and carried him to the house of a great teacher of the day, Proaeresius, who was a friend of the captain's, and whose fame it was which drew the enthusiastic youth to Athens. His companions understand the sort of place they are in, and, with the license of academic students, they break into the philosopher's house, though he appears to have retired for the night, and proceed to make themselves free of it, with an absence of ceremony which is only not impudence because Proaeresius takes it so easily. Strange introduction for our stranger to a seat of learning, but not out of keeping with Athens; for what could you expect of a place where there was a mob of youths, and not even the pretence of control; where the poorer lived anyhow, and got on as they could, and the teachers themselves had no protection from the humors and caprices of the students who filled their lecture-halls? However, as to this Eunapius, Proaeresius took a fancy to the boy, and told him curious stories about Athenian life. He himself had come up to the university with one Hephaestion, and they were even worse off than Cleanthes the Stoic; for they had only one cloak between them, and nothing whatever besides, except some old bedding; so when Proaeresius went abroad, Hephaestion lay in bed, and practised himself in oratory; and then Hephaestion put on the cloak, and Proaeresius crept under the coverlet. At another time there was so fierce a feud between what would be called 'town and gown' in an English university that the professors did not dare lecture in public for fear of ill treatment.

But a Freshman like Eunapius soon got experience for himself of the ways and manners prevalent in Athens. Such a one as he had hardly entered the city when he was caught hold of by a party of the academic youth, who proceeded to practise on his awkwardness and his ignorance. At first sight one wonders at their childishness; but the like conduct obtained in the mediaeval universities; and not many months have passed away since the journals have told us of sober Englishmen, given to matter-of-fact calculations, and to the anxieties of money-making, pelting each other with snowballs on their own sacred territory, and defying the magistracy when they would interfere with their privilege of becoming boys. So I suppose we must attribute it to something or other in human nature. Meanwhile, there stands the new-comer, surrounded by a circle of his new associates, who forthwith proceed to frighten, and to banter, and to make a fool of him, to the extent of their wit. Some address him with mock politeness, others with fierceness; and so they conduct him in solemn procession across the Agora to the baths; and as they approach they dance about him like madmen. But this was to be the end of his trial, for the bath was a sort of initiation; he thereupon received the pallium, or university gown, and was suffered by his tormentors to depart in peace. One alone is recorded as having been exempted from this persecution; it was a youth graver and loftier than even St. Gregory himself. But it was not from his force of character, but at the instance of Gregory, that he escaped. Gregory was his bosom friend, and was ready in Athens to shelter him when he came. It was another saint and another Doctor—the great Basil, then (it would appear), as Gregory, but a catechumen of the Church.

But to return to our Freshman. His troubles are not at an end, though he has got his gown upon him. Where is he to lodge? Whom is he to attend? He finds himself seized, before he well knows where he is, by another party of men, or three or four parties at once, like foreign porters at a landing who seize on the baggage of the perplexed stranger, and thrust half a dozen cards into his unwilling hands. Our youth is plied by the hangers-on of Professor This, or Sophist That, each of whom wishes the fame or the profit of having a houseful. We will say that he escapes from their hands—but then he will have to choose for himself where he will put up; and, to tell the truth, with all the praise I have already given and the praise I shall have to give to the city of mind, nevertheless, between ourselves, the brick and wood which formed it, the actual tenements where flesh and blood had to lodge (always excepting the mansions of the great men of the place), do not seem to have been much better than those of Greek or Turkish towns, which are at this moment a topic of interest and ridicule in the public prints. A lively picture has lately been set before us of Gallipoli. Take, says the writer,[2] a multitude of the dilapidated outhouses found in farmyards in England, of the rickety old wooden tenements, the cracked, shutterless structures of planks and tiles, the sheds and stalls, which our by-lanes, or fish-markets, or river-sides can supply; tumble them down on the declivity of a bare bald hill; let the spaces between house and house, thus accidentally determined, be understood to form streets, winding, of course, for no reason, and with no meaning, up and down the town; the roadway always narrow, the breadth never uniform, the separate houses bulging or retiring below as circumstances may have determined, and leaning forward till they meet overhead;—and

---

[2] Mr. Russell's letters in the *Times* newspaper (1854) [April 26, p. 9].

you have a good idea of Gallipoli. I question whether this picture
would not nearly correspond to the special seat of the Muses in
ancient times. Learned writers assure us distinctly that the houses
of Athens were for the most part small and mean; that the streets
were crooked and narrow; that the upper stories projected over
the roadway; and that staircases, balustrades, and doors that
opened outwards, obstructed it—a remarkable coincidence of description. I do not doubt at all, though history is silent, that that
roadway was jolting to carriages, and all but impassable; and that
it was traversed by drains, as freely as any Turkish town now.
Athens seems in these respects to have been below the average cities
of its time. 'A stranger,' says an ancient, 'might doubt, on the
sudden view, if really he saw Athens.'

I grant all this, and much more, if you will; but, recollect, Athens
was the home of the intellectual and beautiful; not of low mechanical contrivances and material organization. Why stop within your
lodgings, counting the rents in your wall or the holes in your tiling,
when nature and art call you away? You must put up with such
a chamber, and a table, and a stool, and a sleeping-board, anywhere else in the three continents; one place does not differ from
another indoors; your *magalia* in Africa, or your grottos in Syrià,
are not perfection. I suppose you did not come to Athens to swarm
up a ladder, or to grope about a closet; you came to see and to hear
what hear and see you could not elsewhere. What food for the
intellect is it possible to procure indoors, that you stay there looking about you? Do you think to read there? Where are your
books? Do you expect to purchase books at Athens?—You are
much out in your calculations. True it is, we at this day who live
in the nineteenth century have the books of Greece as a perpetual
memorial; and copies there have been, since the time that they
were written. But you need not go to Athens to procure them,
nor would you find them in Athens. Strange to say, strange to
the nineteenth century, that in the age of Plato and Thucydides
there was not, it is said, a bookshop in the whole place; nor was
the book trade in existence till the very time of Augustus. Libra-
ries, I suspect, were the bright invention of Attalus or the Ptole-
mies;[3] I doubt whether Athens had a library till the reign of
Hadrian. It was what the student gazed on, what he heard, what

---

[3] I do not go into controversy on the subject, for which the reader must have
recourse to Lipsius, Morhof, Boeckh, Bekker, etc.; and this, of course, applies
to whatever historical matter I introduce, or shall introduce.

he caught by the magic of sympathy, not what he read, which was the education furnished by Athens.

He leaves his narrow lodging early in the morning, and not till night, if even then, will he return. It is but a crib or kennel, in which he sleeps when the weather is inclement or the ground damp—in no respect a home. And he goes out of doors, not to read the day's newspaper, or to buy the gay shilling volume, but to imbibe the invisible atmosphere of genius, and to learn by heart the oral traditions of taste. Out he goes; and, leaving the tumble-down town behind him, he mounts the Acropolis to the right, or he turns to the Areopagus on the left. He goes to the Parthenon to study the sculptures of Phidias; to the temple of the Dioscuri to see the paintings of Polygnotus. We, indeed, take our Sophocles or Aeschylus out of our coat-pocket; but if our sojourner at Athens would understand how a tragic poet can write, he must betake himself to the theatre on the south, and see and hear the drama literally in action. Or let him go westward to the Agora, and there he will hear Lysias or Andocides pleading, or Demosthenes haranguing. He goes farther west still, along the shade of those noble planes which Cimon has planted there; and he looks around him at the statues and porticoes and vestibules, each by itself a work of genius and skill, enough to be the making of another city. He passes through the city gate, and then he is at the famous Ceramicus. Here are the tombs of the mighty dead; and here, we will suppose, is Pericles himself, the most elevated, the most thrilling of orators, converting a funeral oration over the slain into a philosophical panegyric of the living.

Onwards he proceeds still; and now he has come to that still more celebrated Academe, which has bestowed its own name on universities down to this day; and there he sees a sight which will be graven on his memory till he dies. Many are the beauties of the place—the groves, and the statues, and the temple, and the stream of the Cephissus flowing by; many are the lessons which will be taught him day after day by teacher or by companion; but his eye is just now arrested by one object: it is the very presence of Plato. He does not hear a word that he says; he does not care to hear; he asks neither for discourse nor disputation; what he sees is a whole, complete in itself, not to be increased by addition, and greater than anything else. It will be a point in the history of his life; a stay for his memory to rest on, a burning thought in his heart, a bond of union with men of like mind, ever afterwards. Such is the spell which the living man exerts on his fellows, for good or for evil. How nature impels us to lean upon others, making virtue, or genius, or name, the qualification for our doing so! A Spaniard is said to have traveled to Italy, simply to see Livy; he had his fill of gazing, and then went back again home. Had our young stranger got nothing by his voyage but the sight of the breathing and moving Plato, had he entered no lecture-room to hear, no gymnasium to converse, he had got some measure of education, and something to tell of to his grandchildren.

But Plato is not the only sage, nor the sight of him the only lesson to be learned in this wonderful suburb. It is the region and the realm of philosophy. Colleges were the inventions of many centuries later; and they imply a sort of cloistered life, or at least a life of rule, scarcely natural to an Athenian. It was the boast of the philosophic statesman of Athens that his countrymen achieved by the mere force of nature and the love of the noble and the great what other people aimed at by laborious discipline; and all who came among them were submitted to the same method of education. We have traced our student on his wanderings from the Acropolis to the Sacred Way; and now he is in the region of the schools. No awful arch, no window of many-colored lights, marks the seats of learning there or elsewhere; philosophy lives out of doors. No close atmosphere oppresses the brain or inflames the eyelid; no long session stiffens the limbs. Epicurus is reclining in his garden; Zeno looks like a divinity in his porch; the restless Aristotle, on the other side of the city, as if in antagonism to Plato, is walking his pupils off their legs in his Lyceum by the Ilissus. Our student has determined on entering himself as a disciple of Theophrastus, a teacher of marvelous popularity, who has brought together two thousand pupils from all parts of the world. He himself is of Lesbos; for masters, as well as students, come hither from all regions of the earth—as befits a university. How could Athens have collected hearers in such numbers unless she had selected teachers of such power? It was the range of territory, which the notion of a university implies, which furnished both the quantity of the one and the quality of the other. Anaxagoras was from Ionia, Carneades from Africa, Zeno from Cyprus, Protagoras from Thrace, and Gorgias from Sicily. Andromachus was a Syrian, Proaeresius an Armenian, Hilarius a Bithynian, Philiscus a Thessalian, Hadrian a Syrian. Rome is celebrated for her liberality in civil matters; Athens was as liberal in intellectual. There was no narrow jealousy directed against a professor because he was not an Athenian. Genius and talent were the qualifications; and to bring them to Athens was to do homage to it as a university. There was a brotherhood and a citizenship of mind.

Mind came first, and was the foundation of the academical polity; but it soon brought along with it, and gathered round itself, the gifts of fortune and the prizes of life. As time went on, wisdom was not always sentenced to the bare cloak of Cleanthes; but, beginning in rags, it ended in fine linen. The professors became honorable and rich; and the students ranged themselves under their names, and were proud of calling themselves their countrymen. The University was divided into four great nations, as the mediaeval antiquarian would style them; and in the middle of the fourth century, Proaeresius was the leader or proctor of the Attic, Hephaestion of the Oriental, Epiphanius of the Arabic, and Diophantus of the Pontic. Thus the professors were both patrons of clients, and hosts and *proxeni* of strangers and visitors, as well as masters of the schools; and the Cappadocian, Syrian, or Sicilian youth who came to one or other of them would be encouraged to study by his protection, and to aspire by his example.

Even Plato, when the schools of Athens were not a hundred years old, was in circumstances to enjoy the *otium cum dignitate*. He had a villa out at Heraclea; and he left his patrimony to his school, in whose hands it remained, not only safe, but fructifying, a marvelous phenomenon in tumultuous Greece, for the long space of eight hundred years. Epicurus, too, had the property of the gardens where he lectured; and these, too, became the property of his sect. But in Roman times the chairs of grammar, rhetoric, politics, and the four philosophies were handsomely endowed by the State; some of the professors were themselves statesmen or high functionaries, and brought to their favorite study senatorial rank or Asiatic opulence.

Patrons such as these can compensate to the Freshman, in whom we have interested ourselves, for the poorness of his lodging and the turbulence of his companions. In everything there is a better side and a worse; in every place a disreputable set and a respectable, and the one is hardly known at all to the other. Men come away from the same university, at this day, with contradictory impressions and contradictory statements, according to the society they have found there. If you believe the one, nothing goes on there as it should be; if you believe the other, nothing goes on as it should not. Virtue, however, and decency are at least in the minority everywhere, and under some sort of a cloud or disadvantage; and this being the case, it is so much gain whenever an Herodes Atticus is found, to throw the influence of wealth and station on the side even of a decorous philosophy. A consular man, and the heir of an ample fortune, this Herod was content to devote his life to a professorship, and his fortune to the patronage of literature. He gave the sophist Polemo about eight thousand pounds, as the sum is calculated, for three declamations. He built at Athens a stadium six hundred feet long, entirely of white marble, and capable of admitting the whole population. His theatre, erected to the memory of his wife, was made of cedar wood curiously carved. He had two villas, one at Marathon, the place of his birth, about ten miles from Athens, the other at Cephissia, at the distance of six; and thither he drew to him the élite, and at times the whole body of the students. Long arcades, groves of trees, clear pools for the bath, delighted and recruited the summer visitor. Never was so brilliant a lecture-room as his evening banqueting-hall; highly connected students from Rome mixed with the sharp-witted provincial of Greece or Asia Minor; and the flippant sciolist, and the nondescript visitor, half philosopher, half tramp, met with a reception, courteous always, but suitable to his deserts. Herod was noted for his repartees; and we have instances on record of his setting down, according to the emergency, both the one and the other.

A higher line, though a rarer one, was that allotted to the youthful Basil. He was one of those men who seem by a sort of fascination to draw others around them even without wishing it. One might have deemed that his gravity and his reserve would have kept them at a distance; but, almost in spite of himself, he was the centre of a knot of youths, who, pagans as most of them were, used Athens honestly for the purpose for which they professed to seek it; and, disappointed and displeased with the place himself, he seems nevertheless to have been the means of their profiting by its advantages. One of these was Sophronius, who afterwards held a high office in the State; Eusebius was another, at that time the bosom friend of Sophronius, and afterwards a bishop. Celsus, too, is named, who afterwards was raised to the government of Cilicia by the Emperor Julian. Julian himself—in the sequel, of unhappy memory—was then at Athens, and known at least to St. Gregory. Another Julian is also mentioned, who was afterwards commissioner of the land-tax. Here we have a glimpse of the better kind of society among the students of Athens; and it is to the credit of the parties composing it that such young men as Gregory and Basil, men as intimately connected with Christianity as they were well known in the world, should hold so high a place in their esteem and love. When the two saints were departing, their companions came around them with the hope of changing their purpose. Basil persevered; but Gregory relented, and turned back to Athens for a season.

VI

THE AGE OF PERICLES [1]

By Sir Richard Jebb

The debt which the modern world owes to the best age of ancient Greece is well summed up in some words which the late Professor Green wrote in his *Prolegomena to Ethics:* 'When we come to ask ourselves what are the essential forms in which, however otherwise modified, the will for true good—which is the will to be good—must appear, our answer follows the outlines of the Greek classification of the virtues. It is the will to know what is true; to make what is beautiful; to endure pain or fear; to resist the allurements of pleasure (i.e., to be brave and temperate)—if not, as the Greek would have said, in the service of the State, yet in some form of human society;—to take for oneself, and to give to others, of those things which admit of being given and taken, not what one is inclined to give or take, but what is due.'

Accepting this as a concise description of the Hellenic ideal, we find that the period during which it was most fully realized was that which we are accustomed to call the age of Pericles. The period so named may be roughly defined as extending from 460 to 430 B.C. Within those thirty years the political power of Athens culminated; the Athenians developed that civic life which, as sketched in the great oration attributed to Pericles by Thucydides, made Athens, as the orator says, the school of Greece, and, as we moderns might add, the teacher of posterity; within those thirty years were created works of art, in literature, in architecture, and in sculpture, which the world has ever since regarded as unapproachable masterpieces. This period, so relatively short and yet so prolific in varied excellence, followed closely on the war in which united Greece repelled the Persian invasion. It immediately

[1 This lecture was delivered at Glasgow in March, 1889, and was posthumously published from the author's manuscript in Jebb's *Essays and Addresses* (Cambridge, England, 1907). It is here reprinted from that volume (pp. 104-126) with the consent of the Cambridge University Press.—EDITOR.]

preceded the war of the two leading Greek cities against each other, in which Sparta ultimately humbled Athens. Athens, as it appears in the national struggle against Persia, is not yet the acknowledged head of Hellas. The formal leadership belongs, by common consent, to Sparta; and though Athens is already pre-eminent in moral qualities—in unselfish devotion to the national cause, and in a spirit which no reverses can break,—these qualities appear as they are embodied in a few chosen men, in a Themistocles and an Aristides; the mass of Athenians whom they lead is still a comparatively rude multitude, not yet quickened into the full energy of conscious citizenship. If, on the other hand, we look to the close of the age of Pericles—if we pass to the opening years of the Peloponnesian war—we find that the Athenian democracy already bears within it the seeds of decay. The process of degeneration has already begun, though a century is still to elapse before Philip of Macedon shall overthrow the liberties of Greece at Chaeronea.

The interval between the Persian war and the Peloponnesian war—the space which we call the age of Pericles—is a space of comparative peace and rest, during which all the faculties of the Hellenic nature attain their most. complete development in the civic community of Athens. Yet this interval is the only period in Athenian history of which we have no full or continuous record from a contemporary source. Herodotus leaves us at the end of the Persian invasion. Thucydides becomes our guide only at the beginning of the Peloponnesian war. It is true that in the opening of his work he glances rapidly at the intervening years. But his hints serve rather to stimulate than to appease our curiosity. We learn from him little more than a few external facts which, taken by themselves, tell us little. With regard to the inner life of Athens in the age of Pericles—the social and the intellectual life—he is silent. Among the names which are nowhere mentioned by him are those of the poets Aeschylus, Sophocles, Euripides, Aristophanes; the philosopher Anaxagoras; the sculptor Phidias; the architect Ictinus. He incidentally notices the Parthenon—but only as a treasury; he notices the Propylaea—but only as a work which had reduced the balance in the treasury. This silence, however tantalizing it may be for us, admits of a simple explanation. His chosen subject, as he conceived it, was a purely political one—the Peloponnesian war; and he did not regard such matters as pertinent to it. The art and poetry of the day, the philosophy and the social life, were, in his view, merely decorations of the theatre in which the great drama of the war was being enacted. One thing, however, he allows us to see clearly—viz., that the 'age of Pericles' is fitly so called. Even in his slight sketch, a central and commanding figure is brought before us. And it is significant that the famous Funeral Oration sums up all that Thucydides tells us as to the life of Periclean Athens. It is as if he felt that his own silence on that subject should be broken by no voice save that of Pericles.

Thus it comes to pass that, in regard to the age of Pericles, we have to rely mainly on two sources of information. On the one hand, we have the surviving monuments of its literature, and some fragments of its art. On the other hand, we have that description of its general tone and spirit which Thucydides has embodied in the Funeral Oration. But this description is only in general terms. To those who heard it, of course, its abstract statements were full of vivid meaning, suggesting a thousand familiar details of their daily life. We moderns, however, have to reconstruct that life as best we may, by piecing together scattered bits of evidence. The questions for us are: What were the aims which Pericles set before him? By what means did he succeed in so impressing his own ideas upon his age that the period has ever since been distinctively associated with his name? And what was it in the civic life thus developed which made its atmosphere so incomparably favorable to the creative energies of the intellect? We cannot hope to answer these questions fully; but it is possible to suggest some considerations which may assist clearness of thought in regard to them.

First of all, we must remember the idea which lay at the root of Greek education generally in the period before the Persian wars. That idea was a free cultivation of the mental and bodily powers, not limited or specialized by a view to any particular occupation in after life. The main instruments of mental cultivation were poetry and music, both of them in a close connection with the traditional popular religion. The instruments of physical training were the exercises of the palaestra. When the youth had become a man, his mental education was tested in public counsel and speech, his physical training in military service for the State. This harmonious education of mind and body on certain prescribed lines created a general Hellenic tradition, which was constantly confirmed by the influence of the festivals, with their recitations of poetry and their athletic contests. Hellenes, to whatever part of Hellas they belonged, felt themselves united by a common descent, a common religion, a common language, and a common type of social life. The first two of these ties—descent and religion—were, for a Greek, interdependent; for Greeks conceived themselves as sprung from heroes, and these heroes as sprung from the gods; thus, in Mr. Grote's phrase, the ideas of ancestry and worship coalesced. It was only about a century before the Persian wars that this primitive Hellenic tone of mind began to be troubled by the new scepticism which had its birth in Ionia. The Ionian thinkers, in their attempts to solve the problem of the universe, gave the first shock to the old uncritical acceptance of the popular theology. People began to ask whether gods could do such things as they were said to do; whether these gods were more than symbols or fictions. Athens does not seem to have been much affected by Ionian philosophy before the Persian wars; though, in that earlier time, the social life of Athens was externally more Ionian than it afterwards became. And the effect of the Persian wars on Athens was, in one way, such as to confirm Athenian adherence to traditional modes of thought. Those wars had brought the sturdy Attic husbandmen to the front—the men in whom the old Attic beliefs were strongest; while at the same time Athenians had become conscious of their superiority to the Ionians, the vassals of Xerxes, whom they had routed at Salamis. A feeling was thus generated strongly antagonistic to innovation, especially when it appeared irreligious, and when it came from Ionia. This, however, was not the only effect which the Persian wars left behind them. In those struggles, the Athenian powers of mind and body had been strained to the uttermost. When the effort was over, the sense of stimulated activities remained; it was no longer easy to acquiesce in the routine of ancestral usage; there was a desire for an enlargement of the mental horizon, an eagerness to enter new fields of endeavor, corresponding to the new consciousness of power. Thus, especially in minds of the higher order, a welcome was prepared for intellectual novelties. It is significant that the Ionian Anaxagoras, the foremost speculative thinker of the time, chose Athens as the most congenial abode that he could find. We note also how eagerly Athens received from Sicily the new art of rhetoric, and from Ionia the practical culture brought by the so-called Sophists.

This sympathy with innovation, and on the other hand a newly reinforced conservatism, were the forces which divided Athens at the moment when Pericles entered public life. His father, Xanthippus, belonged to the old nobility of Attica, the Eupatridae. His mother, Agaristè, was a member of a family who belonged to the younger nobility, the Alcmaeonidae, and had latterly been identified with the popular party; Agaristè was a niece of the great reformer Clisthenes. Thus, while the maternal descent of Pericles would recommend him to the party of progress, his lineage on the father's side was a claim to the respect of their opponents. In his character, from youth onwards, one of the strongest traits seems to have been an unceasing desire of knowledge; he sought knowledge, however, not as Goethe did—to whom, in some aspects, he might be compared—with a view merely to satisfying his own intellectual needs, but rather from the point of view of a statesman—in order to strengthen the mental powers by which he aspired to guide the course of the city. Another quality which distinguished him was self-restraint. In pursuing his aims, he showed the highest degree of patience, moderation, and self-denial. The natural fire of his temperament, which flashed out at times in his oratory, was perfectly under the control of his judgment. His career may be divided into two parts. During the first, down to 444 B. C., Pericles appears as a party man—as the leader of the reformers. From 444 B. C. to his death in 429 B. C. he occupies a position raised above party, and has the government of Athens virtually concentrated in his hands. Let us consider the nature of the reforms with which he was associated, or which he initiated, during the earlier part of his career. First of all, the Council of the Areopagus was deprived of certain general powers which rendered it a stronghold of the party opposed to change. Next, it was provided that the State should make a small payment to every citizen for each day on which he served as a juror in the law-courts, or attended the meetings of the public assembly; also, that the State should supply to every citizen who required it the sum needful to procure his admission to the theatre at the public festivals. In modern eyes these measures may not seem very important. But in reality they constituted a revolution of the most momentous kind. In order to see this, we have only to recall a broad difference between the ancient and modern conceptions of the State. A British citizen does not feel himself the less so if he happens to have no direct share in the central conduct of public affairs. When he speaks of the State in its active capacity, he commonly means the Executive Power. He may fully recognize that he ought to live, and, if need be, die, for his country; but, unless he is a person of exceptional temperament, the thought of the State as a parent thus entitled to his devotion is not habitually present to him in everyday life; it is in a colder and more prosaic aspect that the State is chiefly familiar to his thoughts—viz., as an institution to which he owes certain duties, and from which he receives certain rights. But in the theory of the ancient Greek State, the citizen's whole life was most intimately identified with the life of the city. The city was a larger family, to which every member was bound by a supreme obligation, overriding all private considerations of every kind. Further, a citizen was not regarded as enjoying full citizenship unless he had a direct personal share in public affairs—either continuously, or at least in his turn. No such thing as representative government was known; the civic assembly was open to all citizens, and a citizen could use his franchise only by speaking or voting in person. Such was the theory; in practice, however, it was modified in various ways by various circumstances. If we look back to the earlier days of Greece, before the age of Pericles, we perceive the prevalence of a feeling which tended practically to disfranchise many of those who, by birth, were citizens—a feeling, namely, that the possession of independent means, up to a certain point, should be a qualification for taking part in public life.

At Athens, in the time of the Periclean reforms, there does not seem to have been much civic pauperism. A hundred and fifty years or so before, Solon's great agrarian reform had taken a load of debt off the cultivators of the soil, and had done much to limit the size of landed estates. In the days of Pericles probably more than one-half of the Attic citizen-body were owners of land. It was a law that every Athenian citizen should bring up his son to some calling or trade by which he could subsist. With its harbors and its fleet, Athens had unrivaled opportunities for commerce. But Pericles saw that, if the encouragement of industry and commerce was truly to strengthen the city, the artisan and the merchant must feel that they were in deed, and not merely in name, citizens. The unity of the State must be realized as far as possible according to the Greek idea; that is, every citizen must have some personal share in public business. Here, however, a grave difficulty encountered him. A poor citizen could not be expected to serve as a juror in the law-courts, or to attend the public assembly, if such public duties were to suspend the pursuit of his private calling. This difficulty was met by the proposal of Pericles to pay the citizen for the time which he gave to the State. The payment was extremely small; at first it was one obol, a little more than 1½d. for each day in the law-courts or in the assembly; it was afterwards raised to about 4½d. At this time the average day's wage of an Athenian artisan was about ninepence. The public assembly met, as a rule, only four times a month. The jury-courts

sat almost every day. Every year 5000 citizens, with a further
reserve of 1000, were chosen by lot, as the body from which the
juries for that year should be drawn; and a man who was in that
body could do but little work at his trade during that year. Thus,
notwithstanding the small payment from the State, he was serving the State at a sacrifice. Neither in that case, nor in regard
to the public assembly, was he under any temptation to abandon his
trade, and to live on the State bounty. Pericles had foreseen that
danger, and had guarded against it by the scale of payment. A
century later, the public pay had become a mischief; but that mischief was rather the result than the cause of social disorganization.
Now, then, we can understand the full significance of the words
which Thucydides puts into the mouth of Pericles. 'An Athenian
citizen,' he says, 'does not neglect the State because he takes care
of his own household; and even those who are engaged in business
(ἔργα) can form a very fair idea of politics. We regard a man
who takes no interest in public affairs as a useless man; and if few
of us are originators of a policy, we are all sound judges of it.'[2]
Not less essential to the statesman's purpose was the measure which
ensured the presence of the poorer citizens at the public festivals,
when tragedy or comedy was performed in the theatre of Dionysus.
This theatre-money has rightly been compared to modern grants
in aid of education, or to the remission of school-fees. At these
festivals, which were religious ceremonies animated by the noblest
poetry, the citizen felt himself a sharer in the best spiritual inheritance of the city. The Thucydidean Pericles alludes to this when
he says: 'We have provided for a weary mind many relaxations
from toil, in the festivals and sacrifices which we hold throughout
the year.'[3] If we are inclined to be surprised at the extreme
smallness of the State-payments above noticed, and to ask how
they could make any appreciable difference, we must remember
three things: first, that the purchasing power of money was immensely greater then than it is now; next, that ancient civilization rested on a basis of slavery, without which the full development of the Attic democracy would have been impossible; lastly,
we must remember the genuine frugality and simplicity of Athenian life—greatly favored, as it was, by a happy climate—the simplicity to which Pericles refers when he says: 'We are lovers of the
beautiful, yet simple in our tastes, and we cultivate the mind without loss of manliness.' In the same Funeral Oration, indeed, Peri-

[2] Thucydides 2. 40.
[3] *Ibid.* 2.38.

cles speaks of the beautiful objects which surrounded Athenians in their private houses—objects of which the daily delight, as he says, banishes gloom; but it would be an error to imagine that these words could apply only to the homes of the richer citizens; nothing was more characteristic of Greek art than the skill with which it gave lovely forms to the cheapest and homeliest articles of daily use.

The great work, then, which Pericles achieved during his period of political struggle might be briefly characterized as follows. He realized the essential idea of the Greek city more fully than it had ever been realized before, or was ever realized after; and he did this by enabling every citizen, poor no less than rich, to feel that he was a citizen indeed, taking his part in the work of the city without undue sacrifice of his private interests, and sharing in the noblest enjoyments which the city had to offer.

The second part of the career of Pericles dates from the banishment of Thucydides, son of Melesias, in 444 B. C. That event marked the final triumph of the reformers, and left Pericles without even the semblance of a political rival. The contemporary historian describes the position of affairs by saying that Athens was now nominally governed by a democracy, but really by her foremost citizen. The position of Pericles was now, in fact, such as would be that of an immensely popular Prime Minister who not only commanded an overwhelming majority in Parliament, but who could look forward to a tenure of power limited only by his own vitality. The recent defeat of the party opposed to Pericles was only one of the facts which help to explain this unique ascendancy. It is certain that he must have possessed one of the greatest and most versatile intellects ever given to man. On no other hypothesis can we explain the extraordinary impression which he made on the ablest of his contemporaries, and the unequaled reputation which he left behind him. Then his moral qualities were not only great in themselves, but peculiarly fitted to impress his countrymen. He was, as Thucydides says with emphasis, of stainless personal integrity. His private life was entirely free from ostentation. He was rarely seen at public festivals; indeed, he was seldom seen at all, except at his public work, or on his way to it. He was compared by contemporary wits to the 'Salaminia'—a ship, employed in State service, which appeared only on great occasions. He gave no opening to the jealousy of fellow-citizens, and at the same time never risked his hold on their respect—acting in the spirit of Henry the Fourth's advice to his son:

Had I so lavish of my presence been,
So common-hackneyed in the eyes of men,
So stale and cheap to vulgar company,
Opinion, that did help me to the crown,
Had still kept loyal to possession.[4]

In manner, we are told, he was grave and reserved; his public speaking was marked by a studious terseness, which, however, did not prevent him from rising, when strongly moved, into majestic eloquence, adorned by bold and striking imagery, of which a few examples remain. His quick-witted and excitable fellow-citizens were held in awe by the massive mind which they felt under his grave calm—a calm which sometimes gave place to the rushing impulse of great thoughts, but never to irritation, even when the provocation was sorest. Hegel says of him: 'To be the first man in the State, among this noble, free, and cultivated people of Athens, was the good fortune of Pericles. Of all that is great for humanity, the greatest thing is to dominate the wills of men who have wills of their own.'

At the time when Pericles became thus virtually supreme, Athens had reached a position wholly different from that which she had held before the Persian wars. Then, she was merely the chief town of Attica, a small district, of little natural wealth. But in the course of the last thirty years she had become an imperial city, the head of a great confederacy which embraced the islands and coasts of the Aegean Sea. The common treasury of the league had been removed from the Island of Delos to Athens, and located in the temple of Athena on the Acropolis. This transfer—a bold step which Pericles had strongly advocated—was a formal recognition of Athens as the capital of a wide empire. Almost all the cities which had originally been her free allies had now become her subjects; year by year their tribute flowed to the temple on her citadel. And these revenues were administered by Athenian officials, subject to the authority of Athens. The revenues proper to Athens herself had been greatly enlarged by the development of the silver mines of Laurium in Attica, and by the acquisition of gold mines in Thrace. Thus the organization of finance had assumed a new political importance. It should be noticed that the idea of a public treasure—a permanent store on which the State could draw in emergencies—had not hitherto been fully worked out in a Greek democracy. The economical basis of the old Greek commonwealth

[4] [Shakespeare, *1 Henry IV* 3. 2. 39-43.—EDITOR.]

was different from that to which we are accustomed. The Greek city was, in this aspect, more like a corporation possessing property, and paying its current expenses out of that property. The Greek citizens were like joint administrators of a trust fund, for the common benefit. To take a modern illustration on a small scale, we might compare them to the Fellows of a College, in whom is vested the administration of the College property. The Greek city depended very little on direct taxation of the citizen. Hence it had small opportunities of forming a public reserve fund of any magnitude. That would have had to be done mainly out of its annual income, and at the cost of retrenchments which would not have been generally popular. Of course, where a despot had contrived to obtain the supreme power in a Greek city, he could exact from his subjects the means wherewith to form a public treasure. Pisistratus did so, when he was despot of Athens; so also did the Sicilian despots, and many more. Thus, a power based on money had hitherto in Greece been characteristic of a tyranny, not of a free commonwealth. But Pericles saw that the imperial position of Athens, and the naval power on which her empire rested, could be secured only by creating a public reserve fund on an adequate scale. And since the tribute paid by the subject allies was now at the absolute disposal of Athens; since, further, in any emergencies that might arise, the interests of Athens would be identified with those of her dependents; it was now comparatively easy for a statesman to effect this object. He was further assisted by the peculiar relation which existed between public finance and religion. The temples were the public banks of ancient Greece; the safest places of deposit. Under the provisions made by Pericles, the public funds lodged in the temple of Athena on the citadel were of three kinds. First, the fund designed to meet the current expenses of the State, which were consigned merely to the temporary guardianship of the goddess. Secondly, there were moneys which were formally consecrated to Athena, and which were made her own property. These could not be touched, except by way of loan from the goddess, and under a strict obligation to repay her; to take them in any other way would have been sacrilege. Thirdly, there were certain definite sums, also consecrated to her, which could not even be borrowed from her, except in certain specified cases of extreme need— as if, for example, a hostile fleet threatened the Piraeus. The care of these funds, and the administration of all the other sources of Athenian revenue, were organized under Pericles on a complete and elaborate system. Thus it was his merit to secure for a free

State that financial stability which had elsewhere been only a pillar of despotism. We see an immediate result of this in the simple fact that the Peloponnesian war lasted twenty-seven years. Without the treasure on the Acropolis, the naval resources of Athens must have collapsed in a very much shorter time.

I can but touch briefly on the part which colonization played in the policy of Pericles. His principle was to avoid enlarging the empire, but to bind the existing empire together as strongly as possible. When cities which had revolted against Athens had been subdued, their territory was in some cases confiscated by Athens. Such land was then divided into a certain number of allotments. Athenian citizens of the poorer class, who wished for allotments, were then asked to send in their names, and the holdings were assigned by ballot. A successful applicant could do either of two things. He could go out and farm the land himself; in which case the State helped him with his outfit. Or he could stay at Athens, and make the former owner of the foreign land his tenant. In either case he retained his full rights as an Athenian citizen; whereas in an ordinary colony the Athenian emigrant became a citizen of the new settlement. Moreover, the ownership of the allotment was hereditary.

All things naturally conspired at this period to make Athens the great Hellenic centre of industry and of commerce. The Piraeus, the harbor town of Athens, with its magnificent port, was the market to which all commodities flowed from East and West. From the Euxine came cargoes of fish or of hides; papyrus came from Egypt, frankincense from Syria, dates from Phoenicia, ores from Cyprus, silphium from Cyrene; Thrace sent timber; Sicily and the Aegean islands sent their fruits, wines, and other luxuries. Athens itself had a special repute for earthenware, for some kinds of metal work, and for work in leather. It is not surprising, then, that Athens began to suffer from an inconvenience which at the present day is felt on a greater scale in the United States—viz., the influx of aliens, anxious to share in the advantages of citizenship. Pericles checked this evil by reviving the old rule, which had long fallen into disuse, viz., that full citizenship could be enjoyed only by a person, both of whose parents were of Attic birth. A reinforcement of this rule, though unpopular at first, was made comparatively easy by the favorable conditions granted to aliens who wished to fix their abode at Athens.

Thus far we have been considering Periclean Athens chiefly as the most perfect example of Greek civic life; as an imperial city,

in which the fullest individual freedom was enjoyed without prejudice to the strength of the State; as a great seat of industry and
a focus of commerce. The memorials of all these things have well-
nigh vanished; but the modern world still possesses monuments of
the literature, and at least fragments of the art, which proclaim
Athens to have been, above all, the great intellectual centre of that
age. The influence of Periclean Athens is deeply impressed on the
History of Herodotus, and moulded the still greater work of
Thucydides; Athens was the home of the philosopher Anaxagoras,
and the astronomer Meton; it was at Athens that prose composition, which had hitherto been either colloquial or poetical, was first
matured; at Athens, too, oratory first became the effective ally of
statesmanship; both tragedy and comedy were perfected; the
frescoes of Polygnotus, the architecture of Ictinus, the sculpture of
Phidias, combined to adorn the city; and when we think of these
great writers and artists, we must remember that they are only
some of the more eminent out of a larger number who were all
living at Athens within the same period of thirty years. How far
can this wonderful fact be directly connected with the influence
of the political work done by Pericles, or with the personal influence of the man? We must beware of exaggerating such influences.
Statesmanship may encourage men of genius, but it cannot make
them. When we look back on that age, we seem to recognize in
its abounding and versatile brilliancy rather the golden time of a
marvelously gifted race, than merely the attraction which a city
of unique opportunities exercised over the rest of the world. The
great national victory over Persia had raised the vital energy of
the Greek spirit to the highest. But we must also recollect that,
owing to the very nature of Greek literature and art, such a city
as the Athens of Pericles could do more for it than any modern
city could do for modern art or literature. Greek literature was
essentially spontaneous, the free voice of life, restrained in its
freedom only by a sense of measure which was part of the Greek
nature; the Greek poet, or historian, or philosopher, was not merely
a man of letters in the narrower modern meaning of the term; he
was first, and before all things, a citizen, in close sympathy, usually
in active contact, with the public life of the city. For a Greek,
therefore, as poet or historian or philosopher, nothing could be
more directly important than that this public life should be as
noble as possible; since, the nobler it was, the higher and the more
invigorating was the source from which he drew his inspiration.
Among the great literary men who belonged to the age of Pericles,

there are especially two who may be regarded as representative of it—its chief historian and its most characteristic poet—Thucydides and Sophocles. The mind of Thucydides had been moulded by the ideas of Pericles, and probably in large measure by personal intercourse with him. We recognize the Periclean stamp in the clearness with which Thucydides perceives that the vital thing for a state is the spirit in which it is governed; and that, apart from this spirit, there is no certain efficacy in the form of a constitution, no sovereign spell in the name. In Sophocles, again, we feel the Periclean influence working with the same general tendency as in the plastic arts; he holds with the ancient traditions of piety, but invests them with a more spiritual and more intellectual meaning. With regard to the fine arts, it was the resolve of Pericles that they should find their supreme and concentrated manifestation in the embellishment of Athens. Thucydides, with all his reticence as to art, is doubtless a faithful interpreter of the spirit in which that work was done, when he makes Pericles speak of the abiding monuments which will attest to all posterity the achievements of that age. This feeling was not prompted merely by Athenian patriotism; Athens was the city which the Persian invader, bent on avenging Sardis, had twice laid in ruins. The fact that Athens should have risen from its ashes in unrivaled strength and grace was, as Pericles might well feel, the most impressive of all testimonies to the victory of Hellene over barbarian.

When Pericles reached his full power the port of Athens was already a handsome town, with regular streets, spacious porticoes, large open spaces and perfectly equipped harbors. But the Upper City—Athens proper,—with which the Piraeus was connected by the long walls, remained comparatively poor in ornament. It still showed some traces of the haste with which it had been rebuilt after the Persian wars. Now, under the guiding influence of Pericles, architects, sculptors, and painters combined in adorning it. That which gave its distinctive stamp to their work was, ultimately, the great idea which animated them. Its inspiration was the idea of the imperial city, Athens, as represented and defended by the goddess Athena; the Athens which, with the aid of gods and heroes, had borne the foremost part in rolling back the tide of barbarian invasion.

In no other instance which history records, has art of a supreme excellence sprung from a motive at once so intelligible to the whole people, and so satisfying to the highest order of minds.

It is well to remember that the story of Greece was not closed when the Greek genius reached the brief term of its creative activity. It is well to follow the work of the Greek mind through later periods also; but those qualities which were distinctive of its greatness can best be studied when the Greek mind was at its best. That period was unquestionably the Fifth Century before Christ— the Age of Pericles.

VII

THE ATTIC AUDIENCE [1]

By Arthur Elam Haigh

Another point which was required from ancient actors was great distinctness in the articulation of the separate words, and a careful observance of the rhythm and metre of the verses. In this respect the Athenians were a most exacting audience. Cicero speaks of their 'refined and scrupulous ear,' their 'sound and uncorrupted taste.' Ancient audiences in general had a much keener ear for the melody of verse than is to be found in a modern theatre. A slovenly recitation of poetry, and a failure to emphasize the metre, would not have been tolerated by them. Cicero remarks on the fact that, though the mass of the people knew nothing about the theory of versification, their instinctive feeling for rhythmical utterance was wonderfully keen. He says that if an actor should spoil the metre in the slightest degree, by making a mistake about a quantity, or by dropping or inserting a syllable, there would be a storm of disapproval from the audience.[2] No such sensitiveness is to be

[1 These three passages are taken from *The Attic Theatre* (pp. 275-276; 323-325; 343-348) by A. E. Haigh. Third edition, revised and in part rewritten by A. W. Pickard-Cambridge, Oxford, 1907. They are reprinted with the consent of the Delegates of the Clarendon Press, grateful acknowledgment being made also to the family of the late author. The footnotes of Haigh have been omitted as of no immediate value here.—Editor.]

[2 Compare what Milton says of the relation between the habit of utterance and the national character (letter to Bonmattei, quoted by Lord Morley, *Studies in Literature*, pp. 223-224): 'Whoever in a state knows how wisely to form the manners of men, and to rule them at home and in war with excellent institutes, him in the first place, above others, I should esteem worthy of all honor. But next to him the man who strives to establish in maxims and rules the method and habit of speaking and writing received from a good age of the nation, and, as it were, to fortify the same round with a kind of wall, the daring to overleap which let a law only short of that of Romulus be used to prevent. . . . The one, as I believe, supplies noble courage and intrepid counsels against an enemy invading the territory. The other takes to himself the task of extirpating and defeating, by means of a learned detective police found in modern theatres. It is common enough at the present day to hear blank verse declaimed as if it were prose. But among the ancient Greeks the feeling for correctness of rhythm in poetical recitations was just as instinctive as is the feeling for correctness of tune among ordinary musical audiences at the present time. If an actor in a Greek theatre made a slip in the metre of his verses, it was regarded in much the same way as a note out of tune would be regarded in a modern concert-room. . . .

[The theatre of Dionysus at Athens, during the period of the Lenaea and the City Dionysia, presented a spectacle which for interest and significance has few parallels in the ancient or the modern world.] The city kept universal holiday. The various proceedings were in reality so many religious celebrations. But there was nothing of an austere character about the worship of Dionysus. To give freedom from care was his special attribute, and the sincerest mode of paying homage to his power was by a genial enjoyment of the various pleasures of life. At this time of universal merriment the dramatic performances formed the principal attraction. Each day soon after sunrise the great majority of the citizens made their way to the southern slopes of the Acropolis, where the theatre of Dionysus was situated. The tiers of seats rising up the side of the hill were speedily filled with a crowd of nearly twenty thousand persons. The sight of such a vast multitude of people, gathered together at daybreak in the huge open amphitheatre, and dressed for the most part in white, or in red, brown, yellow, and other rich colors, must have been exceedingly striking and picturesque. The performances which brought them together were not unworthy of the occasion. The plays exhibited at the festivals of Dionysus rank among the very noblest achievements of Greek genius. For beauty of form, depth of meaning, and poetical inspiration they have never been surpassed. It would be difficult to

of ears, and a light band of good authors, that barbarism which makes large inroads upon the minds of men, and is a destructive intestine enemy of genius. Nor is it to be considered of small consequence what language, pure or corrupt, a people has, or what is their customary degree of propriety in speaking it. . . . For, let the words of a country be in part unhandsome and offensive in themselves, in part debased by wear and wrongly uttered; and what do they declare but, by no light indication, that the inhabitants of that country are an indolent, idly-yawning race, with minds already long prepared for any amount of servility? On the other hand, we have never heard that any empire, any state, did not at least flourish in a middling degree as long as its own liking and care for its language lasted.'—EDITOR.]

point to any similar example of the whole population of a city meeting together each year to enjoy works of the highest artistic beauty.
It is seldom that art and poetry have penetrated so deeply into the
life of the ordinary citizens. Our curiosity is naturally excited in
regard to the tone and composition of the audiences before which a
drama of such an exceptional character was exhibited. . . .

At the Lenaea, which was held in the winter, when traveling was
difficult, the audience consisted almost exclusively of natives of
Athens. The City Dionysia came about two months later, at the
commencement of the spring, and attracted great crowds of
strangers from various parts of Greece. Representatives from the
allied states came to pay the annual tribute at this season of the
year. It was also a favorite time for the arrival of ambassadors
from foreign cities; and it was considered a mere matter of politeness to provide them with front seats in the theatre, if they happened to be in Athens during the celebration of the City Dionysia.
In addition to these visitors of a representative character, there
were also great numbers of private individuals, attracted to Athens
from all parts of Greece by the magnificence of the festival, and the
fame of the dramatic exhibitions. Altogether the visitors formed
a considerable portion of the audience at the City Dionysia. One
of the great aggravations of the offense of Midias was that his
assault upon Demosthenes was committed in the presence of 'large
multitudes of strangers.' Apparently the natives of foreign states
were not allowed to purchase tickets for the theatre in their own
name, but had to get them through an Athenian citizen.

The composition of the purely Athenian part of the audience is
a subject upon which a great deal has been written, the principal
difficulty being the question as to the admittance of boys and women
to the dramatic performances. In the treatment of this matter
scholars appear to have been unduly biased by a preconceived
opinion as to what was right and proper. Undoubtedly Athenian
women were kept in a state of almost Oriental seclusion. And the
old Attic comedy was pervaded by a coarseness which seems to make
it utterly unfit for boys and women. For these reasons some writers have gone so far as to assert that they were never present at
any dramatic performances whatsoever. Others, while not excluding them from tragedy, have declared that it was an impossibility
that they should have been present at the performances of comedy.
But the attempt to draw a distinction between tragedy and comedy,
in regard to the admission of boys and women to the theatre, will

not bear examination. If they were present at one, they must have
been present at both. The tragic and the comic competitions frequently took place upon the same days, and succeeded one another
without any interval; and it is difficult to suppose that, after the
tragedies were over, a large part of the audience had to be turned
out before the comedies could begin. Moreover, if women and boys
had been present at the tragedies, they would of necessity have been
spectators of the satyric dramas, which were nearly as coarse as
the comedies. It is useless therefore to endeavor to separate tragedy
from comedy in the consideration of this question.

As a matter of fact, the evidence upon the subject, if considered
without prejudice, makes it practically certain that there were no
restrictions of the kind suggested. The audience at the dramatic
performances, whether tragic or comic, was drawn from every class
of the population. Men, women, boys, and slaves were all allowed
to be present. The evidence from ancient authors is too copious to
be accounted for on any other supposition. . . .[3]

The Athenians were a lively audience, and gave expression to
their feelings in the most unmistakable manner. The noise and
uproar produced by an excited crowd of twenty thousand persons
must have been of a deafening character, and is described in the
most uncomplimentary language by Plato. It was exceedingly difficult for the judges to resist such demonstrations, and to vote in
accordance with their own private judgment. The ordinary modes
of signifying pleasure or disgust were much the same in ancient as
in modern times, and consisted of hisses and groans on the one hand,
and shouts and clapping of hands on the other. The Athenians had
also a peculiar way of marking their disapproval of a performance
by kicking with the heels of their sandals against the front of the
stone benches on which they were sitting. Stones were occasionally
thrown by an irate audience. Aeschines was hissed off the stage,
and 'almost stoned to death,' in the course of his theatrical career.
There is an allusion to the practice in the story of the second-rate
musician, who borrowed a supply of stone from a friend in order
to build a house, and promised to repay him with the stones he
collected from his next performance in public. Country audiences
in the Attic demes used figs and olives, and similar missiles, for
pelting unpopular actors. On the other hand, encores were not

[3 B. B. Rogers forcibly argues against the assumption that women attended
performances of the Old Comedy. See his edition of the *Ecclesiazusae* of Aristophanes, Introd., pp. xxix-xxxv.—EDITOR.]

unknown, if particular passages took the fancy of the audience. Socrates is said to have encored the first three lines of the *Orestes* of Euripides.

If the Athenians were dissatisfied with an actor or a play, they had no hesitation about revealing the fact, but promptly put a stop to the performance by means of hisses and groans and stamping with the heels. They were able to do so with greater readiness, as several plays were always performed in succession, and they could call for the next play, without bringing the entertainment to a close. In this way they sometimes got through the program very rapidly. There is an instance of such an occurrence in the story of the comic actor Hermon, whose play should naturally have come on late in the day; but, as all the previous performers were promptly hissed off the stage, one after another, he was called upon much sooner than he expected, and in consequence was not ready to appear. If the tale about the comic poet Diphilus is true, it would seem that even the authors of very unsuccessful plays were sometimes forcibly ejected from the theatre.

A few scattered notices and descriptions, referring to the spectators in the Athenian theatre, show that human nature was very much the same in ancient times as at the present day. Certain types of character, which were generally to be met with among an Attic audience, will easily be recognized as familiar figures. There was the man of taste, who prided himself upon his superior discernment, and used to hiss when every one else was applauding, and clap when every one else was silent. There was the person who made himself objectionable to his neighbors by whistling an accompaniment to tunes which happened to please him. There were the 'young men of the town,' who took a malign pleasure in hissing a play off the stage. There were the people who brought out their provisions during the less exciting parts of the entertainment. There was the somnolent individual who slept peacefully through tragedies and comedies, and was not even waked up by the noise of the audience going away. Certain indications show that the employment of the clâque was not unknown to Greek actors and poets. The parasite Philaporus, who had recently taken up the profession of an actor, and was anxious about the result of his first public appearance, writes to a friend to ask him to come with a large body of supporters, and drown with their applause the hisses of the critical part of the audience. Philemon, in spite of his inferior talents as a comic writer, is said to have frequently won victories from Menander by practices of this kind.

The character of the Athenian audience as a whole is well exemplified by the stories of their treatment of individual poets. Although they were willing to tolerate the utmost ribaldry upon the stage, and to allow the gods and sacred legends to be burlesqued in the most ridiculous fashion, they were at the same time extremely orthodox in regard to the national religion. ⌊Any atheistical sentiments, and any violations of their religious law, were liable to provoke an outburst of the greatest violence.⌋ Aeschylus on one occasion was nearly killed in the theatre itself, because he was supposed to have revealed part of the mysteries in the course of a tragedy. He was only saved by flying for refuge to the altar of Dionysus in the orchestra. Euripides also caused a great uproar by beginning his *Melanippe* with the line: 'Zeus, whoever Zeus be, for I know not save by report,' etc. In a subsequent production of a revised version of the play he altered the line to: 'Zeus, as is reported by truth,' etc. In the same way sentiments which violated the moral feeling of the audience were received with intense indignation, and sometimes resulted in the stoppage of the play. The *Danaë* of Euripides is said to have been nearly hissed off the stage because of a passage in praise of money. On the other hand, wise and noble sentiments excited great enthusiasm. Aristophanes was rewarded with a chaplet from the sacred olive because of the splendid passage in which he counsels mercy to the disfranchised citizens. ⌈Sophocles is said to have been appointed one of the generals in the Samian expedition on account of the excellent political wisdom shown in certain passages of the *Antigone*.⌋ The partiality of the Athenians for idealism in art is shown by the reception which they gave to Phrynichus' tragedy of the *Capture of Miletus,* an historical drama in which the misfortunes of the Ionians were forcibly portrayed. So far from admiring the skill of the poet, they fined him a thousand drachmas for reminding them of the miseries of their kinsfolk, and passed a law forbidding the reproduction of this particular play.

The enthusiasm of the Athenians for the drama was unbounded. Nowhere was the theatre more crowded. In the words of one of the old historians, they 'spent the public revenues on their festivals, were more familiar with the stage than with the camp, and paid more regard to verse-makers than to generals.' The speeches of Demosthenes are full of complaints in the same strain. The eagerness with which dramatic victories were coveted, and the elaborate monuments erected to commemorate them, have already been referred to. . . . It was not, however, till the middle of the fourth

century that the devotion to this and similar amusements grew to
such a height as to become a positive vice, and to sap the military
energies of the people. The Athenians of the fifth century showed
that enthusiasm for art and music and the drama was not inconsistent with energy of character. As a matter of fact, the very
greatest period of the Attic drama is also the period of the political
supremacy of Athens.

As far as intelligence and discrimination are concerned, the
Athenian audiences were probably superior to any audience of the
same size which has ever been brought together. Their keen and
rapid intellect was a subject of frequent praise among the ancients,
and was ascribed to the exhilarating influence of the Attic climate.
They were especially distinguished for the refinement of their taste
in matters of art and literature, and for the soberness of judgment with which they rejected any sort of florid exuberance. That
they were keenly alive to the attractions of beauty of form and
chastened simplicity of style is proved by the fact that Sophocles
was by far the most successful of their tragic poets. Though Euripides became more popular among the later Greeks, Sophocles in
his own lifetime obtained far more victories than any other tragic
writer. At the same time, it is easy to form an exaggerated idea
of the refinement of an Attic audience. They were drawn from all
classes of the people, and a large proportion were ignorant and un-
cultured. Plato speaks in the most disparaging terms of them, and
charges them with having corrupted the dramatic poets, and
brought them down to their own level. His evidence is perhaps
rather prejudiced. But Aristotle, who had much greater faith in
popular judgment, is not very complimentary. He divides the
theatrical audience into two classes, the refined and cultured class
on the one hand, and the mass of rough and ignorant artisans on
the other. One of his objections to the profession of an actor or
musician is that he must accommodate himself to the level of the
ignorant part of his audience. He mentions examples in the *Poetics*
of the low level of popular taste, from which it appears that the
average spectator in ancient times was, like his modern counterpart,
fond of 'happy terminations.' He cared little for the artistic
requirements of the composition; his desire was to see virtue rewarded, and vice punished, at the end of a play. Then again, a
large part of the audience, Aristotle remarks, were so ignorant as
to be unacquainted with the ordinary facts of mythology, which
formed the basis of most tragedies. In judging a play, they paid

more regard to the actor's voice than to the poet's genius. At the same time, in spite of depreciatory criticisms, it must be remembered that the true criterion of a people's taste is to be found in the character of the popular favorites. The victorious career of Sophocles, lasting over more than fifty years, is a convincing proof of the fact that, at any rate during the fifth century, the dramatic taste of the Athenians was altogether higher than that of an ordinary popular audience.

VIII

THE GREEK RACE AND ITS GENIUS [1]

By Maurice Croiset

If we wish to trace the intellectual and moral evolution of a people in the history of its literature, it would seem indispensable to determine first of all, as precisely as may be, its original point of departure. What was the people, before it so much as had a literature? What elemental and distinctive qualities did it possess within itself during those times of ignorance and childlike simplicity, when, from afar, and unconsciously, it was preparing for its great achievements to come? To what degree of perfection had these qualities advanced when it saw fit to turn them to account in its first poetical productions?

These questions naturally suggest themselves to us. But with respect to Greece we lack the documents that would give us satisfactory answers. Before there was a nation that could properly be called Hellenic, the ethnic elements which were one day to constitute it had each a separate existence; then, by a series of combinations which still remain obscure, they were gathered into groups, or superimposed one upon another. Even the names of these primitive stocks are imperfectly known to us; and, in spite of the daily disclosures of archaeology, the glimpses we catch of the state of their morals and the characteristics of their civilization amount to very little. We discern these pre-Hellenic races of Asia Minor and the islands through a sort of haze; the Pelasgians scattered here and there, the Danai, and the Achaeans, whose name reappears on ancient Egyptian monuments. Their temples, their tombs, and their fortresses have been partially restored for us by the unceasing research of scholars. One may assemble and study the more or less rude products of the industry of these early people,

[1 This extract is translated from the *Histoire de la Littérature Grecque* (1. 1-19) of Alfred and Maurice Croiset (Paris, 1896); and the translation is published by an arrangement with Fontemoing & Cie., of Paris. Of the admirable French work, in five volumes, it is hardly too much to say that, on the whole, it is the best history of any literature in any language.—Editor.]

and examine the objects that were for them works of art, in an attempt to discover some indication of their taste, of their mental culture, and of the foreign influences they underwent. Such investigations are full of interest and of promise, but as yet they have been carried only a little way. Not until that day when science can demonstrate with certainty the order in which these races or these tribal groups followed each other, and can distinguish the peculiar characteristics of each of these prehistoric societies, will the history of Greek literature be in possession of its real starting-point. Then we shall be able to see the Greek genius come into being and grow, to enumerate the essential elements of which it is composed, and to comprehend what it owes to its remote origins, to foreign influences, to the mingling of races, and to its own vigor. It is thus that modern peoples are studied; let us hope that in a not distant future Greece may be known and described in the same way. For the present, an application of this method would be too conjectural. We should bewilder our readers with prolonged discussions, or involve them in pure hypothesis; and they would be little aided in their understanding of the subject we are about to consider with them.

Let us therefore defer these hopes, and content ourselves with briefly setting forth such things as are certain. Whatever the manner of its formation, we know that the Greek genius had taken shape before the birth of the *Iliad*. Let us try to represent it for ourselves here in its most essential and, consequently, most primitive features, and let us ignore the subsidiary traits, which revealed themselves only at certain times and under special conditions.

The first thing that strikes one in the Hellenic race is the variety of its talents. The old Roman, Juvenal, bitterly assailed, by the mouth of Umbricius, the versatility of the Greeks of the decadence who overran Rome, and deemed themselves fit for any occupation.[2] Though it must not be taken too seriously, this sally of a satirical poet in a fit of anger undeniably contains an element of truth. What the Roman ridiculed, so serious an observer as Thucydides admired in the Athenians of his day;[3] and in versatility, as in

2 Juvenal, *Satires* 3. 73 ff.:

> Ingenium velox, audacia perdita, sermo
> Promptus et Isaeo torrentior. Ede quid illum
> Esse putes; *quemvis hominem secum adtulit ad nos:*
> Grammaticus, rhetor, geometres, pictor, aliptes,
> Augur, schoenobates, medicus, magus: omnia novit
> Graeculus esuriens; in caelum, jusseris, ibit.

3 Thucydides 2. 41. 1.

many other qualities, the Athenians were the most Greek of all
Greeks. Aristotle, in his turn, pointed out that, generally considered, the Europeans, dwelling in the cold countries, had energy,
but were wanting in swift intelligence; the Asiatics, on the contrary, dwelling in the warm countries, had a swift intelligence, but
lacked energy; whereas the Greeks, thanks to their temperate
climate, combined energy of character with intelligence.[4] This
even development of diverse faculties brought about that happy
balance and harmony which mark the great literary as well as the
great artistic works of Greece. The Hellene always possessed judgment in imagination, intellect in sentiment, reflection in passion.
One never sees him entirely carried away in one direction. He has,
so to speak, a number of faculties ready for every undertaking,
and it is by a combination of these that he gives to his creations
their true character.

For the same reason, too, he is in contact, in a thousand ways at
once, with nature and with his fellows. Stolid and sluggish races,
at least in their beginnings and before they become educated, are
capable of only a limited number of unvarying impressions, which
give to their ideas a certain solidity. They think little, they
imagine little; their thoughts are firmly fixed, and their conceptions seem to be inflexible. The Greeks, an alert and active race,
are altogether different. Innumerable impressions are constantly
taking shape in their minds. Nature speaks to them an infinitely
varied language, always heard, and ever new. They are interested
not only in her great phenomena, but also in her changing aspects,
in the delicate and fleeting phases of her endless life. And this is
not the special privilege of the Ionian of Asia Minor, or of the
dweller in Attica; it is not even exclusively that of the seaboard
people, who combine the life of the fisherman or the merchant with
that of the husbandman. The Boeotian or Locrian laborer, as we see
him in the *Works and Days* of Hesiod—he who toils heavily in the
district of Ascra, 'cold in winter and scorching in summer'—even
he has impressions of astonishing vividness, and, as it were, a thousand visions so light and transparent that the gaiety or sadness of
the things shines through them. The cry of the birds of passage,
the strident note of the cicada, the blossoming of the thistle, all
these familiar little things touch him like the communications,
at once mysterious and clear, of so many neighboring spirits. And
this is the reason why all the Greeks everywhere peopled the earth
with gods who are neither mere names nor unknown powers, but

[4] Aristotle, *Politics* 7. 7.

living and almost familiar beings. And, in thus transforming
nature, they did no more than return to her what she had given
to them. The life of the external world had come to them full of
images and sensations; it departed again from them and reverted
to external objects, full of gods.

And if the spectacle of the world thus moved, enchanted, and
taught them, that of humanity did not profit them less. The Greek
is eminently sociable. He joyfully seeks out his fellow because he.
has much to give him and much to receive from him, and because
this exchange is one of his keenest pleasures. Hesiod, whom we are
fond of quoting as the earliest source of information on the life of
the people, bids the industrious peasant pass by the forge and the
lesché without stopping. It is there that people hold long conversa-
tions in winter, and he knows how strong is the temptation to
enter. He does not fear for his laborer gross allurements such as
wine and debauchery; he fears those which one might call delicate,
those of the spirit rather than the flesh. The Hellenic mind, in
general, is too open, too approachable from all sides, to shut itself
up in a dark and dominating passion; and hence comes that great
and precocious experience of life which is already obvious in the
most ancient epic poems. In them man shows himself full of contrasts, with unexpected shades of feeling and distinctions in ideas,
with reverses of passion which are wonderful; in them he conforms
to every rôle, and adapts himself to all situations; he is master or
subject, conquered or in revolt; he is father, husband, son, friend,
or enemy, each and all, not only with truth and propriety, but with
great variation. Never, perhaps, in any other people, has the play
of human faculties been so free, so ready, so wide in scope.

Without doubt it is to this that we must attribute one of the
most remarkable qualities of the Greeks, the lively and inexhaustible
curiosity which manifests itself in so many ways in everything that
race has created.[5] In the natural or moral sciences, in history, in
geography, in philosophy, and in mathematics, the Greeks were,
in the best sense of the word, inquisitive; and, because of that, they
were the first to propound almost all the great questions and to
inaugurate almost all good methods. An enigma, under whatever
form it was presented, always tempted them, and, above all, the
enigma of the universe. Always and everywhere they wished to see
and to know. This craving to question everything that could give
an answer comes to light in the first natural philosophers of Ionia.

---

5 Plato, *Republic* 4. 435 E: τὸ φιλομαθές, ὃ δὴ περὶ τὸν παρ᾽ ἡμῖν μάλιστ᾽ ἄν τις
αἰτιάσαιτο τόπον.

It is revealed with wonderful artlessness and dignity throughout the profoundly Hellenic work of Herodotus; and in the history of all the sciences it remains one of the glories of the Peripatetic school, which threw open so many avenues to research and bestowed so much honor upon learning. In poetry, too, this bent of mind shows itself from the earliest times. Part of the charm in the *Odyssey* for its first auditors lay in its disclosing to their inquisitive minds so many remote and unknown things. The two great primitive poems of Greece are, in a sense, two revelations: the *Iliad* displays the depths of human nature; the *Odyssey* discloses the immensity of the world.

From the literary point of view quite as much as from the moral, it is true, grave faults were connected with these superior qualities. A facility in understanding everything and in lending oneself to everything is at times a dangerous privilege. The maxim of Theognis[6] is well known: 'Learn to imitate the polypus, which takes the aspect of the stone to which it clings; sometimes follow that course, and sometimes change your color; wisdom is worth more than inflexible rigidity' (κρέσσων τοι σοφίη γίγνεται ἀτροπίης). The thought had already been expressed in an old epic or didactic poem, in which the hero Amphiaraus says to his son Amphilochus, at the moment of parting from him: 'Amphilochus, my child, be guided by the example of the polypus, and contrive to accommodate yourself to the customs of those people to whom you will come; now under one aspect, now under another, show yourself like the men among whom you will live.'[7] To tell the truth, this piece of advice did not belong to any particular individual, but expressed one of the tendencies of the national character. The supple and cunning Ulysses was one of the chief heroes of epic poetry, and Hermes represented the same type among the gods. Now in the history of literature, the dangerous element in this native versatility will show itself quite as clearly as the advantageous. The race will take possession of art with remarkable ease; it will turn its facility to account in a brilliant way, but often it will be too complacent in the exercise of its faculties. Cicero tells us in one of his letters that Posidonius of Rhodes (one of the most weighty of the philosophers), and some others, whom he does not name, wrote to him with the request that he would send them some notes concerning his consulate, promising to embellish the same without delay:

6 Theognis 215-218 (*Poetae Lyrici Graeci*, ed. Bergk, 4th ed., vol. 2).

7 Athenaeus 7.102. See the commentary of Bergk in regard to the passage just quoted from Theognis.

'*Instabant ut darem sibi quod ornarent.*'[8] No doubt one may see
in this a sign of the decadence; yet it should not be forgotten that
times of decadence do not bring to light in the character of a race
things which were not latent there. As reported by Thucydides,[9]
Cleon had long since reproached the Athenians with being 'spectators of words and auditors of actions'; that is to say, with regarding the oratorical contests at the tribune as a spectacle, and historical events as an affecting drama. And there we have the natural
defect of the most Hellenic quality. When a people is in possession of faculties so ready and so diverse, the danger lies in making
use of them after the manner of a virtuoso instead of adapting them
seriously to the work of human life.

And now, if, in addition to this general aptitude, we try to single
out more precisely some of the qualities of mind, of imagination,
or of feeling, in the Greeks, our principal observations are the
following.

The Hellenic race is essentially keen of intellect.[10] 'From ancient
times,' says Herodotus, 'the Hellene has been distinguished from
the barbarian because he is more wary and more free from foolish
credulity.'[11] This is true neither of one particular period nor of
one special group of individuals. Intellectual acuteness may be
observed in the oldest epic poets as well as in the great tragic
writers of the fifth century, and as far down as the sophists of the
decadence. And in the very life of the nation it is as evident as in
the literature. It finds its way into the social life, where it maintains and excites a taste for ridicule, for discussion, for anecdote,
for fable, for the neatly turned sentence; it seeks and discovers
an outlet in affairs, notably in finance and commerce; finally, it
dominates political life; for not only in Athens, but in every town
of Greece, wherever the light of history penetrates, we see men
who manipulate their interests with acumen.

In this connection we must not allow ourselves to be deceived by
certain bits of ancient testimony which have been too quickly
accepted, and which need some explanation. Often, and not without reason, one hears the gravity of the Dorian nature contrasted
with the delicate subtlety of the Ionian; a jest is still made, upon
the authority of one of Aesop's fables, on the simplicity of the

---

[8] Cicero, *Ad Atticum* 2. 1.
[9] Thucydides 3. 38. 4.
[10] *Ingeniorum acumen*—Cicero, *Pro Flacco* 4.
[11] Herodotus 1. 60: Ἀπεκρίθη ἐκ παλαιτέρου τοῦ βαρβάρου ἔθνεος τὸ Ἑλληνικὸν ἐὸν
καὶ δεξιώτερον καὶ εὐηθείης ἠλιθίου ἀπηλλαγμένον μᾶλλον.

Greeks of Cyme; and the dulness of the Boeotians is proverbial. Here we are dealing either with relative truths greatly exaggerated, or with silly taunts maliciously spread abroad. People with keen, and consequently satirical, wits naturally are the most prone to disparage themselves in that way as a result of certain local differences in customs or language. One must guard against believing these things when they are merely asserted. Not to mention here the great names in literature and politics of Boeotia, no one to-day could be persuaded that the unknown artists who unpretentiously shaped the beautiful little figures of Tanagra were boors or blockheads. And it would be a singular mistake to conceive of the Dorian gravity as a sort of mental ponderousness incompatible with delicacy. The witty sayings of the Spartans were justly famous throughout Greece; we still possess an ample collection of them in the moral writings of Plutarch.[12] Less graceful and less delicately ironical than those of the Athenians, they are more concise and vigorous. Several wise men, famous for their maxims, belonged to the Dorian section of Greece; and when Cicero in his *De Oratore* wished to teach the method of pointing those clever expressions which furnish eloquence with a weapon, he sought examples from all the Greeks without distinction of tribe. 'I have found among the Greeks,' he says, 'a multitude of witty sayings. The Sicilians excel in this sort of thing, and also the Rhodians and Byzantines, but above all the Athenians.'[13] The Sicilian Greeks, in general, seem to him 'a nation acute and able in discussion' (*Acuta illa gens et controversa natura*).[14] 'A Sicilian,' he says, 'is never in so bad a plight that he cannot find some witty thing to say.'[15] Moreover, in order to realize how truly Hellenic is the quality of which we have been speaking, it is only necessary to contrast the native genius of Greece with that of an alien people, as, for example, that of Rome. The Roman mind is wise and powerful, naturally judicious and precise; but not even its very precision has the acuteness of the Greek mind. Though for that reason more safe from the bold fascinations of logic and the subtle refinements of argument, how dearly does the Roman pay in his corresponding lack of penetration!

It is due to this keenness of mind that the Greeks were so early

[12] Plutarch, *Apophthegmata Laconica* and *Lacaenarum Apophthegmata*.
[13] Cicero, *De Oratore* 54.
[14] Cicero, *Brutus* 12.
[15] Cicero, *In Verrem* 2. 43: Nunquam tam male est Siculis, quin aliquid facete et commode dicant.

and so long masters in moral analysis as well as in the art of
reasoning. It is through this, too, that they so easily turned sophists during certain periods of their history, and that there was
often an element of excessive ingenuity in their greatest writers.
It was always easier for them than for others to make nice vital
distinctions in ideas, and to perceive and bring to light the least
obvious aspects of things; but they had always some difficulty in
refraining from the discussion of what was unworthy of discussion, and from searching out what was not worth the search.

As they thought with penetration, so they executed with clearness. The Greeks were a people of imagination, but they shared
that quality with many other races. It certainly is safe to believe
that in the head of a Hindu, a Scandinavian, or a German, there
have generally been as many images, and images as strong and
lively, as in the head of a Greek. But the peculiarity in the latter's
manner of conceiving is that all the images which he carried within
his mind, and which were constantly renewed, presented simple
forms and settled outlines. Nothing that was vague, obscure,
indefinable, had any place there, so to speak. All things were, if not
equally, at least adequately, clarified. One might properly say
that it was never night in the imagination of a Greek. And since
measureless things are necessarily in some part obscure, it is only
natural that every Greek conception was measured. Not that moderation in all things was, much as it has at times been asserted, an
essential trait of the Greek genius. In their philosophical speculation, as well as in their political life, the Greeks lacked it often
enough. But in works of the imagination they preserved it without effort. If this faculty more than any other in man is under
the direct influence of the senses, it would seem that the habit of
living beneath a sky frequently clear, and of having before one's
eyes horizons almost always sharply defined, might be regarded as
the primary cause of this truly national characteristic. Never
from his infancy accustomed in looking about him to encounter
either infinity or vagueness, the Greek put neither into the mental
images which he formed.[16] The world of his recollections, his

16 The beautiful lines in Euripides' *Medea* [828-830] in regard to the Athenians are familiar: Φερβόμενοι κλεινοτάταν σοφίαν, ἀεὶ διὰ λαμπροτάτου βαίνοντες
ἀβρῶς αἰθέρος, κ. τ. ἑ.   Cicero, *De Nat. Deor.* 2. 16: 'Etenim licet videre
acutiora ingenia et ad intelligendum aptiora eorum qui terras incolant eas in
quibus aer sit purus ac tenuis, quam illorum qui utantur crasso caelo atque
concreto.'—E. Reclus, *Nouvelle Géogr. Univ., Europe Méridionale,* p. 59: 'In
the country about the gulfs of Athens and Argos, it is not only the blue of
the sea, the infinite smile of the waves, the transparency of the sky, the reced-

fictions, and his fancies, naturally resembled the world of reality which he saw about him.

Nothing is more instructive in this respect than his mythology. Since it belongs to all the Greek tribes simultaneously and during the earliest period of their history, it serves especially well to show the turn of imagination which from the most distant times prevailed throughout the race. Now is it not remarkable to observe how the great natural phenomena which are the basis of their fables immediately took on distinct and simple forms, restrained alike in feature and outline? The greater number of the gods appear as human beings. If perchance any element of indefiniteness is to be found in them at their origin, poetry instinctively strives to eliminate it. They are represented as surrounded with light. Far from remaining half plunged in the unknown and mysterious, they emerge fully to offer themselves in their sensible beauty to the minds of those who have faith. And even when their original nature least lends itself to such transformation, it is, just as far as possible, forced upon them. When the Greek imagination personifies the lightning and the thunder, tempests, whirlpools, and volcanic eruptions, that is to say, immense and unbridled forces, it simplifies and limits them as much as it can. In Greek mythology one finds absolutely nothing analogous to the immense and fantastic conceptions of India, or to the dark dreams of the Scandinavians. The Cyclopes, the Hecatonchires, Aegeon and Briareus, Typhoeus and the Titans, in their struggle against the Olympians, certainly offer the closest resemblance to them; but it is evident that Greek poetry, when it represents these, does everything in its power, short of being too unfaithful to their original creative idea, to render them easy to conceive; and it must be added that as a general rule Greek poetry, far from delighting in such images, on the contrary more and more neglected them. The gods whom the poets most loved were the most human.

This plastic distinctness of conception is one of the most attractive qualities of Hellenic literature. For the Greeks, everything in the realm of imagination is clear, everything open to the senses; and as these pure forms are in addition full of vitality, so they contain something that charms us intensely and gives us satisfaction. These qualities, however, necessarily exclude others, or at least re-

ing stretches of the shores, and the bold relief of the promontories, that entrance the artist; it is, likewise, the pure, sharp outline of the mountains with their strata of limestone or marble. One thinks of them as great architectural piles, and many of the temples that crown them seem only to repeat the design.'

strict them. The obscure, as well as the luminous, has its poetry, and what a man fancies he dimly descries through shadows is often the thing that most deeply stirs him. Perhaps the Romans had more of this sense of the invisible and intangible than the Greeks. In Lucretius and Virgil we may discover profound lines that make us feel what we cannot see, and open to the imagination mysterious distances full of illusion or terror:

Impiaque aeternam timuerunt saecula noctem.[17]

And yet the Romans were not by nature poets of the mysterious. This wonderful faculty of dreaming outside the realm of precise forms, and of feeling what lies beyond definite and limited sensations, we find far more in the poems of India; and the Germanic and Scandinavian races have communicated more or less of it to almost all modern peoples.[18] Among the Greeks, on the contrary, the faculty is relatively weak. But, to compensate, their distinctness of conception follows them into the field of abstractions—and there, too, it has its advantages as well as inconveniences. No people has given to metaphysics a greater measure of concrete reality. Not only do the philosopher-poets of the earliest times make for themselves a mythology which they substitute for the popular one, but, in the full supremacy of prose, the disciples of Socrates do precisely the same thing. Plato creates for himself a world of gods with his Ideas; he sees them reclothed in marvelous forms, and he describes them to us. Thus the most unsubstantial generalizations become animated; they take on a physiognomy, so to speak, and are rendered familiar. Assuredly there is pleasure in this— but is there no danger to science and sound reason? The Greeks alone put into the world more metaphysical entities than all other peoples together. How many of these phantoms there are which have the air of being something, and are nothing! You may say, if you like, that their intellectual keenness and curiosity are chiefly at fault; but has not their method of invention also been in large measure responsible?

In the study of Greek literature, moreover, it is necessary to take serious account of a trait of character which is not simple, but is the result of nearly all the special qualities already described.

[17] Virgil, *Georgics* 1. 468.—EDITOR.]
[18] Victor Hugo, *Feuilles d'Automne* 31:
    For the soul of the poet, a soul of shadow and love,
    Is a flower of the night, which opens when day is done,
    And unfolds itself to the stars.

Although tradition is very powerful in Greek literature, individual liberty everywhere shines forth. The same subjects are handed down through many generations of poets, but almost never are the newcomers enslaved by the authority of their predecessors. If they readily accept the given models, they also accept them in the right way; for example does not in any fashion cramp them. They have a way of employing these models which is their own, and which implies nothing that could be called slavishness. The use of old subjects, and even of established forms, is for them like the use of language; every one avails himself of it without a thought that he is thereby imitating any one else. Above all, one scarcely encounters in Greek literature those dominant influences which, among almost all peoples, have more or less permanently substituted a conventional moral truth for the truth of nature. The Roman usually possesses a certain senatorial or consular dignity which he exhibits in all that he writes. He assumes a part suited to the loftiness of his worldly position, and utters only the sentiments that are in accord with it. One might inscribe at the beginning of a history of Latin literature:

Tu regere imperio populos, Romane, memento.[19]

In all our modern literatures, without exception, the same circumstance reappears. The Middle Ages are mystical, chivalrous, and scholastic. The sixteenth century is erudite and at times pedantic. The seventeenth, be it in France, in England, or in Spain, experienced the vogue of refined gallantry, of pretty wit, and often of Castilian punctiliousness. The greatest geniuses themselves, Shakespeare, Calderon, Corneille, were more or less subject to these conventions. But in Greece it is difficult, down to the Alexandrian age, to point out anything analogous. And even in the decadence, when the Hellenic genius was no longer so clearly conscious either of its power or its originality, how this innate independence on occasion once more flashes out! In contrast with Pliny and Tacitus, both of them so completely Roman, there stands Plutarch, with his fine and charming Hellenic spirit, so natural and human under the slightly mannered forms which his time imposed upon him. Finally, when a Syrian like Lucian has, by his entire education and reading and mode of life, rendered himself Greek, what freedom he finds in the Hellenism which has become second nature to him! The Greeks, in fact, were constantly nearer than any other people to the simple human truth. It was they who most rarely lost sight

[19 Virgil, *Aeneid* 6. 851.—EDITOR.]

of it, and who always most easily found it again. By his bold-
ness of judgment, by the whim of his imagination, by the naïve or
reflective sincerity of his feelings, the Greek escapes everything
that might curb the swing of his nature.[20] Nothing artificial is
superimposed upon the pure humanity in him. The special characteristics which this humanity takes on in his works are those of
which he could not divest himself, since he actually carries them
within his being. They appertain neither to one accepted rôle nor
to any discipline whatsoever.

In conclusion, we must say something of what one might call
the predominant moral characteristic of the Hellenic race, since in
point of fact nothing is of greater importance for its literary history. On this matter differences of opinion that are worth considering have appeared among eminent critics. For some, carelessness and gaiety are at the foundation of the Hellenic character.
'The Greeks,' says M. Renan, 'children that they were, took life
so merrily that it never occurred to them to curse the gods, or to
find nature unjust and treacherous to man.'[21] And in another
place the same writer tells us of 'the eternal youth and gaiety
which have always characterized the true Hellene, and which to-
day still make the Greek a stranger to the heavy cares that prey
upon us.'[22] On the other hand, the author of *Le Sentiment Religieux en Grèce*, M. Jules Girard, who has so profound a sympathy with the Greek spirit, takes an altogether contrary view.
'In reality there was in the Greek,' he says, 'an anxiety about himself, about his condition, and about his destiny, which awoke at the
same time as his brilliant imagination, and which put into his
first works, no matter how vigorous they might otherwise be, a
note of melancholy, the pathetic force of which has never been
surpassed by anything in the writings of the moderns.'[23] No one
can seriously disregard the measure of truth in this last opinion.
But if it emphatically expresses the result of an erudite and careful examination, the first opinion sums up in broad outline, and
with an exaggeration undoubtedly intended, a general impression
which, in spite of the necessary corrections, remains on the whole
accurate. Surely the Greeks had too keen an intelligence, and too
much freedom of judgment, to fail in perceiving very early all that

[20] This explains the great personal originality of some of the distinguished
men of Greece. There is no Socrates or Diogenes to be found in Rome. Compared with them, Cato the Censor seems stiff and formal.

[21] Renan, *Les Apôtres*, p. 328.

[22] *Ibid.*, p. 339. Cf. E. Reclus, *op. cit.*, p. 64.

[23] Girard, *Le Sentiment Religieux en Grèce*, 2nd ed., Paris, 1879, p. 6.

there is of darkness in man's condition, and of injustice and pain sometimes in the march of events. And it was at the same time impossible that their quick sensibilities should be exempt from suffering over the calamities of life. But if the question is one of determining the moral characteristic that predominated in them, and that is most often observable in their literature, it seems very evident that this is not finally to be identified with the mournful conception of things to which the moderns have frequently given expression, and which shows itself also in certain Latin authors. In a moment of affliction or revolt, they might doubtless have exclaimed with Theognis: 'The best thing for a man is not to be born, never to see the shining light of the sun; once born, the best thing is to break through the gates of Hades as soon as possible, and to lie down in the tomb, heaping earth upon his head.'[24] But it is a long way from chance lamentations, which now and then escape from the least melancholy natures, to a gloomy habit of thought and feeling. All the poetry of the Greeks is, in a word, the poetry of life. Their constant ideal is an ideal of youth and beauty, which they ceaselessly strive to realize, and upon which they love to fix their thoughts. The great cause of habitual sadness—that is to say, a profound sense of the constant disproportion between what we conceive and what we accomplish, between what we desire and what we obtain—this inward cause of the modern lament, the Greeks scarcely knew. Certain thinkers among them may have had some notion of it, but the Greek race, in its entirety, delighting in its own thoughts and feelings, and prompted by nature to an ever active optimism, has been, more than any other, a friend to life.[25]

Such, in its general traits, is the Hellenic type as we conceive it. The history of Greek literature, when viewed from above and as a whole, is simply a development of these fundamental observations.

[24] Theognis 425-428, Bergk.

[25] Aristotle (*Problems* 30. 1) asks himself why it is commonly true that men who are superior in philosophy, politics, poetry, or the arts, are melancholy. Doubtless his observation chiefly concerned the Greeks; yet it was not confined to them. If it is quite correct—and that may be doubted,—the conclusion drawn from it should simply be that the great men of Greece did not wholly escape a natural law; but one must be careful not to regard melancholy as a trait of the national character.

IX

THE NATURE OF ANTIQUITY [1]

By August Boeckh

It is obviously hard to define the general character of an age or a nation, and indeed almost impossible to represent it in precise concepts; for the intuitive grasp of the whole, that clearly is demanded, can hardly be given in such terms. But as science can work only with definite terms, our sole resource is, through these, to stimulate an appreciation of the whole, approaching it from various sides. First of all, then, we must discover the appropriate concepts; and as consistency forbids our abandoning the philological standpoint, we may not borrow them, say, from the philosophy of history; rather, this last should acquire them by the philological method, so as not to lose itself in empty formulas and fancies. On the other hand, if philosophers often stretch and strain the facts to suit preconceived notions and fit into a system, this does not warrant us in following certain philologists who deem all historical speculation useless—the needful thing is the rigorous grounding of speculation in fact. But again, nothing is more faulty than the attempt to characterize a race or a period directly from individual facts. The procedure will generally result in a one-sided and biased estimate; for, the motion of life being free, the spirit of the whole and of the

[1 Professor Gildersleeve says of Boeckh (*Hellas and Hesperia*, p. 42): 'His teaching made a passionate classicist out of an amateurish student of literature. Boeckh was a great master, the greatest living master of Hellenic studies, and if I became after a fashion a Hellenist, it was due not merely to the catalytic effect of his presence, but to the orbed completeness of the ideal he evoked, and though the fifty odd years that have elapsed since I sate in his lecture-rooms have witnessed the elimination of many of the results of his studies, the human results abide.' No results of Boeckh's activity are more permanent than his *Encyclopädie und Methodologie der Philologischen Wissenschaften*, a posthumous publication containing his theory of literary and linguistic scholarship. Herein is evoked his ideal in its 'orbed completeness.' His general characterization of antiquity (*Encyclopädie*, pp. 263-300) has not been surpassed. The translation appears with the consent of Messrs. B. G. Teubner. Leipzig.—EDITOR.]

general does not find uniform expression in all the particulars. Thus the idea of cosmopolitanism occurs in Socrates and the Stoics, but is not characteristic of antiquity; it anticipates the modern conception of life. Again, the thought expressed by Socrates at the end of the Platonic *Symposium,* that a good tragic poet will be a good comic poet, too, is similarly isolated in antiquity. These examples show how mistaken is the attempt to derive the ruling ideas of antiquity from single instances; we must draw our inferences from the entire body of facts. And the sources are easily found. One should try to comprehend the great spheres of life in their proper nature—the State, private life, art, and learning—each for itself, and each in relation to the others. The characteristic element will in every case be found by an induction based upon all the included forms, just as the character of these forms will be inferred from the individual phenomena. Now induction is never complete, so that this in itself makes the problem only approximately soluble. Furthermore, the particulars themselves can be rightly understood only in the light of a general survey of antiquity; thus we are again confronted by the circle inherent in the nature of philological investigation, a circle which in turn can be only approximately avoided. In characterizing antiquity we cannot, of course, make explicit the inductive process that has led to each several thought.

Now it might not in general seem admissible to speak so sweepingly and without distinction of a character of antiquity, when this term embraces the most varied nationalities. In the ancient Orient, in so far as it is historically related to the Occident, we find highly civilized peoples, such as the Indians, Persians, Babylonians, Phoenicians, and Jews. To these must be added the Egyptians and Carthaginians and the barbarians of the West. And in the province of classical antiquity itself, as the term is commonly used, we have to reckon with the difference between Greek and Roman. How can one detect a common character in this variety? But a closer inspection tells us that ancient civilization reached its high-water mark in Hellenism, and here attained to classic perfection. Hellenism represents the real character of antiquity, which in essentials, though stamped with a definite bias, appears again among the Romans. To gain an understanding of antiquity, therefore, we must begin with the culture of the Greeks as a basis. On the one hand, Greece stands opposed to the Orient, from which the Greeks, like the rest of the Indo-Germanic peoples, took their origin; there the character of antiquity did not come to full development, but may nevertheless be seen in the germ. On the other hand, we have a contrast in modern civilization, with Roman civilization as the intermediary link. . . .

The Greek spirit, like spirit in general, developed gradually, and when we go back to the earliest times of which we have any knowledge, the divergence of Greek culture from Oriental is very slight. In the first period, commonly called Pelasgic, the religion of the Hellenes—cult as well as myth,—and also their communal and family life, has many analogies with the Orient. At this point we find primitive relations containing the germ of all possible developments; here are the beginnings of what is human, fettered in nature to a lower form of consciousness which operates almost entirely as an instinct. The Greeks, however, achieved their freedom from the shackles of nature, while the pertinacious and inflexible Oriental culture remained prisoner. Nevertheless, even among the Greeks the balance in the intellectual life was on the side of nature, and not until modern times did a purely spiritual consciousness finally become predominant. Accordingly, the most general difference between ancient and modern culture is this: relatively speaking, in antiquity it is nature that rules, and in modern times, spirit. Nature develops according to necessary laws; while spirit, though subject indeed to laws, is nevertheless free. The culture of antiquity, then, is characterized rather by necessity, and that of modern times by freedom. In comparison with the Orient, to be sure, the Greeks attained a high degree of freedom; all their culture rests upon the development of the free spirit of man. But the human race makes its escape from necessity by a gradual process, and the Greeks succeeded in raising themselves only to the level of individual freedom; for since in nature everything is individual, and the realm of pure spirit is the universal, the culture of antiquity is predominantly individual, while modern culture strives after universality. But the peculiarity of the Greeks lies in the way they developed human nature to an untrammeled perfection of individuality, apprehending the universal only in so far as it is inseparable from individual culture. And this explains the fact that in every realm of life they produced a great variety and multitude of distinct forms; whereby, indeed, they brought to perfection that culture of antiquity based upon the principle of nature. The multiplying tendency is inherent in nature, since there everything separates into many varied shapes and forms; whereas the principle of unity is spirit, and hence in the development of mod-

ern times a striving after unity is uppermost—the universal can
be brought to pass only when the parts are united. To the contrast between multiplicity and unity corresponds another that has
often been applied to the relation between ancient and modern
times, namely that of the real and the ideal. Ancient culture as
a whole is more realistic than modern, for in antiquity even the
most ideal aspirations assume a realistic form. Analogous is the
distinction between the external and internal, and the subjective
and objective. The natural is external, objective; and the purely
spiritual, internal, subjective. Among the ancients, then, even the
inmost emotions assume an external shape; subjective feeling asserts
itself less than objective perception and representation. Herewith
we have the differences between ancient and modern times reduced
to seven categories:

ANTIQUITY	MODERN TIMES
Supremacy of Nature	Supremacy of Spirit
Necessity	Freedom
Individuality	Universality
Desire for Multiplicity	Desire for Unity
Realism	Idealism
Externality	Inwardness
Objectivity	Subjectivity

By applying these pairs of contrasted concepts to the several
spheres of ancient life, we may present a general view of antiquity,
approaching our object from every angle. Yet we should not forget
that the contrasted ideas are not mutually exclusive, and that in
antiquity particular individuals advanced beyond the limits of the
general development, while modern civilization, on the other hand,
has in more than one respect fallen behind, or indeed on occasion
retrogressed.

I. On its first appearance in the Orient the State seems to have
been wholly under the dominion of nature, being formed by a natural artistic instinct in man (who is a ζῷον πολιτικόν) out of
the family, and upon the model of the family, into the organized
tribe. Larger kingdoms arose when one tribe held a number of
others together by force. In the absence of any free and conscious
principle, occupations undertaken by the individual for society
were handed down as an inheritance. Thus arose castes—for they
were no invention of the priesthood. Among the early Greeks we
find similar conditions. There each state originally consisted of

natural stocks, phratries, and families, and occupations as well as
political functions were inherited. Even when the original principle ceased to be binding, the division continued in existence; only
it was now modified in accordance with the greater freedom of the
individual. In place of phylae came territorial divisions; but the
fiction of stocks was always retained, and in addition the State was
split up into a large number of corporate units. This tendency
toward particular, separate, individual forms may also be seen in
the fact that Greece was always sundered into little states. The
tendency to form larger states is modern, though it has its beginnings in antiquity, in the empires of Macedon and Rome. But
the policy of Alexander the Great oversteps the bounds of what is
characteristically ancient; and the great Roman state differs from
modern states in that it is simply the wide realm of the one city,
Rome. The ancients always conceived of the State in an external
and plastic fashion as a city. Thus the Roman state means the
civitas Romana. Similarly, Athens and Sparta never concentrated
the might of Hellas into a single power; they merely exercised
dominion over other states. Of course, this same particularism has
in the modern State been but gradually overcome. As it caused
the downfall of Greece, so it has repeatedly brought Germany to
the brink of ruin. The principle of individuality in the ancient
State is further illustrated by the fact that each member of the
State represented himself, personally. Representative governments,
where an individual acts for the community, are modern. Among
the ancients, assemblies of the people were a matter of necessity,
taking place even under the tyrants. Indeed, the Greeks in the
Persian empire, like those in Ionia and Caria, had their popular
assemblies. Now this would seem to contradict the statement that
in antiquity necessity, and in modern life freedom, has the predominance—there would seem to have been greater political freedom in ancient times than we have in modern. With the ancients,
however, freedom rested upon the recognition of all individuals,
and hence upon the predominance of individuality and multiplicity
as against the universal and unity. And it had its limits. Beyond
the circle of individual culture there was no freedom, so that a
great proportion of human beings were not free. Slavery is a
necessary presupposition of ancient life; Aristotle, in fact,
attempted to justify it upon scientific grounds. Modern slavery,
on the other hand, runs counter to the spirit of the modern State.
When the American slaveholders asserted that the black race was
designed by nature for the service of the whites, their contention

was precisely the same as that of the Greeks when the latter asserted that the barbarians were born to serve them; save that such a view is wholly out of keeping with modern times, and strikes us as inhuman and godless. Furthermore, in antiquity, though the republican form of government prevailed, nevertheless the State as such, and similarly the individual as such, were less free. Individuals counted as individuals in the State, which was represented by all, not by one or a few; even in relation to the State, however, the particular individual was not on that account more free; nay rather, he entirely lost his identity therein. What would seem to be the highest degree of freedom was but a tyranny of the people. In principle the ancient State was passionate, hard, despotic. Moreover, in comparing the ancient with the modern State one must take corresponding forms of government. An ancient republic was, of course, more free than a modern despotism, but it was less free than a modern republic. In origin, the republics of antiquity were aristocratic; and, judged by our standards, they so remain even in the period of the freest democracy—as, for example, in Athens, where, in a population of 500,000 persons, there were not more than 21,000 enfranchised citizens. An ancient monarchy was either despotic or patriarchal, for constitutional monarchy was not developed in antiquity—there existed only a vague conception of it in the mixed form of government composed of the three fundamental types, and this form almost never appeared. When the modern State has reached the goal of its development, it will, irrespective of its form of constitution, have a degree of freedom far in advance of anything offered by antiquity; but it has not everywhere reached its goal, whereas antiquity lies before us in its entirety. In the evolution of government the freedom of the ancient State appears simply as a middle term between Oriental despotism and the constitutional freedom of modern nations. Noteworthy, too, is the circumstance already touched upon, that throughout antiquity allegiance to a particular state was paramount. A man was fettered to his own government, and few struggled through into cosmopolitanism. The patriotism of the ancients was rooted in a life wholly lived in the actually existing State; whereas modern cosmopolitanism often leads to false theorizing and an indifference to one's immediate surroundings. True cosmopolitanism, however, in no way militates against patriotism, but rather frees it from the narrowness and bigotry with which it was often infected among the Greeks, who were unable to conceive of the State even in terms of its national function—to say nothing of its ideal relation to humanity.

II. Those general interests of mankind which the State is designed to realize, false cosmopolitanism construes subjectively; they are, as it were, made a private concern, and the State then easily appears in the light of a necessary evil—as an instrument of compulsion for the security of private life, this last being the only thing to which any value is attached in and for itself. In antiquity, on the other hand, private life was completely merged in the life of the State, so that the individual seemed to exist merely for the sake of the State; for, as public affairs were carried on in a wholly individual manner, and as state interests are more objective than private, in the prevailing objectivity of ancient times the particular man found his satisfaction, as an individual, in public life. The objective side of private life, the real labor and burden of daily existence, fell to those whom the State did not recognize as individuals—the slaves and the women. The free citizen was the despot of the home. Consequently all domestic and social intercourse was marked by a lack of freedom, a characteristic especially noticeable in the relations between the sexes. Man did not recognize woman as his equal, and her position was more subordinate in proportion as the political freedom of the citizen became greater. In warlike states, during the frequent absence of all able-bodied men, independent management of the household devolved upon the women; only there did they enjoy a greater measure of consideration. In Sparta they were almost emancipated. Absolute intellectual and spiritual equality was first conceded to them by Plato; but not until the advent of Christianity was the foundation laid of that reverence for woman which since the Middle Ages has put the relations of the sexes upon an ever higher plane of freedom and nobility, though women even now have not fully secured their release from an unworthy state of dependence. 'Platonic' love, so-called,—that is, pure spiritual love—is not ancient. Plato merely sought in similar fashion to idealize the love of men for boys. But this last arose from the fact that in social intercourse the sexes were kept apart, the result being that the natural attraction of the adult toward blooming adolescence succumbed to the allurement of external sense, and particularly to the sight of naked figures in the gymnastic exercises. In antiquity sexual love is dominated by the senses. Even in the most beautiful poetry the representation of love lacks the higher spiritual consecration—whereas the sentimental love of modern times often wants the touch of nature. The ancients regarded marriage in its natural aspect, realistically, as instituted for the ends of procreation. The marriage contract originally was limited by natural rela-. tionship; wedlock occurred only between members of related clans. Here again we observe the same multiplicity of natural groups that showed itself in the life of the State. Later, when the right of intermarriage between the citizens of different states existed, it still depended upon express conventions. That the free consent of the bride was not a prerequisite to the validity of the contract may be gathered, for example, from the Attic laws concerning heiresses; by virtue of his descent, the nearest relative had a claim to the hand of an heiress, and could make good his claim before the law. Under such an arrangement the wife might easily appear an unwelcome addition to her dower, and the code of Solon therefore humanely sought to render the natural ends of marriage secure by providing that the husband should fulfil his conjugal duties at least three times a month. Yet it must not be thought that the spiritual bond was wholly lacking in the family life of antiquity. The feminine sex was by no means despised, and in the Greek house the apartment of the women was no harem. If scattered utterances in ancient writers—as, for example, in the misogynist Euripides— reduce woman to a mere machine for child-bearing, this argues nothing as to the general attitude of antiquity; in not a few modern authors the depreciation of woman goes still farther. Greek poetry and sculpture presented high ideals of womanhood, and indeed the rigorous adherence to monogamy evinces the respect accorded to the personal dignity of woman. Upon the basis of the natural appeal to the senses there often grew up in marriage a tender conjugal love, while the great reverence of children for parents was remarkable. Again, the Greek cult of the dead bears witness to the depth and permanence of their fidelity even to the departed. Parental love found its characteristic expression in the manner of educating the children, which eminently well illustrates the individualizing tendency of the Greek spirit. The Greeks introduced the ideal of humanity into education. Their aim was to fashion every free citizen into a complete man by the harmonious development of his spiritual and bodily powers through artistic training and gymnastics. His further education came from life itself, through the public nature of all communal affairs, the friendly intercourse of men and youths, and the spectacle of the rich world of art with which the daily life of the Greeks was surrounded. Choice of occupation followed individual propensity, and every one could become everything. There were no professional castes. But whatever he chose to be, each strove to be that entirely. Precisely on account of their general human culture, the ancients were dominated by an energetic endeavor to excel in special callings. In modern times the idea of general human culture has taken on a wider meaning. The individual is to be formed not simply into a man as such, but at the same time into a useful member of human society, an end that can be attained only through instruction of every sort. Such instruction is therefore the principal thing in modern education, whereas in the genuine antiquity of Greece emphasis was laid upon cultivating skill in the arts and gymnastics. Moreover, instruction has become universal in two senses. First, in modern times the tendency has been to impart it to all, whereas in antiquity slaves were entirely, and women for the most part, excluded. And secondly, with respect to subject-matter, it is not, as with the Greeks, narrowly national, but is meant to introduce the individual historically to the evolution of mankind; for which reason a knowledge of ancient and modern languages is deemed a part of general culture.

III. Greek religion apparently grew out of an aboriginal monotheism belonging to the same stage of civilization as the patriarchal monarchy, though supplanted at a much earlier date. Polytheism arose among all the nations of antiquity as a result of nature-worship, in which the divine power was apprehended under manifold natural symbols, contemplation being mainly directed to the particular and real. In the pre-Homeric age the religion of nature was transformed by priestly minstrels into that profound mysticism which we also note in the religious systems of the Orient. But the result was not, as among the inhabitants of India and the Jews, a priestly religion set down in writing. With the Greeks, it is true, the priesthood originally descended by inheritance within families, yet this gave rise to no priestly caste and no hierarchy. And thus it became possible for the entire body of myth to be metamorphosed through epic poetry; the plastic figures of the divinities created by the poets represented the divine nature of mankind in all its varied manifestations, and the State of the Homeric gods, the serene and free world of Olympus, was an ideal image of the individual freedom won by the efforts of the Greek spirit. But the gods never ceased to be divinities of nature. All nature was divided up among them, and was under their dominion. And the variety and color of the divine world were further diversified by the individual forms given to legend and cult in each several state. Greek religion was not concerned with instruction in spiritual matters; it was poetical, and adorned with all the radiance and charm of art—but for that very reason external and sensuous. Religious feeling and piety, it is true, were by no means lacking in the Hellenes; but their devotion was of a purely practical order. Nor was it moral conduct alone that appeared pleasing to the gods. The most external and sensuous activities and pleasures of life were linked with religious conceptions, so that sense was deified, while the inner religious life was quite in abeyance. This serves to explain the remarkable fact that the age of the Pisistratidae witnessed a revival of the old mystical religion which had lived on in the practice of soothsaying and in the mysteries. This revival was prompted by a craving of the deeper emotions, and under the influence of philosophy there gradually developed a purer form of religious perception. Thus the way was prepared for Christianity. But with Christianity came the dominance of an entirely new principle; for the national barriers of Jewish monotheism were broken down, and the Christian Church aimed at the founding of a universal religion that elevated man not merely into a citizen of the world, but into a citizen of the kingdom of heaven. While paganism strove to reduce spirit to terms of the senses, Christianity would fain make the sensuous spiritual. As a religion of the spirit, it must needs destroy the ancient religion of nature; but in establishing itself upon the ruins, it was obliged to incorporate from paganism much that even now has not been completely eliminated. So in the Christian form of worship there are many outward ceremonies of pagan origin which give the divine service a sensuous quality; and the polytheistic elements in the dogma are likewise pagan. Now this runs counter to the true nature of Christianity, which transcends all ancient religions by attaining to an ideal monotheism drawn from the depths of the human heart. In antiquity, philosophy alone had attained thereto; and hence the very striking utterance of Chrysostom—that the Cross of Christ had turned all peasants into philosophers. Here lie the beginnings of the advance of modern times to spiritual freedom. The change may be seen above all in the transformation of the ancient ideas as to the relation between what was and what was not divine. It was the fundamental notion of antiquity that fate—the εἱμαρμένη— necessarily determined everything, even the will of the gods. Modern religion, on the other hand, rests upon the belief in a free providence, an idea found in antiquity only in certain philosophers. When we penetrate more deeply, of course, we see that fundamentally the two views amount to the same thing, since in God freedom and necessity are identical; but the form of apprehension is after all essentially different. Let it not be supposed, however, that with the Greeks a belief in the law of necessity as governing every occurrence paralyzed their energy of action. Their individual training endued them with a lofty self-confidence, based upon a knowledge of their own power; and without attempting what lay beyond its necessary limitations, they made this power count to the full.

Since ancient art sprang from religion, the two had essentially the same character. The art of antiquity was far less concerned than that of to-day with the inner feelings, but it had more of the truth of nature. This is the distinction Schiller had in mind when he called ancient art 'naïve' and modern art 'sentimental'; though, indeed, there ran through the old nature-worship a strain of sentiment that found expression in music and poetry. And yet in their very sentimentality the Greeks were natural, even sensuous. But the special quality of Greek art was its plastic form. All their artistic conceptions were presented in firm, objective, individually complete figures, which reflected the world of actuality in an idealized image. The clear apprehension of individual forms in their distinct multiplicity enhanced the unity of each work of art, and this very simplicity made it possible to attain more perfectly and effectively to completeness of the whole and harmony of all the parts. The true contrast is that of *plastic* and *romantic;* for it is a mistake to represent *romantic* as the opposite of *classic.* The term classic should be applied to all perfect art and culture, wherever found; but the classic art of modern times—in so far as it is not modeled after, or is not indirectly influenced by, antiquity—is prevailingly romantic, its aim and purpose being to reveal the inner life of the spirit. The unity and totality it strives to compass are of sentiment, which it seeks to arouse in manifold ways; and hence it operates by means of an inclusive universal variety that often runs into profuseness. The harmony of the parts is not addressed to the senses; it is ideal. The forms which this art derives from the world of reality are not strictly delimited, but are freely combined by an imagination that strives toward the infinite; and so their outlines often melt away into a nebulous haze. Since the plastic quality is normal in plastic art itself, the ancients attained supreme excellence in sculpture, creating unsurpassable models for all time. Ancient painting, on the other hand, lacked the romantic perspective. Everything appeared in direct, tangible proximity, often as if done in relief. But in comparison with modern times music especially was backward, since of all the arts this least admits of plasticity. Among the Greeks it was confined in a severe rhythmical form; with us its movement is not constrained. In the age of Pericles it more nearly approached the modern style; but this departure was looked upon as decadent. In poetry likewise it was the epic, the most objective type, that the Greeks developed in the most complete purity of style. The modern epic, on the other hand, has a lyrical coloring, to be seen externally in the employment of the strophic form. The ancient lyric lacked romantic brilliancy of coloring, fantastic play of sentiment and tone, and melody of rhyme and assonance. Even in this most subjective type, where we find the nearest approach to modern poetry, there was a plastic clarity of thought, though considerably less than in the epic. Tragedy, however, exhibited this plastic quality in its utmost perfection. Here the simple, concise action rendered unity of plot more emphatic. So far as possible, even interruptions through change of scene were avoided, in order that unity of time and place might enhance the directness of the spectator's vision. Indeed, all devices for attaining the end and aim of the drama—music, dancing, scenery, delivery, diction, and thought—were so harmoniously conjoined that it is impossible to conceive of anything more perfect. The striking contrast between ancient and modern tragedy will be fully appreciated if we compare Aeschylus with Shakespeare. Shakespearean tragedy has no immediate unity; rather, contrasts of the most glaring sort, gross inconsistencies, follow one another in successive scenes. A colossal dramatic apparatus is set in motion, at first perplexing the spectator's vision—until at length the rich variety fuses in his mind to a beautiful ideal whole. All the chords of sentiment are struck; the serious and comic mingle; and in the end the whole resolves itself into an exalted harmony— which nevertheless is not so distinct as that of the ancient drama. The intermingling of comedy and tragedy in Shakespeare illustrates the general tendency of modern times to obliterate those lines of demarcation between literary types which the ancients rigorously observed. Accordingly, the practice of poetry, as of art in general, was more limited as regards the individual in ancient than in modern times. No eminent Greek poet composed, after the fashion, say, of Goethe, poems of every sort—epic, lyric, and dramatic, including tragedies and comedies. Each strove to excel in a single type.

IV. So far we have characterized Greek poetry only as one of the arts; for it developed in the most intimate relations with the rest of the arts. But its medium of expression, language, in itself illustrates the character of antiquity in classic perfection. The natural element in language—the physical sounds, that is,—has primarily an independent existence, and helps to determine the spiritual content. And so we find in Greek a copious supply of purely phonetic distinctions which makes it possible to express the same idea by various forms. This copiousness was greatest during the earliest period in the formation of the language. So long as the mind is wholly given over to observing nature, the significance of the elements of speech is attached by the free play of the imagination to the widest variety of objects. . . . Thus in each mental representation numerous observations run together, so that the formation of general concepts is hindered. The process of thinking is restrained through the multitude of forms. In the modern languages the striving toward unity is shown in the elimination, so far as possible, of purely phonetic distinctions. But spirit could not have won this superiority over nature in the realm of language, had not the Greeks themselves unshackled the process of forming concepts. In the very basic observations Greek exhibits a depth and clearness surpassed only here and there in Sanscrit. But the individualizing power of the language is most obvious in its wealth of roots and its ductility and flexibility for combination, derivation, and inflection. Thus each several notion can be expressed in sharp outline, and the language gains a truly plastic distinctness. At the same time it possesses a thoroughly original stamp of its own. But the feeling for language among the Greeks had individual limitations; the impulse to acquire foreign tongues, and thus to secure a broader outlook, was rare. Because of this narrowness, antiquity produced no scientific historical grammar, although after the expeditions of Alexander sufficient material was at hand for linguistic comparison. It is true, the more universal feeling for language in modern times has led to a linguistic mixture quite alien to the Greeks, with the result that the national purity of languages has suffered. Language originally expresses real, concrete perceptions that are pictures of the ideas. In antiquity that native significance of words was still more vividly preserved in consciousness, so that even in prose the language remained more poetical. But with the final development of Greek science began the universal spiritualization of language, a process thereupon carried over into Latin, and subsequently into the modern languages. Words became the immediate symbols of ideas, and the original meaning for the senses ceased to be present in consciousness. This change has been accelerated by the taking over of scientific terms from Greek and Latin into the modern languages, where they lose their popular connotation. But the process of spiritualization involves the danger that the meaning of words will fade away into unvisualized abstractions. In Greek even the inner relations of concepts are expressed as clearly as possible by outer symbols, in the form of the sounds; while in modern languages the formal element (as, for example, inflections) tends more and more to disappear, and the structure must be inferred from the inner relation of the concepts. The only clue to this relation is the word-order, which is therefore more rigorously fixed, and has a logical importance, whereas in Greek it mainly served rhetorical and poetical ends. The same is true in the metrical form of language. In Greek the accent depends upon quantity, and the latter is not determined by the meaning, for the relation is purely rhythmical. But in the last, the Christian, stage of antiquity, the firm, plastic, quantitative distinctions of Greek and Latin disappeared, and thereafter quantity depended upon stress and accent, a principle that has become dominant in the nations of modern Europe. Here stress depends in part on logical relations, which in the Germanic languages also determine word-accent. But at the same time in tone and accent we have the melodic element of language, without which subjective feeling in language cannot gain complete expression. Consequently the basis of versification in the sentimental poetry of modern times is a symmetry of stress indicated by accent, aided by the equally melodic unison of rhyme and assonance; whereas in antiquity rhythmical stress very often failed to coincide with word-accent, and the repetition of like sounds was avoided. The German language has shown a capacity for combining the metrical principles of quantity and accent.

In every domain of Greek literature, language, the organ of knowledge, had attained complete artistic perfection before the theoretical life had withdrawn so far into the inmost being of the thinker that science reached its full development; for science did not come into flower until genuine antiquity was departing. Accordingly, it could undergo no such universal diffusion as in modern times. Among the Greeks art had the supremacy over science; with us the situation is reversed. The ancients had relatively as many statues as we have books, and likewise as few books as we have statues. The explanation is that art, as opposed to science, is an objectifying of the theoretical life. We are not justified in tracing the universal spread of scientific education in modern times to external causes like the invention of printing; far rather, the demand for education is itself responsible for such inventions. And this general demand arises from the fact that ever since the scho-

lastic philosophy of the Middle Ages the entire life of modern
Europe has been more and more completely dominated by scientific
theory. The content of this last, however, is to a marked degree
more universal than with the ancients, because the circle of experience in regard to nature and history has grown until our scientific
investigations now take in the entire globe, and consequently stretch
away without bound or limit into the universe. But the ultimate
foundations of things and of knowledge cannot be derived from
experience; from the earliest times they have emerged in the creative activity of thought itself. These foundations Greek philosophy
had already apprehended in full, since individual freedom of consciousness was sufficient thereto. As long as speculation among the
Greeks was unhampered by an excess of unsubdued empirical subject-matter, just so long did they continue to fashion the most
fundamental ideas of philosophy with fresh and youthful inspiration; and, more than any other, Plato displayed them in plastic
perfection. For this reason ancient philosophy has an imperishable
value. But in the empirical sciences, if the individual limitation
of antiquity led to a clear-cut apprehension of particular phenomena, it also encouraged one-sided views. Aristotle was the original
founder of an inclusive polyhistory which aimed to unite the multitudinous particulars of empirical knowledge into one scientific
whole, and which throve and flourished at Alexandria. But the
fund of experience was too limited; the special sciences could not
preserve that unity, and lost themselves in a multiplicity of detailed investigations; and at the same time philosophy became disorganized under the influence of empirical scepticism. For all
that, Alexandrian learning is absolutely modern in character, and
the quality of modern times is also evinced in the universal cultivation of science to which that learning gave rise. Science had
previously been carried on by individual investigators working in
isolation; and in the schools of philosophy and rhetoric a single
teacher was the nucleus of a group of pupils who studied with him
alone; but in the Museum of Alexandria we have the first establishment of a great scientific community, which in turn became the
model for similar foundations elsewhere. These institutions, however, simply mark the first steps in the formation of that *universitas
litterarum* toward which our academies and universities are striving—although the term university at first had by no means the significance which the Germans give it. As the sciences have developed
and become more comprehensive, they have in modern times
tended in a different direction from that of antiquity; they have be-

come fundamentally more spiritual and inward, as well as freer and more ideal. In the beginnings of ancient philosophy the contemplation of nature, and that alone, was paramount. With Socrates and Plato came the addition of ethics; yet no matter what stage of perfection this attained, it seized upon ethical relations rather on the objective side. The concept of spiritual freedom was not clearly apprehended by the ancient philosophers. In modern philosophy the object of knowledge has more and more come to be the process of knowing, and precisely in this way science becomes aware of its own nature, and free. Here again, through the interpretation he gave to γνῶθι σεαυτόν, Socrates encroached upon the modern conception of things. As for the empirical sciences, with the ancients historical investigation was eminently realistic. The sequence of facts was the main concern. The external course of events was portrayed with great clearness, and indeed not without a feeling for inner motives. But the basic psychological analysis was imperfect, and investigation of leading ideas in history was almost wholly lacking. This was quite natural, since everything was particular history, and the facts were not seen in their significance for the history of the world. In the history of philosophy and science—that is, of the inner life of the spirit—the ancients did not advance beyond mere beginnings. In natural science modern times at first glance seem to be more empirical, and hence more external, than antiquity; yet one must not compare the ancient philosophy of nature with our empirical natural science. Ancient empiricism was in the main based upon simple observation, and was therefore more natural and realistic. With the moderns everything is tested by experiment, which rests upon free combination. Our empiricism therefore is more spiritual, more ideal; and the same thing holds true of our speculations about nature in comparison with those of the ancients. Even in mathematics we see the special quality of the ancient attitude. Corresponding to the plastic character of antiquity, ancient mathematics tended to the consideration of geometrical form. Arithmetic was therefore less highly developed, and was itself referred to geometrical schemata. Conversely, the moderns treat geometry more after the fashion of arithmetic, reducing spatial relations to abstract formulas. The beginnings of analytical geometry, it is true, belong to antiquity, but the subject was little developed by the ancients, since for them the constructive procedure was always the principal thing.

Thus far we have considered the Hellenic character as a whole. But Hellenism included important differences which may be classed according to space and time. By virtue of the individualizing tendency of the Greek spirit, each several Hellenic state had its own peculiar stamp, and all these peculiarities had their roots in the characters of the main racial stocks. Differences of stock were of natural origin, and can be explained only as the combined effect of native disposition and climate. They became fixed through habit, and finally, when the stock grew conscious of its special quality, were purposely fostered. The most important difference lay in the contrast between the Doric character and the Ionic; for the Aeolic and Attic can be understood only with reference to these. The Dorians were originally a people of the mountains, and in the narrow highland valleys of Doris and Thessaly, under the most primitive conditions of life, their harsh and rugged disposition grew extraordinarily firm and strong. As a conquering race they later continued to hold a place apart; and while outwardly they appeared hard, severe, and unsusceptible, in them the Greek spirit sank inward to the greatest depth of which it was capable. From the beginning the Ionians were found everywhere on the seaboard in Asia Minor and Hellas. Under the influence of their natural environment and mode of life, their naturally more yielding and flexible disposition became gentle and mobile. They were susceptible to all impressions—graceful and social, but at the same time superficial and pleasure-loving. The name Aeolians originally included all stocks except the Dorians and Ionians. The Aeolic character at first was closely related to the Doric; but as they developed, the Aeolians, generally speaking, united Doric harshness with Ionic superficiality and love of pleasure, carrying the defects of both stocks to the point of eccentricity. Theirs was an overbearing, bombastic, often unwieldy nature, and with them an outward show of culture was often coupled with inward coarseness. On the other hand, the Athenians, who were of the Ionic stock, appropriated the better traits of the Dorians, and the Attic character represented the golden mean between the extremes of the Doric and Ionic.

The influence exerted by these differences of stock upon the entire culture of the Greek nation was duly recognized in antiquity itself. In almost every province of life the ancients characterized their various individual tendencies by the names of the racial stems. Their forms of government were divided into Doric and Ionic; the Doric being the old aristocracy, which the Dorians were the last to give up. It was displaced among the Ionians by the timocracy and democracy, which later found entrance into the remaining states. The genuine Aeolic form was the oligarchy, a mixture of aristocracy and timocracy. In private life also the ancients distinguished an Ionic and a Doric fashion. In matters of housing, food, and raiment, the life of the Dorians was restricted to the bare necessities, whereas the Ionic type was soft and luxurious. Here again the Athenians preserved the golden mean. Systematic hardening in the way of life had its origin with the Dorians; and since with them the women also were made robust by gymnastics, the Dorian woman had a masculine mind. Her social position was correspondingly freer than in the other states of Greece, and certain individuals rose to a high degree of intellectual culture. The Aeolic way of life was ostentatious and extravagant. As the racial character expressed itself especially in the language, the Doric dialect was termed by the ancients the masculine, and the Ionic the feminine. The Aeolic was the most archaic, more cumbrous than the Doric, and remarkably pompous. The Attic was not so wanting in vigor as the Ionic of Asia Minor. There were also rhetorical differences according to stock, Doric 'brachylogy' being opposed to Ionic 'macrology.' In literature the Ionians developed the epic, which was completely in accord with their nature; and their dialect served as a basis for that of the type. As the natural overflow of the feelings, lyrical poetry was cultivated among all stocks. But there was a very characteristic difference between the sentimental Ionic elegy and the passionate Aeolic *melos;* while in the Doric choral odes lyrical poetry reached its high-water mark. From this point on, the Doric dialect prevailed in the lyric, so that even in the drama, which was developed at Athens, and in which epic and lyric elements are fused together, the choral odes take on the Doric character, and even a Doric coloring as to language. Among prose types, history, like the epic, arose in Ionia. Philosophy, like the lyric, is the common property of all the stocks. But from the outset there was a contrast between the systems of the Ionian natural philosophers and those of the Doric schools of Italy; while the antinomy of both was intensified in the Eleatic school (which bore the Aeolic character), and was solved by philosophical criticism, which Socrates founded, and which was genuinely Attic. Rhetoric, too, developed in Attica, its germs, like those of the drama, being Doric. Differences emanating from the stocks were least evident in the mythology. Still, the Doric and Ionic cults may be distinguished in much the same way as the corresponding two manners of life, the Doric being notably less rich, but more profound. In all departments of fine art, on the other hand, the differences between the stocks were of the utmost importance, and the Greeks themselves named the most prominent styles accordingly. In music the oldest genuinely Greek mode was the Doric, which was subsequently imitated in the Aeolic and Ionic. Similarly in dancing the different stocks each developed a thoroughly national style. Of the formative arts, architecture brought the differences of stock to their most complete expression. Doric architecture was the original; the Ionic developed later; and in Athens the spirit of the two was united.

The development of the Greek spirit in point of time was materially affected by the influence of the characters of the stocks. The pre-Hellenic age, during which the Greeks were still thoroughly akin to the Orient, extended approximately to the first Olympiad. This earliest period was marked by the patriarchal form of monarchy, and in literature by the supremacy of the epic. About the time when reckoning by Olympiads began and the genealogies of the sons of Hellen came into existence, the main stocks emerged, and the Hellenic period proper started, which lasted down to Alexander the Great. Aristocracy now became the prevailing form of government, and epic poetry was transcended by the lyric, which flourished as a result of the same heightened consciousness that had overthrown the patriarchal monarchy. Soon after, a strife broke out between the aristocratic and democratic elements, and from this arose a tyranny, when the popular leaders in most of the Greek states overthrew the chief families, and then set themselves up as rulers. The Doric aristocrats, particularly those of Sparta, sought in all parts—including the Ionian states—to bring about the fall of the tyranny; but with the expulsion of the Pisistratidae from Athens there spread through all Greek lands a mighty impetus for freedom. The Ionic timocracy now effected a reconciliation between the ruling families and the people; and democracy did not get the upper hand until after the Persian wars. All that the separate stocks had produced in the way of epic and lyrical poetry had already become common property of the nation in the age of the tyrants, so that in literature the several dialects stood upon an equal footing. Accordingly, from the time when Athens assumed the leadership among the maritime states, all Greek culture flowed together in Attica; and thus the Hellenic character was perfected through the interchange of racial peculiarities. The climax of the entire period was the age of Pericles. After that, the Peloponnesian war disorganized public and private life, until Greece, through her particularism, succumbed to foreign rule. Consequently, the time shortly before Alexander the Great cannot be regarded as the highest point in Hellenic culture—prose literature alone then reached its culmination. With the supremacy of Macedon began the third period of development, which may be termed the Macedonian. The several stocks no longer exercised any influence, although the dialects still persisted in literature. Since Attic culture had prepared for the blending of characteristics from the several stocks, the common written language was formed from the Attic dialect. In the Alexandrian age, it is true, the Greek spirit continued to make great advances in science; yet these exceeded the essential limits of antiquity, and in fact led to its decay. The period of actual decay began with the supremacy of Rome. During this time there was a final epoch in the reign of Hadrian when Hellenic culture was artificially revived.

Those men who founded the history of philosophy thought the essential trait of antiquity to be the note of beauty. But in all times, modern as well as ancient, the ideal of art is the beautiful; while in other realms of ancient life one can speak of a 'beautiful' order only in a metaphorical sense. In characterizing the ancients, we cannot, for example, attribute to them a 'beautiful' State or a 'beautiful' political life. Beauty was so prominent in Hellenic life simply because art was so extraordinarily important in that life, and because, by virtue of the individual culture, all sides of life were developed in wonderful harmony. And an evidence of this harmony was the uniform influence, in every sphere, of the differences of stock; the aims of individuals were in keeping with the surrounding life of the State, where, as we have seen, each separate person counted. Art and politics interpenetrated each other. The several branches did not develop independently, but always in company. In the individual culture of the Greeks lay their originality also. Now true originality is normal, and hence Hellenism became the norm for antiquity as a whole. The civilization of the Greeks vanquished all other civilizations of the ancient world. Their language and customs, art and science, early spread, through the influence of their colonies, over Macedonia and Thrace to the remotest shores of the Black Sea, and yet further over the coast of Libya; and in the West to Spain, Gaul, Sicily, Italy, and Illyria; still later, to the utmost extent of the Macedonian and the Roman Empire.

But in the very nature of Hellenic culture were involved certain defects which to a greater or less extent belonged to all the stocks, and which through our method of characterization become visible in all departments of Greek life. In the first place, Greek individualism had an overbalance of sensuousness—a sensuousness that was entirely frank because natural, and hence even in its excesses less pernicious than the reflective sensuousness of modern times. The latter, though, stands in contradiction to the spirit of our civilization; whereas Hellenic civilization became disorganized when philosophy lifted the spirit of the Greeks to the contemplation of the supersensuous. A second defect was egoism, which arose in antiquity from the particularistic isolation of individuals and states. True, egoism has by no means been eradicated in modern times; but it is deemed unethical because it is opposed to the ideal of a universal love of mankind, and hence in the main it attempts to keep up an appearance of disinterestedness—which means, of course, the fostering of deceit and disgusting hypocrisy. In antiquity, however, the principle of universal philanthropy is foreign to the popular consciousness. There were no rights of man, but only rights of the citizen. Egoism appeared normal. The doctrine of Plato that it is unjust to injure any one, even an enemy, and that it is the task of the good man to reform the bad, is, of course, in harmony with the Christian precept as to loving one's enemy; but it runs counter to the general opinion, enunciated, for example, by Xenophon, that one must injure one's enemies as much as possible. Finally, a third defect in the culture of the Greeks was the narrowness of their conception of life. Says Goethe: 'The modern man, whenever he reflects, almost always projects himself into the infinite, to return at last, if fortune favors him, to a limited sphere; but the ancients went straight to the point, and found their sole satisfaction within the pleasant bounds of the beautiful earth. Here they had been placed, and to this they had been called; their activity here found room, and their passion object and nourishment.' Herewith Goethe distinguishes the point where the culture of the Greeks ceased to be harmonious and became narrow. While they saw each particular thing in its concrete shape, and in all their doing strove for supreme excellence, the vision of all things in a universal interdependence was denied them.

But far narrower than Greek culture was that of the Romans. The limitation of the Greeks did not consist in their seeing only one side of nature and spirit, but in their seeing all sides in only one way. In other words, they saw things from but a few points of view, and so had a less inclusive apprehension of individual objects than the peoples of modern times. The Greeks lived in the joyous exercise and manifold development of their powers, and in an absolute interpenetration of theory and practice. Thus not all that they

did was done for the sake of the necessities of life; but all bears the
stamp of humane culture.   Their tendency was away from the
merely useful.   The beautiful added to the good was their motto.
The original motion of their spirit toward the beautiful was revealed in the shape they gave even to things intended for mere
necessary service.   With this liberal spirit, this innate poetical and
aesthetic sense, it was natural that where they did not actually discover, they at least built up all arts and sciences, and at the same
time constructed wonderfully perfect forms of government.   On the
contrary, from the very first the character of the Romans, who
otherwise were fundamentally allied to the kindred Greeks, tended
only to the practical.   The elemental Roman trait was, not joyous
free play, but practical earnestness, or *gravitas*.   The *virtus Romana*
meant power and rigor in the conduct of life.   The Roman everywhere strove after energetic external activity, together with inward
stability, and herein was most nearly related to the Doric stock,
save that the Doric tendency to inner isolation was greater.   The
harshness and inflexibility of character in the Dorians were more
in the nature of an inward exclusiveness of culture, while with
the Romans the ruling motive was outward activity.   And so the
Dorians were far more concerned with theory, bringing music and
poetry to a high degree of cultivation, while in these arts the
Romans produced nothing original.   In the immediate vicinity of
Rome, in Magna Graecia, there came into existence among the Doric
states of the Pythagorean alliance the most perfect union of scientific theory and political practice.   As for the excessively warlike
temper that distinguished the Dorians from the other Hellenic
stocks, this was intensified in the Romans, and drove them on to
restless enterprise.   As the Greeks disseminated culture throughout the earth, so the Romans carried the sword into every land, and
the Roman Republic aimed at the supremacy of the world.   But
this, as we have noted, was exceeding the limits of what was
characteristic in antiquity.   And besides, the republicanism of
Rome was more apparent than real; for that paramount leaning
toward aristocracy which the Romans likewise had in common with
the Dorians steadily made for autocracy.   The true democratic
impulse was wanting, which among the Greeks gained the ascendancy through the Ionic stock.

   With their practical bias, the Romans were eminent in the mould-
ing of public and private life.   As for the State, their quality was
above all evinced in their peculiar development of things military.
The Greeks were not unwarlike.   Military tactics and strategy with

them became an art. But this gifted race did not possess the rigor of the Roman manly training; even in Sparta the discipline was less binding. Roman army regulations, methods of camping, and so on, became the models for all time. The maintenance of standing armies was quite in the modern spirit, and so was the centralized strategy, which was an absolute departure from Greek methods, since it allowed the least possible room for individual discretion. As for statecraft, the Romans were the first to exhibit real diplomacy in the modern sense. The policy of Rome was consistently cold, calculating, and inflexible. Once Italy had been subdued by the Roman *virtus,* that policy pursued, abroad, the most extensive plans of conquest with the utmost tenacity and endurance, and the most refined cunning. At home, it meant a concatenation of shifts and wiles practiced by the nobility so as to extend their rights over the whole State, and to hold the people by the shortest possible leash. The Greeks were far less consistent; their policy was more natural. They could not attain to the Roman *prudentia,* since with them all that was done for the guidance of the State proceeded from the centre of national feeling and popular consciousness, whereas at Rome the guiding principle of the State was the intelligence of the magistrates, and the manner of government was therefore more external and mechanical. The greatest achievement of Roman policy was the extraordinary development of civil law. Cicero maintains[2] that the *ius civile* of the Greeks—even the codes of Lycurgus, Draco, and Solon—was 'artless, well-nigh ridiculous.' Such was necessarily the view of the practical Roman, who strove to discriminate all legal relations sharply and firmly, when he considered Greek law, wherein the pedagogical element played a great rôle. From the outset the patricians desired to regulate all relations, greatest and least, by fixed statutes, and the law thus became so involved that they alone understood it. As a result came the ominous shackles of the *clientela,* and the production of a special class of jurists. Among the Greeks there were interpreters in sacred law only; . . . the πραγματικοί were not highly esteemed. It seems to have been very fortunate for Greece that philosophers and statesmen there took the place of jurists. The form of legal process was much more free; and the laws, with all their variety, were much simpler and more purely human, so that any one with a political training could administer them. The entire practical wisdom of the Romans was juridical, while from the beginning that of the Greeks had a philosophical and poetical cast, revealing a religious

2 Cicero, *De Oratore* 1. 44.

spirit that transcended common affairs. Cicero, who seeks to exalt his own race as far as possible in comparison with the Greeks, in praising the Romans always falls back on their practical ability, and if we listen to the statesmen speaking in the dialogue *De Oratore*, we gain a very vivid idea of the Roman character. Among the men whom the Romans compared with the seven sages of Greece were Tiberius Coruncanius, the first teacher of law; Publius Sempronius, whose legal knowledge brought him the surname *Sophus;* Fabricius and Mannius Curius, the representatives of incorruptible justice; and Appius Claudius Caecus, who built the Appian Way and the Roman aqueducts. Along with political wisdom, Cicero praises the Romans[3] for their superiority in the management of household affairs: 'As for the manners and customs of life, and domestic and family affairs, we certainly manage them with more elegance, and better than they did.' In point of fact, Greek family life was likewise without that discipline which was made possible among the Romans by the almost unlimited *patria potestas;* and the free and easy ways that went with their genius prevented the Greeks from attaining in their household affairs to the exemplary order for which the Romans were distinguished.

On the other hand, the entire theoretical life of the Romans remained on a lower plane because it stood at the service of the practical. Religion was with them, even more than in Crete and Sparta, a state religion, a civil institution. Augury was a tool in the hands of the patricians. The cult did not have the pure beauty and speculative value in the Greek worship of the gods, but included considerably more of superstitious usage and much Etruscan jugglery. Yet it was most intimately linked with every act of domestic life, and was the expression of deep and earnest religious feeling; whereas with the Greeks the practice of religion became in many respects a graceful pastime. The noblest forms of the ancient Roman cult, however, the institutions of Numa, were the result of Greek influences; for Magna Graecia arose in the time of Numa, and the story, untenable on chronological grounds, which made the king a Pythagorean, at all events pointed to an acquaintance on his part with the Greek civilization of lower Italy. But the serene spirit of Greek religion Numa could not transplant to Rome. Further, Roman mythology, a mixture of old Italian and Greek elements, was far less ideal than the Hellenic, which itself was in a state of utter decay when Greek culture found entrance among the educated at Rome. From that time on, the Roman official religion

[3] Cicero, *Tuscul.* 1. 1. 2.

became nothing more than a political tool, and hence its development as *theologia civilis*, in the service of practical demands, was
purely external.   According to Augustine,[4] Varro distinguished
between *theologia mythica, physica,* and *civilis*—that is, between
poetical, philosophical, and civil theology,—while the Greeks had
only the first two divisions, since with them the civil religion was
in fact the poetical. The underlying reason was that the Romans
lacked the poetical bent. In art and science generally they were not
original, and what they took from the Greeks they developed independently only in so far as it subserved practical needs. Cicero
himself is forced to admit this, though he thinks that the Romans
could have excelled the Greeks in art and science as well, if only
they had desired to. 'It has always been my opinion,' he says,
'that, with regard to the subjects they have deemed worth their
attention, our countrymen have in some instances made wiser discoveries than the Greeks, and in others have improved upon their
discoveries, so that we surpass them in every point.'[5] The practical sense of the Roman, of course, disdained everything unpracti-
cal, for the very reason that his gifts did not tend that way.
Cicero, on the contrary, believes that if the artistic genius of a
Fabius Pictor had been appreciated, the Romans could have pointed
to their Polycletus and Parrhasius. In his opinion music flourished
among the Greeks simply because of universal appreciation, since
even the greatest statesmen had received a musical education.[6] The
truth is that the Romans, lacking the talent, had no desire, either,
for theoretical pursuits. Consequently art and science were not
honored, and this in turn reacted to hamper them. In point of
fact, at Rome a poet like Sophocles, who took part in the acting
of his own plays, could never have been appointed a general. Since
a *levis notae macula* attached to the artist, the nobler spirits could
hardly apply themselves to art. But even when Greek culture came
into vogue, and the prejudice was to some extent overcome, the
Romans, however great their zeal, could not equal the Greeks.
They were weakest on the side of music, standing far behind Crete
and Sparta. Greek music was introduced as a luxury, as a form
of entertainment, and the Romans simply turned it over to Greek
musicians. Similarly the art of gymnastics, something purely
Greek, in spite of all artificial attempts, never became domesticated
at Rome. For its purpose—the harmonious development of body

4 Augustine, *De Civitate Dei* 6.5.
5 Cicero, *Tuscul.* 1.1.1.
6 Compare the *Proem. in Cornel. Nep.*

and soul—the Romans had no appreciation. Their recreations were of a different order—swimming, ball-playing, the warlike *ludi Circenses*, gladiatorial contests, and beast-baiting. In the art of building they showed independence only in the construction of roads and fortresses. The really artistic element in architecture was originally as foreign to them as were sculpture and painting; but when they had developed a taste for it through the Greeks, they did produce a style of building corresponding to their own character. Even in the art of poetry they made no independent progress beyond the first rude beginnings. To this stage belonged the old religious songs, which, aside from the artless and unchanging ritual chants, were in the main oracular, and hence in their very nature did not aim at artistic representation, having rather the practical end of guiding and determining the actions of men through predicting the future; and hence the Greek Sibylline books were an early dower for the Roman State. In addition, from early times festival occasions in public and private life were attended with singing, to which the tibia most commonly formed the accompaniment. To this class also belonged the songs in praise of ancestors, sung by the youths at banquets. Niebuhr's view that an old national epic developed out of these songs has, however, been proved untenable. Rome never possessed on its native soil an infancy of culture; it had no mythical tale of heroes. From the outset its heroes were statesmen. Thus all the conditions essential to the rise of an epic were missing. Nor was there, as in the heroic age of Greece, a class of minstrels; and so there was no folk-poetry—for this lives in the mouth of the minstrels. It is true, the Romans were always intent upon preserving the memory of the deeds done by their forefathers; but from the earliest times this was accomplished through written records. Noteworthy political and religious events were registered in the *annales pontificum* and the *commentarii magistratuum;*[7] furthermore, the patricians kept domestic and family chronicles. Accordingly, whereas the writing of history among the Greeks developed out of epic poetry and mythology, unhampered by any influence from the State, among the Romans it was by its origin in the strictest sense of the word pragmatical, and the records, being devised for necessary ends, were meagre and prosaic. They were supplemented by the documents of sacred and civil law, including the *libri* and *commentarii pontificum*, the *fasti*, the *leges*, the *libri lintei*, and so on. These

[7] K. W. Nitzsch, *Die Römische Annalistik*, pp. 189-242; *Geschichte der Römischen Republik* 1. 191-203.

earliest writings comprised the fundamentals of Roman national knowledge—the *doctrina civilis*.

The year 240 B. C. marks the beginning of an artistic literature at Rome, for in that year Andronicus, a Greek captured at the fall of Tarentum, brought upon the stage the first tragedy translated from the Greek. Scenic plays, the *ludi Fescennini*, the Romans had at a very early date; but these were improvised farces in which Roman gravity displayed itself in a cumbersome and grotesque form of raillery. Tragedy must have been particularly congenial to the seriousness of the people; and how well the enterprise of Andronicus was received may be inferred from the honor bestowed upon him of corporate rights as poet. From this time on, the Romans rapidly acquired a taste for Greek literature. With tragedy they also appropriated comedy, and native materials from Roman tradition were employed in both. The *fabula praetexta*, especially in the form given to it by Pacuvius, was truly sublime and powerful, even though it lacked the harmonious structure of Greek tragedy. Comedy, too, the *palliata* as well as the *togata*, was originally in the high style, like that of Attic comedy, only far more cumbrous; for the Greek παιδιά always remained foreign to the Romans. The epic, which Andronicus introduced by translating the *Odyssey*, was similarly employed without delay upon materials from the national history. After the *Bellum Poenicum* of Naevius came the *Annales* of Ennius, dealing with the entire history of Rome, which was continued by subsequent poets. Still, the more familiar the Romans became with Greek literature, the more they imitated it. The great achievements of the Greeks encumbered the Roman spirit with examples, and hampered the further development of those achievements in any original way; the more so as poetry never ceased to be regarded superficially, as merely entertaining and diverting, and hence, though it was duly encouraged by munificent patrons, found no abiding-place in the artistic sense of the nation. One literary type only was the special property of the Romans, namely, satire, in which the old burlesque chaffing and joking songs of Rome were transformed into something artistic. Horace justly calls it[8] a *Graecis intactum carmen*. In Greek literature there was nothing even approximately like it except the *silloi;* to the satyric drama—the similarity of name is purely accidental—it is in no way related. This literary form, half poetry, half prose, the Roman poets succeeded in filling with a profusion of ideas on life, of wit, and of mordant lampooning and

8 Horace, *Serm.* 1. 10. 66.

ridicule. Jest is here in true Roman fashion seriously employed upon life. Further, in two types of prose literature the Romans, under the influence of Greek models, accomplished significant results—that is, in history and oratory. Even before Ennius reclothed the old state chronicles in the garb of poetry, Quintus Fabius Pictor had portrayed all Roman history, in the Greek language, for the circle of educated patricians. In the face of this, the elder Cato began a system of compiling annals in Latin that was independent of the State. But with Sallust, Roman history for the first time assumed an artistic form entirely modeled after the Greek, though it never attained to the character of an art independent in its manner of presentation, such as that of the Greeks. It is precisely the most original Roman historians, Sallust and Tacitus, that depart the farthest from the genuinely plastic manner of antiquity, and do so through the subjective and sentimental coloring they give to their facts. As for oratory, it formed the essential basis for Roman prose. Appius Claudius Caecus, Quintus Fabius Cunctator, and after them the elder Cato, had recorded their speeches; and soon the Greek models were studied with such success that Cicero[9] could declare the Romans to be little or not at all inferior to the Greeks. Cicero himself, it is true, in comparison with Demosthenes often seems like a tattler in the presence of a true orator. But then, with all his gifts and culture, Cicero was not a great, genuinely Roman character—he lacked the *virtus Romana*. In weight and dignity the genuine eloquence of the Romans actually surpassed that of the Greeks. And herein the language of Rome likewise had the advantage; for no other language in the world permits one to speak and write with more nobility and vigor than does Latin. From the first it had the general character of antiquity—in tone and accent, too; for the supposition is untenable that in the earliest period the accent was like that of the modern languages, and not dependent upon quantity. But whereas Greek had every tone, running the whole gamut of expression from the utmost sweetness and flexibility to the greatest power and austerity, Latin developed in a single direction, namely that represented in Greek by the harsh but powerful Aeolic dialect, to which, in tone and accent, Latin itself is most nearly related. Precisely by virtue of this one-sidedness, however, the language became the most adequate form of expression for the Roman *gravitas*. The stress itself serves to illustrate this, since all polysyllabic words were barytones. For all the practical rela-

[9] Cicero, *Tuscul.* 1. 3. 1.

tions of life the language produced the most significant forms; on the other hand, it had a very limited range of expression for more general concepts, without circumlocution, and offered very imperfect forms for speculative ideas. In philosophy and pure theoretical science, again, the Romans did not increase the fund of knowledge derived from the Greeks. Philosophy is something over and above the necessities of life, and requires a mind intent upon the hidden depths of things—which the Romans never possessed. They were friendly to energetic action, and not susceptible to the lure of speculation, in which the Greek spirit found its highest satisfaction. The Roman *gravitas* was not the seriousness of the thinker, but that of a man immersed in affairs. Philosophy leads to *otium*, but the Roman prized only *negotium*. Consequently all men of austere convictions saw in the introduction of Greek science a danger to good morals. Such Greek philosophers and rhetoricians as came to Rome were banished from the city by decrees of the Senate. At first not even grammarians were tolerated, nor Greek physicians, either. Had not the fathers got along for five hundred years without medical science? Decrees of the Senate, it is true, were of no avail. Yet the pursuit of science at Rome long remained virtually in the hands of the Greeks. On account of their practical value, philological studies were the first to be pursued by Romans after the fashion of the Greek grammarians, and the body of ancient law underwent a scientific investigation. In all other sciences only the practical side was taken up. Thus mathematics, for example, which the Greeks had developed into an admirable theoretical system, was cultivated at Rome only for the art of computing and surveying. Cicero significantly remarks:[10] 'Geometry was in high esteem with them, and so none were more honorable than the mathematicians; but we have confined this art to useful measuring and calculating.' On that showing, the Romans stand on the level of Strepsiades in the *Clouds* of Aristophanes, for he takes geometry to mean the practice of measuring the lands of the *cleruchi*. Of course the great Greek mathematicians were notable also for practical mechanical inventions, but they attached far less value to these than to their theoretical discoveries. At Rome the pursuit of philosophy was for most persons a matter of fashion, and was looked upon as a form of amusement. In the number of the servants it was quite proper to keep a house-philosopher along with the Greek cook and the paedagogus. It just suited Roman

10 Cicero, *Tuscul.* 1. 2. 5.

taste when Terence[11] mentioned *canes, equi,* and *philosophi* together—though Terence probably borrowed the joke from Menander, since in Athens narrowly practical statesmen evinced the same
contempt for philosophy as is expressed by Anytus in Plato's *Meno.*
Only a few Romans sought in philosophy a deeper culture. Nobler
natures accepted Stoicism, the philosophy of activity and endurance, since this was most in keeping with the Roman temper. But,
like other Greek systems, it was popularized; and the sole philosophical achievement of the Romans, when all is said, was an
eclectic popular philosophy. Under the empire there grew up with
a diminished participation in the life of the State a taste for the
sciences, and from the time of Hadrian this was encouraged by the
establishment of numerous public academies. Even so, philosophy
and the purely theoretical disciplines were still valued only as a
means to an encyclopedic education, whose highest aim was a
shallow declamatory art of rhetoric. And at the imperial schools,
particularly the great academies founded in the year 425 by Theo-
dosius the Second and Valentinian the Third in Constantinople and
Rome, attention was more and more restricted to bread-and-butter
studies. Thus through the Roman principle of utility the advance
of science was hindered, and was gradually limited to the trans-
mission of extant knowledge, until finally the most needful information was brought together in compendiums, which in the Middle
Ages continued for over five hundred years to be the only source of
Western scientific culture.

Roman civilization lacked the rich variety which Greek civilization owed to the combined influence of the different racial stocks.
Apart from the Celtic admixture in the North, and the Greek in the
South, the Italic stocks were related to one another like those of
Greece, although a general Italic national character can hardly be
demonstrated. But save for the Etruscans, whose influence upon
the Roman spirit was marked, no stock in Italy rose to equal importance with the Roman; and through political supremacy, the language and culture of the city of Rome became the norm for all her
subjects. In comparison with what was *urbanum,* every deviation
was disdained as *rusticum* and *peregrinum.* In every part of the
extensive Roman empire, except where Greek prevailed, through
the skill of the Roman government the tongue of Latium became
current; and here again the *lingua urbana* was everywhere the
speech of the educated. Provincialisms in language and custom
first made headway in the time of the decadence. Then, after the

11 Terence, *Andria* 1. 30.

fall of the Western Empire, the Romance languages were formed, not from the literary language, but from the *lingua rustica* as modified in the several provinces. Thus the varieties of Roman civilization according to nationalities acquired no historical significance until the birth of the peoples of modern Europe.

Accordingly, the main differences to be observed in the Roman character in the order of time lay simply in its different relations to Greek culture. The first period was the Italic-Etruscan, in which the ancient national civilization prevailed, and which came down to the end of the first Punic war. Here the Etruscan influence was at first most powerful, and then gradually decreased. With the second Punic war began the period of Graeco-Latin civilization:

In the second Punic war did the Muse with pinioned flight
Speed to Romulus' rude race, who in warfare take delight.[12]

In this period the real nature of Rome most truly flourished; the *virtus Romana* was married to genuine Roman eloquence, and poetry enjoyed relatively its greatest independence and vigor. But the Greek influence steadily gained at the expense of what was distinctively Roman. The third period embraced the golden and silver ages of Latin literature. From then on, after the State had been subjugated to the autocracy through bloody civil wars, Roman culture was wholly occupied in imitating Greek; from the over-refined form the ancient national vigor disappeared. And then, after the time of the Antonines, complete decay set in.

Taken as a whole, the history of mankind represents the universal unfolding of the powers implanted in the human spirit. Spirit, whose essence is cognition and that moral will which is founded upon knowledge, operates only in connection with the vegetative and animal functions; and corresponding to the favorable or unfavorable influence of these, the capacity for cognition is extremely variable. In sleep, where the animal functions of sensation and movement are at rest, we see cognition reduced to a minimum, since consciousness lives only in the imaginative creations of dreaming. In the child we see cognition begin with the feeblest efforts, because the vegetative functions, whose end is the preservation and

[12 Porcius Licinius, in Gellius 17. 21. 44-45. The translation of the two lines is adapted from that in *A Literary History of Rome* by J. Wight Duff, p. 119.—EDITOR.]

development of the organism, entirely occupy the feeble consciousness. But even as its strength increases, this consciousness, in waking hours, can be wholly absorbed in sensory images, and at the same time desire can be completely determined by them. This was the level on which the human spirit stood in the earliest Oriental period, which one may describe as the vegetative and dreaming age in the life of man. At this stage cognition and the moral will operated without any consciousness on man's part that they were active; that is, they operated after the fashion of a natural impulse. But the impulse was the instinct of reason, which, before reason attained to self-consciousness, in prehistoric ages slowly accomplished the most difficult steps, herein performing, as it were, miracles. Although the cognition of the Eastern peoples remained prisoner in a twilight of mythical imagination, they nevertheless produced the germs of all knowledge respecting God, nature, and mankind; and their artistic impulse found expression in works of power and admirable technique. But civilization itself, conjoined with the luxuriance of nature, exercised an enervating influence upon those races. They lost moral energy, and hence could not rouse themselves to free and conscious action. Their very cognition was stifled by a riotous imagination, so that art and science, while they had their beginnings in the East, never throve there to the point of classic perfection. Yet the several Eastern races approached in different degrees the height of spiritual freedom attained by the Greeks. The barbarians of the West developed in the opposite direction. Their energy was steeled by war and privation; but they built up no civilization, because with them the intellectual life lagged behind the powerful activity of an unfettered animal nature. More than one stock thus degenerated to complete brutality. Others—in particular the Germanic peoples—preserved the treasure of primitive mythical cognition inherited from their aboriginal home in the East, and with it moral will-power. Like the Greeks of the heroic age, they acted according to the wild impulses in their hearts, but a deep religious spirit without compulsion held their passions within certain limits. Between the two extremes of the Eastern civilized nations and the Western natural races, the Greeks and Romans constituted the mean, spiritually as well as geographically. And since with them the energy that raises man above the vegetative life was joined to a constructive mind and artistic impulse that prevent him from sinking to the life of a beast, spirit here attained to the stage of complete humanity. This position of the classic culture of antiquity was properly indicated in their time by Plato[13] and Aristotle.[14]

When the ancient world had fulfilled its own true nature, and, surpassing and transcending itself, cast forth in germ the forms of a new culture, the seed again was brought to maturity through the union of Oriental profundity and Occidental energy. In a small, despised, and subjugated people of the Orient, under the influence of Greek speculation, Christianity arose, whose function it was to make the consciousness of the nations soar to the supersensuous, and to tear the spirit free from its roots in the life of nature. The Roman world-supremacy had prepared the way for the spread of the world-religion; but this religion was itself involved in the corruption of a falling civilization, and bore its part in the destruction of pagan art and science. Yet precisely in its disfigurement Christianity found easier access to the Germanic peoples, mollifying their hardy independence, and thus making them capable of producing a new civilization. In the Middle Ages were laid the foundations of all modern culture. So far as the barbarity of the nations and the ignorance of the clergy allowed, public and private life were permeated by the Christian spirit. Christian art bore splendid fruit; and science, in spite of pressure from the hierarchy, finally led to free investigation, which in the fifteenth century, assisted by truly providential events, gave the impulse to the development of modern times. These began when the experimental sciences were founded wholly anew. In this way, as time went on, speculation was purified, being relieved by natural science and history of many false assumptions upon which it had rested in antiquity, and still more in the Middle Ages. Along with this, Christianity itself experienced after the Reformation a progressive scientific rectification; and under the constant influence of free investigation the true consequences of the Christian view of life became more and more active in art, society, and the State. At present we are still in the midst of this movement, and cannot survey its further course in advance. But the ideal of the future can only be a civilization which shall take up into itself the genuine elements of antiquity. Spiritual freedom cannot consist in such a striving after the supersensuous as shall turn us away like enemies from nature. Rather must spirit penetrate into the laws of nature in order to subdue her; and the life of reason cannot be unnatural or opposed to nature. Accordingly, the harmonious

13 Plato, *Republic* 4. 435E.
14 Aristotle, *Politics* 7. 7.

individual culture of the ancients will always remain for us a glorious prototype; for the universality of modern times has life and strength only when the particular is not effaced by the general, but elevated and idealized by it. And so, in general, the problem is to reconcile and compose all that is at variance in ancient and modern culture.

X

FATE AND FREE WILL IN GREEK LITERATURE [1]

By Abby Leach

To the minds of the many, emphatic iteration and reiteration of a statement have all the force of truth; for people in general are prone to avoid the trouble, exertion, and close thinking that result in logical conclusions, and take instead the easier course of accepting ready-made opinions. When a popular belief, however at variance with fact, has thus become fairly established, being asserted many times by many writers,[2] to dislodge it is no easy task; and there may be difficulty even when we have to do with so evident a perversion of the truth as the widespread notion that the Greeks were fatalists.

What do we mean by fatalism? We mean that man is not master of his fate, but that his fate masters him—that, do what he may, he cannot escape his destiny. Fate is irresistible, unconquerable; and its decrees are absolute. The Turk is a fatalist; he goes into battle with the conviction that, if death is to be his portion, be he brave man or coward, death will come all the same. For him, this fatalism is brightened and cheered by a hope which is an incentive to deeds of daring, for he believes that if he meets his doom with heroic valor, he will be amply rewarded in the world to come; in itself, however, the doctrine tends to inaction and despair. Of Napoleon the Third as a fatalist, Zola has given a wonderful por-

[1 This article, which first appeared with the title, *Fatalism of the Greeks,* in the *American Journal of Philology* 36. 373-401, is reprinted with the consent of the editor of that journal, Dr. Gildersleeve. The author, Miss Leach, is Professor of Greek in Vassar College. With her kind permission, certain changes have been made in the selection so as to bring it into conformity with the rest of the present volume. In particular, numerical references have been relegated to the footnotes, and passages in Greek replaced by English. Here and there, the material has been slightly condensed or abridged.—EDITOR.]

[2 Compare, for example, Moulton, *The Ancient Classical Drama* (1898), p. 93: 'Destiny is the main idea inspiring Ancient Drama; whatever may have been the religion of Greek life, the religion reflected in Greek Tragedy is the worship of Destiny.'—EDITOR.]

trayal in *The Downfall*. Whether Zola represents Napoleon truth-
fully or not is beside the point; what concerns us is the description
of a fatalist in the person of the hero.   Take the passage where the
Emperor presents himself on the battlefield: 'Entirely unattended,
he rode forward into the midst of the storm of shot and shell,
·calmly, unhurriedly, with his unvarying air of resigned indifference, the air of one who goes to meet his appointed fate. . . . He
rode forward, controlling his charger to a slow walk. For the space
of a hundred yards he thus rode forward, then halted, awaiting the
death he had come there to seek. The bullets sang in concert with
a music like the fierce autumnal blast; a shell burst in front of
him and covered him with earth. He maintained his attitude of
patient waiting. His steed, with distended eyes and quivering
frame, instinctively recoiled before the grim presence who was
so close at hand and yet refused to smite horse or rider. At last
the trying experience came to an end, and the Emperor, with his
stoic fatalism, understanding that his time was not yet come,
tranquilly retraced his steps.'[3]

G. H. Lewes thus defines fatalism: 'Fatalism says that something *must be;* and this something cannot be modified by any
modification of the conditions.'[4]

The *Century Dictionary* says: 'Fatalism . . . does not recognize
the determination of all events by causes, in the ordinary sense;
holding, on the contrary, that a certain foreordained result will
come about, no matter what may be done to prevent it.'

John Stuart Mill thus writes on the subject: 'A fatalist believes,
or half believes (for nobody is a consistent fatalist), not only that
whatever is about to happen will be the infallible result of the
causes which produce it, . . . but, moreover, that there is no use
in struggling against it, that it will happen however we may strive
to prevent it.'[5]

The natural outcome is as Milman has described it: 'It was vain
to resist the wrath of God; and so a wretched fatalism bowed to a
more utter prostration the cowed and spiritless race.'[6]

Fatalism benumbs and paralyzes the will, until apathy and stoical
submission are the only resource. To accept the inevitable without
a murmur, with passionless calm to wrap one's mantle around oneself, and with bowed head to say impassively: 'Kismet'—'It is

[3] Zola, *The Downfall (La Débâcle)*, Part 2, Ch. 1.
[4] Lewes, *Problems of Life and Mind* (Boston, 1880) 1. 284.
[5] Mill, *A System of Logic* (1872) 2. 425.
[6] Milman, *History of Latin Christianity* 5. 9.

ordered'—this is fatalism, and this is what a fatalistic belief engenders.

That so deadening a doctrine as this can be attributed to a people like the Greeks seems more than strange. When we look at the Hellenes, and especially the Athenians—for Athens represented to Hellas, and represents to us, the highest reach of Greek thought and feeling—what do we find as their characteristics? Are they not alertness of mind, power to make independent judgments, a spirit of adventure and unresting activity, a proud self-confidence that made them dare and do what seemed impossible, and a courage buoyant after direst disaster? We turn to the matchless description given by Thucydides in what purports to be the funeral oration of Pericles over those who had fallen in battle in the first year of the Peloponnesian war:

'The great impediment to action is, in our opinion, not discussion, but the want of that knowledge which is gained by discussion preparatory to action; for we have a peculiar power of thinking before we act, and of acting, too; whereas other men are courageous from ignorance, but hesitate upon reflection. And they are surely to be esteemed the bravest spirits, who, having the clearest sense both of the pains and pleasures of life, do not on that account shrink from danger.'[7] 'We have compelled every land and every sea to open a path for our valor, and have everywhere planted eternal memorials of our friendship and of our enmity.'[8] 'They resigned to hope their unknown chance of happiness, but in the face of death they resolved to rely upon themselves alone.'[9]

The emphasis here is upon the intelligent calculation that entered into Athenian warfare. The deity of these Greeks is Athena, the goddess of wisdom and skill, who teaches men to put their strength and energy at the service of intelligence, to plan and contrive, to measure dangers and resources, and to count the cost, not rushing into battle in blind fury or with the desperation of those who feel themselves driven on by an unswerving doom. To anything like fatalism their spirit is diametrically opposed. Connoting untiring energy, hopeful courage, belief in one's own powers, confidence in skill and foresight, it has nothing in common with a belief that depresses effort and darkens the soul, giving only the courage of despair, or at best a stoical fortitude.

[7] Thucydides 2. 40. Jowett's translation.
[8] *Ibid.* 2. 41.
[9] *Ibid.* 2. 42.

According to Simonides: 'It was due to the valor of these men that smoke did not go up to heaven from the burning of spacious Tegea. Their choice was to leave their children a city flourishing in freedom, and to lay down their own lives in the front of the battle.'[10] That is the Greek note, the noble choice that sets life at naught against the priceless treasure of freedom. No fatalism is this, surely.

Demosthenes in his matchless speech *On the Crown,* after according to the Athenians of other days the high praise that they were willing to give themselves to dangers for glory and honor, adds: 'Choosing what was noble and right, for all men's lives have a fixed limit in death, even if they should shut themselves up in a chamber and keep guard; but good men ought to put their hand to all that is noble on every occasion, holding before themselves as a shield the hope of good, and to bear whatever the god gives, nobly.'[11] How does this differ from what we should say?—'Do what is right, and leave the issue with God.' Not once throughout the eloquent speech is there a word of a fate that held the Athenians in its firm grip, and relentlessly doomed them to defeat and overthrow. Instead: 'If Thessaly had had only one man, and Arcadia one, who had adopted the same policy as I, none of the Hellenes on the further or on the hither side of Thermopylae would have experienced the present evils, but all would have dwelt in their countries, free and autonomous, in perfect fearlessness, in safety and happiness.'[12] Are these the words of a man who believes in the resistless oncoming of a dread doom?

Again he speaks even more plainly: 'The man who feels he has been born only for his parents awaits the death of fate and the natural death, but he who feels he was born for his country will die that he may not see her suffer slavery, and will count the insults and loss of honor that he must bear in an enslaved state more to be feared than death.'[13] In other words, the patriot is ready to sacrifice his life on the altar of his country's need, while the stay-at-home will not risk his personal safety on any battlefields, but waits ingloriously for death, which comes to all, to come even to him. In no way are we made to feel that the Athenians were foredoomed to defeat, being but puppets in the iron clutch of fate. Instead, Demosthenes portrays in vivid speech the conditions that favored

10 Simonides, fr. 102 (Bergk).
11 Demosthenes, *On the Crown* 18. 97.
12 *Ibid.* 18. 304.
13 *Ibid.* 18. 205.

Philip in his aggressions, and in his analysis of the causes that contributed to the final triumph of Macedonia shows himself a statesman of the keenest insight.

Of Thucydides Croiset says: 'First of all, he is a philosopher, a man who believes . . . that the events of nature are brought to pass in accordance with regular laws . . . If he speaks of fortune (τύχη), nowhere has he made it a divinity. It signifies for him only the unforeseen and unknowable. In politics, as in nature, he believes in intelligible causes, purely human, which need to be discovered.'[14]

Even in the *Odyssey*, what do we find? In the First Book, beginning with line 32: 'Lo, now, how falsely mortals blame the gods; for they say evils come from us, whereas they, even of themselves, have woes beyond fate ['contrary to fate,' ὑπὲρ μόρον] through their own follies.' Then Zeus tells how he had sent Hermes to warn Aegisthus not to slay Agamemnon or to wed Clytemnestra, lest punishment come to him from Orestes later on, and says that it was because Aegisthus paid no heed, though the warning was given by Hermes himself, that he had to suffer the consequences.[15]

In the *Oedipus at Colonus* of Sophocles, a direful threat is pronounced by Oedipus upon Polynices if he should make the intended attack upon Thebes, and Antigone adds her plea:

> Turn back thy host to Argos with all speed,
> And ruin not thyself and Thebes as well.

Polynices replies to his sister:

> That cannot be. How could I lead again
> An army that has seen their leader quail?

Seeing that she pleads in vain, Antigone then asks:

> Wilt thou then bring to pass his prophecies,
> Who threatens mutual slaughter to you both?[16]

That is, Polynices, having the power of choice, willed to go, and so sealed his own doom. It is true that he makes the charge:

> Of this I hold thy Erinys to be the cause.[17]

---

[14] Croiset, *An Abridged History of Greek Literature* (tr. Heffelbower), pp. 296, 297.

[15] *Odyssey* 1. 32-43.

[16] Sophocles, *Oedipus at Colonus* 1416-1425. Storr's translation.

[17] *Ibid.* 1299.

But it is worthy of note that these are the words of a man who of his own volition has come with foreign aid against his native city; and Oedipus on his part heaps the bitterest reproaches upon him for his cruel lack of filial feeling: ' 'Tis thou that hast brought my days to this anguish, 'tis thou that hast thrust me out; to thee I owe it that I wander, begging my daily bread from strangers. And, had these daughters not been born to be my comfort, verily I had been dead, for aught of help from thee.'[18] With this compare his earlier reference to the two brothers: 'But now, moved by some god, and by a sinful mind, an evil rivalry hath seized them.'[19]

Of the futility of warning, and even of sure prophecy, Hawthorne has given a good illustration in *The Prophetic Pictures*. An artist of marvelous insight paints the portraits of two young people who have just been wedded, and, discerning a taint of madness in the young man, gives it subtle expression in the portrait. The bride detects it, and is filled with horror. Years pass, and the artist comes back after a long absence, and goes to this house to see his pictures. Just as he reaches the room, a tragedy is impending. The curtain over the portraits has been drawn aside, and before them stand the hapless pair, the man in his frenzy grasping his victim's hair with one hand, while in the other he holds an uplifted knife to slay her. The artist interposes, and saves her life; then with a stern look he cries: 'Wretched lady! Did I not warn you?' 'You did,' answers Elinor calmly. 'But—I loved him!' 'Is there not a deep moral in the tale?' continues Hawthorne. 'Could the result of one, or all our deeds, be shadowed forth and set before us—some would call it Fate and hurry onward—others be swept along by their passionate desires—and none be turned aside by the Prophetic Pictures.' The portentous knowledge of the oracle does not save the man; as with Oedipus, the impulsive nature flashing out in wrath brings upon him the very doom he sought to escape. Does not the Greek drama, in its treatment of oracles, express something similar to the profound truth here uttered by the American novelist?

Take the *Antigone* of Sophocles. Tiresias earnestly and solemnly warns Creon, but to no purpose. Stubbornly entrenched in his purpose, the king will not heed, but insults the prophet with base suspicion, and brings down upon himself the full weight of woe. Too late he sees himself in the true light—his own self-will, and not Heaven, the agent of his doom—and over his dead son he cries out from a broken heart:

18 Sophocles, *Oedipus at Colonus* 1362 ff. Jebb's translation.
19 *Ibid.* 371.

'Woe for the sins of a darkened soul, stubborn sins, fraught
with death! Ah, ye behold us, the sire who hath slain, the son
who hath perished! Woe is me, for the wretched blindness of
my counsels! Alas, my son, thou hast died in thy youth, by a
timeless doom, woe is me!—thy spirit hath fled—not by thy folly,
but by mine own!'[20]

And the commonly neutral chorus, which had found its voice to
condemn Creon with the words,

'Lo, yonder the King himself draws near, bearing that which
tells too clear a tale—the work of no stranger's madness, if we may
say it,—but of his own misdeeds,'[21]

now rejoins:

'Ah me, how all too late thou seemest to see the right!'[22]

Finally, at the woeful news of his queen's death, with heart-
rending cry the hapless king exclaims:

'Ah me, this guilt can never be fixed on any other of mortal
kind, for my acquittal! I, even I, was thy slayer, wretched that
I am—I own the truth. Lead me away, O my servants, lead me
hence with all speed, whose life is but as death!'[23]

But what of the great ethical teaching of the Greek drama? Is
not such a function inconceivable if a Greek play is merely the
spectacle of men and women moving like automata to a destined
end? In the *Poetics,* Aristotle says: 'The right thing, however, is,
in the characters, just as in the incidents of the play, to endeavor
always after the necessary or the probable; so that whenever such
and such a personage says or does such and such a thing, it shall
be the probable or necessary outcome of his character; and whenever this incident follows on that, it shall be either the necessary
or the probable consequence of it.'[24] Conversely, what a personage
says or does, reveals a certain moral purpose. Thus, it is because of
the nobility of her nature that Antigone cannot leave her dearly

[20] Sophocles, *Antigone* 1261-1269. Jebb's translation.
[21] *Ibid.* 1257-1260.
[22] *Ibid.* 1270.
[23] *Ibid.* 1317-1325.
[24] *Poetics* 1454 ª 33-36, Bywater's edition, p. 43.

loved brother to be a wretched outcast in the world below; unhesi-
tatingly she gives him burial, well knowing though she does that
the price of her act will be her own young life. There is no fatalism
in her unwavering choice; she feels in her heart the binding con-
straint of those unwritten laws 'that are not of to-day or yesterday,
but live on for ever';[25] and so she will obey the decree of no man,
even an all-powerful king, if it conflicts with them, choosing instead
to fulfil the sacred obligations prescribed by her own loving heart.
Character interpreted by action and in action—this is the Greek
drama; and out of the far-reaching consequences of acts that are
the logical outcome of character, its structure is formed. So in a
single house we see crime followed by crime and punishment by
punishment, as in that of the ill-fated Atridae, until at last comes
one pure and undefiled to do the god's behest and so stay the curse;
but always the beginning of the evil is in the sin of one man.
Laius sins through his passion for Chrysippus, and receives as his
punishment the sentence of childlessless.[26] But though warned of
his doom if he beget a child, he forgets the oracle when inflamed by
passion and flushed with wine. He then tries to prevent the fulfilment of the prophecy by exposing the hapless Oedipus; but such
an attempt is now folly, and Oedipus fulfils the oracle by slaying
his father where the three roads meet, on the way to Delphi. This is
not fatalism, however. Laius was forewarned, but disobeyed the
warning. Is this not one of the great truths of life? Do we not
know—know to a certainty—the outcome of such and such an act,
and yet perform that act, hoping in some vague way to contrive an
escape from the consequences? And so, 'the fate that overtakes
the hero is no alien thing, but his own self recoiling upon him for
good or evil.'[27] That 'A man's character is his destiny' ($\mathring{\eta}\theta o\varsigma$
$\mathring{a}\nu\theta\rho\acute{\omega}\pi\psi\ \delta a\acute{\iota}\mu\omega\nu$), as Heraclitus says, is a principle clearly recognized
indeed by the Greek drama; but nowhere do we find this principle
better illustrated than in the English tragedy of King Lear, who
pays for his folly as inexorably as any character in any Greek play.

Among those who maintain that the Greek drama was a drama
of destiny is De Quincey. 'Man,' he says, 'no longer the representative of an august will—man, the passion-puppet of fate—could
not with any effect display what we call a character. . . . The will
is the central pivot of character; and this was obliterated,
thwarted, canceled, by the dark fatalism which brooded over the

25 *Antigone* 456-457.
26 Cf. Euripides, *Phoenissae* 16-25.
27 S. H. Butcher, *Aristotle's Theory of Poetry and Fine Art* (1907), p. 355.

Grecian stage. . . . Powerful and elaborate character . . . would have interrupted the blind agencies of fate.'[28]

Butcher replies: 'It is strange that the Greeks of all people, and Aeschylus of all poets, should have been accused of depriving man of free agency and making him the victim of a blind fate. The central lesson of the Aeschylean drama is that man is the master of his own destiny: nowhere is his spiritual freedom more vigorously asserted. The retribution which overtakes him is not inflicted at the hands of cruel or jealous powers. It is the justice of the gods, who punish him for rebellion against their laws.'[29]

Pindar has the same moral code. Prosperity engenders pride, pride lifts up a man's heart within him to commit sin, and sin brings punishment. The genealogy is ὄλβος, κόρος, ὕβρις, ἄτη: prosperity, satiety, insolence, vengeance. 'The prosperity that produces pride and fullness of bread culminates in overweening insolence and outrage, and brings on itself mischief sent from heaven,' as Professor Gildersleeve phrases it in his edition of Pindar.[30] 'If ever the watchers of Olympus honored any man,' says Pindar, 'that man was Tantalus. But the high honor of friendly intercourse with the gods proved too much for Tantalus. He grasped after more than mortal might, and so brought down upon himself unmeasured woe.'[31] In similar strain Bacchylides denounces ὕβρις: 'Insolence . . . who swiftly gives a man his neighbor's wealth and power, but anon plunges him into a gulf of ruin,—she it was who destroyed the giants, overweening sons of earth.'[32] Excess the Greeks condemned and deplored. Their cardinal virtue was σωφροσύνη ('measure,' 'moderation'), and they rang the changes on μηδὲν ἄγαν ('nothing too much,' 'the golden mean'). Consciously or unconsciously, they made this the canon of their art and literature, and so they wrought the perfect work. In line with σωφροσύνη is the oft-repeated injunction to remember that we are mortals and cannot venture too far. 'Seek not to become Zeus'; 'mortal things befit mortals'; 'the brazen heavens are not to be mounted.'[33] True, Aristotle reaches a loftier note: 'Let us not listen therefore to

[28] De Quincey, *Shakespeare. The Collected Works of Thomas De Quincey*, ed. Masson (1897), 4. 74-75.

[29] Butcher, *Aristotle's Theory of Poetry and Fine Art*, pp. 356-357. Compare Aeschylus, *Agamemnon* 750-781.

[30] Gildersleeve, *Pindar: the Olympian and Pythian Odes.* Introductory Essay, p. xxxi.

[31] Pindar, *O.* 1. 54-57.

[32] Bacchylides 14 [15]. 59 ff. Jebb's translation.

[33] Pindar, *I.* 5. 14; *I.* 5. 16; *P.* 10. 27.

those who tell us that, as men and mortals, we should mind only the
things of man and mortality; but, so far as we may, we should bear
ourselves as immortals, and do all that in us lies to live in accord
with that element within us, that sovereign principle of reason,
which is our true self, and which in capacity and dignity stands
supreme.'[34] Yet Aristotle defines virtue as the mean between the
two extremes of excess and deficiency, and condemns alike the too
much and the too little.   Courage is a virtue; it is the mean between
the extremes of rashness and cowardice, which are both vices.
'Pride goeth before a fall,' is the teaching of Herodotus.   'He
believes in the existence of a law governing events. . . . Every
sin draws upon man a punishment, but, above all, pride, which is
the unpardonable sin.   The defeats of Xerxes have no other cause
but this.'[35]   Bury says that the Persian overthrow according to
Herodotus is 'a divine punishment of the insolence and rashness
that are often born of prosperity.'[36]   The Greek dramatists, too,
show presumptuous pride ($\H{v}\beta\rho\iota\varsigma$) punished, and heavily punished,
by the gods.   Ajax, the bravest of the Greeks after Achilles, over-
confident in his strength and bravery, dares to set the gods at
naught; and this presumption Sophocles makes the central thought
in his play of that name:

' "Yea," said the seer, "lives that have waxed too proud, and avail
for good no more, are struck down by heavy misfortunes from the
gods, as often as one born to man's estate forgets it in thoughts too
high for man.   But Ajax, even at his first going forth from home,
was found foolish, when his sire spake well.   His father said unto
him: 'My son, seek victory in arms, but seek it ever with the help
of heaven.'   Then haughtily and foolishly he answered: 'Father,
with the help of gods e'en a man of naught might win the mastery;
but I, even without their aid, trust to bring that glory within my
grasp.'   So proud was his vaunt.   Then once again, in answer to
divine Athena,—when she was urging him onward and bidding
him turn a deadly hand upon his foes—in that hour he uttered a
speech too dread for mortal lips: 'Queen, stand thou beside the
other Greeks; where Ajax stands, battle will never break our line.'
By such words it was that he brought upon him the appalling
anger of the goddess, since his thoughts were too great for man.'' '[37]

[34] Aristotle, *Nicomachean Ethics* 10. 7.
[35] Croiset, *Manuel d'Histoire de la Littérature Grecque*, p. 393 (cf. the same
authors' *Abridged History of Greek Literature*, tr. Heffelbower, p. 270).
[36] Bury, *The Ancient Greek Historians*, p. 68.
[37] Sophocles, *Ajax* 758-777.   Jebb's translation.

And to Odysseus Athena speaks the clearest words of warning because of the wretchedness and disgrace Ajax has brought upon himself:

'Therefore, beholding such things, look that thine own lips never speak a haughty word against the gods, and assume no swelling port, if thou prevailest above another in prowess or by store of ample wealth; for a day can humble all human things, and a day can lift them up; but the wise of heart are loved of the gods, and the evil are abhorred.'[38]

But though Ajax deserves his fate at the hands of Athena, yet the poet, in meting out to him the doom his haughty pride has brought upon him, has not failed to set forth most beautifully the other side of his nature; so that, with mingled emotions of pity, admiration, and blame, we mourn the sad end of one who, with all his faults, still was a man cast in heroic mould. But this only illustrates what Aristotle meant by putting the emotions of pity and fear in the forefront of tragedy, and maintaining that by the interplay of these the most tragic effects are produced. The haughty pride and fierce resentment of the hero, his murderous onslaught foiled by Athena, his ungovernable nature that cannot brook with patience a wrong, his terrible humiliation, all fill us with awe and fear. In him we see portrayed human nature in its pride and arrogance calling down upon itself, in its own act, utter ruin. On the other hand, our hearts are filled with pity at the injustice dealt out to him which has embittered his soul, at the moving spectacle of this mighty man of valor brought thus low, at his deep sense of shame and his pathetic resolve not to survive his disgrace. And there are other figures on the canvas: the narrow-minded Menelaus, with his angry resentment and hatred; the loving Tecmessa, with her tender and unselfish devotion; the magnanimous Odysseus, who sees beyond the limits of his own feelings into the great truths of human experience; and the blunt, loyal Teucer, who makes his brother's cause his own.

It is strange that any one should have made the word 'classic' synonymous with something cold and formal. Greek drama is all aglow with life and feeling; the men and women have like passions with ourselves; the red blood courses through their arteries; their pulses are set throbbing with the emotions that sweep over their souls; and because they make real to us the passion of grief and the

[38] Sophocles, *Ajax* 127-133.

agony of distress and sorrow, our own hearts vibrate in sympathetic accord with their every mood. In these wonderful creations of the poet's fancy, we see before us real people, baffled or triumphant, suffering or rejoicing, receiving the just recompense of their acts, with righteousness vindicated and wrong punished. The Greek drama makes a profound appeal to human feelings; and so it is ageless for ever; for, though the seasons wax and wane, and the revolving years swiftly roll on in their course, year giving place to year, yet human nature does not change, and always the poet who knows how to reach its deep springs has lasting power to charm and delight. The Greek imagination was greatly stirred by the sight of greatness brought low, of a king in the moment of his triumph struck down, of great prosperity changed in the twinkling of an eye to extreme adversity. The vicissitudes of fortune, the brevity of life, the insecurity of high place and station—these are their constant theme. Not man doomed, but man vital, acting with passion and vigor, loving life and exulting in his powers and strength, in his very exuberance of life and joy provoking fortune to his undoing—this is what the Greeks give us again and again. Take Hippolytus, whom Euripides has portrayed with exquisite charm. All the freshness and buoyancy and loveliness of youth are his while his pure soul, abhorring all that is evil, worships only at the shrine of the virgin goddess. But though he honors with every honor his beloved Artemis, from Aphrodite he turns away in scorn and loathing, and is punished by the goddess for his contemptuous neglect. His faithful retainer, wise with the experience of years, utters a warning word, but the youth is too confident in himself to pay any heed. It is an altogether human document, this drama, though gods intervene and play their part with the rest.

Here, again, is a fertile field for misconception. It must be remembered that the Greeks lived on terms of familiar intercourse with their gods and goddesses, and conceived of them as beings like themselves, only moving on a higher plane, and greater and grander than mortals of daily life. Then, too, the Greeks with their vivid personifying power create a divinity of major or minor importance for all that we see or feel. So with them Phaedra is the victim of Aphrodite, where we should say that she was under the spell of a mad passion for Hippolytus, or was infatuated with the beautiful youth, or was a lovesick queen, or was driven to distraction by the conflicting emotions in her soul. Moreover, the Greek divinities never hold themselves far aloof from mortals; they sometimes even fight with them on the battlefield, and appear to them in visible presence to advise and direct. That is why the *deus ex machina* in a Greek play is sometimes so far from what it is represented to be, the poet's device in a situation that has become too complex to be solved otherwise. The appearance of the god or goddess is not alien to actual experience—as in the story Herodotus tells of Pan before the battle of Marathon; and the final word spoken by a divinity is by no means the last resort of a poet tangled up in a plot too intricate to be unraveled; rather it gives the seal and impress of divine sanction for the issue desired, and the word of prophecy for the happy outcome in the future. Calm after storm, subsidence of emotion into a sense of peace and harmony, strife and turmoil followed by quiet acquiescence in the universal law—this is the rule of tragedy, and for this the god or goddess comes with authority that cannot be gainsaid.

Yet the Greeks are perfectly consistent no more than we, and the *Hippolytus* will illustrate their somewhat contradictory views as to free will and divine agencies. Phaedra has brooded over the cause of the misery in the lives of mortals, and her conclusion is that 'We know and understand the good, but do not carry it out in action, some from sloth, and some because they set some pleasure before the good,' etc.[39] She is admirably portrayed. Right-minded, holding up to herself right standards, but weak and vacillating, she is ready to succumb to her passion. It is noteworthy that the god or goddess who influences any particular character, and holds sway over him, is the one that is in accord with his own nature. Phaedra is peculiarly fitted to be the victim of Aphrodite, and Hippolytus has the chaste Artemis for his companion and the object of his worship. In the prologue, Aphrodite tells how she will punish the chaste but haughty Hippolytus through Phaedra; yet throughout the play we forget all about the goddess, so vividly do we see Phaedra yielding and resisting, ashamed and yet secretly consenting to the base plan of her loyal nurse, whom she covers with reproaches only when the withering scorn of Hippolytus has burnt into her soul. Then the nurse shrewdly, and a little bitterly, knowing her mistress all too well, replies: 'If I had succeeded, then I should be reckoned with the wise, for our wisdom is measured by our success.'[40] And in the end, when Phaedra,

> ere she perished, blasted in a scroll
> The fame of him her swerving made not swerve,[41]

[39] Euripides, *Hippolytus* 380 ff.
[40] *Ibid.* 700-701.
[41] Browning, *Artemis Prologizes* 29-30.

there is no mention of any god or goddess. Phaedra herself, and by herself, made the plan and executed it. Again, when Hippolytus is dying, Artemis does say that the Cyprian willed for this to happen, in order to fill up the measure of her wrath for his haughty neglect of her worship; but she condemns Theseus because he destroyed his son without first weighing evidence, or consulting seers, or waiting for time to prove or disprove the baleful charge.

No one can read the Greek dramas in their entirety without feeling that, whatever outside forces are at work, whatever the inheritance may be, after all, man is a free agent, who makes his choice for weal or woe—and this moral responsibility is the opposite of fatalism. Man has his chance, but so dull is he, or so perverse, that rarely does he seize the golden opportunity; and hence the maxims, γνῶθι σεαυτόν, γνῶθι καιρόν, were put forth by the Wise Men of Greece as the primal need for true living: 'For a brief span hath opportunity [καιρός] for man, but of him it is known surely when it cometh, and he waiteth thereon, a servant but no slave.'[42] This word, καιρός, Butcher thus defines: 'Time charged with opportunity; our own possession, to be seized and vitalized by human energy; momentous, effectual, decisive; Time the inert transformed into purposeful activity.'[43] With this definition compare Sophocles:

For opportunity is the best captain of all enterprise.[44]

Plato, in his tale of Er, in which he represents the souls choosing each a life for himself, says emphatically: 'The responsibility is with the chooser—God is blameless';[45] but once the choice is made, they must abide by it. Plato sounds his note of warning: the most earnest study and thought must be given in order that the choice may be wise, since everything is involved in it. Is this fatalism? Looking at life as we see it, do we not say virtually the same thing?—'Whatsoever a man soweth, that shall he also reap.' 'They have sown the wind, and they shall reap the whirlwind.' Is it not the law of life that to us has been entrusted the choice in great measure of what our lives shall be, and do we not pay the penalty or reap the reward accordingly? Perhaps the Greeks press home the truth more strongly than we, because Christian teaching emphasizes the possibility of reform even for one deeply dyed in

42 Pindar, *P.* 4. 286-288. Myers' translation.
43 S. H. Butcher, *Harvard Lectures on Greek Subjects*, p. 119.
44 Sophocles, *Electra* 75-76. Storr's translation.
45 Plato, *Republic* 10 (617E).

sin; yet we know that the consequences of wrongdoing are inevitable, and that no repentance or change of conduct will make the
character and life what it would have become through the choice
of the beautiful and good. But though the Greeks emphasize the
punishment that waits upon sin and folly, yet, if the offense is not
too great, there comes relief from the punishment, and a new
chance. In the seventh Olympian ode of Pindar one finds the Greek
conception of life clearly expressed; Nemesis is the thing dwelt
upon, not fate. Those who have sinned, who have forgotten, who
were absent, paid the penalty; but, even so, there came 'sweet
recompense for grievous disaster.' 'Yet the Titans were set free
by immortal Zeus.' 'The heavy stone that from the hand is
hurled we cannot check, nor word that leaves the tongue.'[46]

I do not for a moment deny that fate and fortune play a part in
Greek literature and life; but that is quite different from saying
that the Greeks were fatalists. Even where some god or goddess
lays a heavy hand upon a hero, as upon Heracles in the *Trachiniae*
of Sophocles—Heracles, the type of the man of toils and burdens—
yet after all, it is his own folly that destroys him; for with time,
according to the play, he would have had release from his relent-
less taskmaster, had not his passion for Iole worked his undoing.
And moreover, his patient endurance and hard-won conquests are
shown in the *Philoctetes* to have received rich reward in the apotheo-
sis of the hero.

There is a passage in the *Prometheus* of Aeschylus often brought
forward to prove that the Greeks held fate to be supreme over the
gods—even Zeus himself,—and cited as conclusive evidence of their
fatalism. In this play Prometheus says: 'Fate, the all-fulfiller, has
otherwise decreed the end of these things.' The Chorus asks: 'Who
then holds the helm of necessity?' Prometheus replies: 'The triple
Fates and the mindful Erinyes.' 'And is Zeus weaker than these?'
they ask. 'Yes,' Prometheus answers, 'and therefore he cannot
escape what is fated.'[47] This positive statement of the supremacy
of the fates is the more remarkable, because elsewhere Aeschylus
exalts the power of Zeus in no uncertain terms as supreme. To cite
a few passages out of many, in the *Suppliants* we have: 'There is
no o'erstepping the mighty impassable will of Zeus.'[48] Again: 'And
regard thy suppliants, O almighty Zeus that swayest the earth!'

---

[46] (1) Pindar, *O.* 7. 77; (2) Pindar, *P.* 4. 291; (3) Menander, *Incert. Fab.*
fr. 1092 (Kock).

[47] Aeschylus, *Prometheus Bound* 511-518.

[48] Aeschylus, *Suppliants* 1016. Tucker's translation.

'Yet thine wholly is the beam of the balance, and without thee what cometh to pass for mortals?'[49] 'King of Kings, most blessed of the blest, and most absolute of absolute powers, all-happy Zeus!'[50] Clearly in these passages there is no subordination of Zeus to fate; on the contrary, he is represented as wielding all power, the supreme ruler of the universe. Can we reconcile the passage in the *Prometheus* with this? In the first place, we must remember that Prometheus, who says these words, is the bitter opponent of Zeus, stubborn in his resistance, implacable in his resentment, with unbending will enduring more than mortal agony rather than yield to the god's authority. His haughty defiance kindles our admiration, even though the poet through the Chorus shows us that he has sinned, and is suffering justly for his deed, however proudly he may refuse to recognize the fact. We must remember, too, that this is but one play of the trilogy. There was also a *Prometheus Unbound*, of which only a few fragments have come down to us, but from these we find that in the end Zeus triumphs, and Prometheus confesses his sin. Thereafter he takes his place among the gods of Olympus, but henceforth he wears upon his brows a willow wreath, the token of repentance.[51]

However, I am far from saying that the Greeks were consistent in their utterances or beliefs. While in general Zeus is exalted to the supreme place, sometimes we find passages that seem to give predominance to fate; and while in general man is free to work out his own destiny, sometimes there is a doom upon him which he cannot escape.[52] But do we not see precisely this in life? However we may explain it, do we not sometimes feel the futility of human endeavor? Have we not the proverb: 'Man proposes, but God disposes'? And Shakespeare says:

> There's a divinity that shapes our ends,
> Rough-hew them how we will.[53]

[49] Aeschylus, *Suppliants* 815 ff. Theognis (157) uses the same figure: 'Zeus inclines the balance now one way, and now another.'

[50] *Ibid.* 503 ff.

[51] Athenaeus 15. 672E, 674D.

[52] Compare Bacchylides 16. 24-28: 'Whatever the resistless doom given by the gods has decreed for us, and the scale of Justice inclines to ordain, that appointed fate we will fulfil when it comes.' (Jebb's translation.) On the other hand, see Bacchylides 14. 51-56: 'Zeus, who rules on high and beholds all things, is not the author of grievous woes for mortals. No, open before all men is the path that leads to unswerving Justice, attendant of holy Eunomia and prudent Themis.' (Jebb's translation.)

[53] Shakespeare, *Hamlet* 5. 2. 11.

And again:

What fates impose, that men must needs abide.[54]

And:

But O vain boast, who can control his fate?[55]

Or compare Cowper:

Fate steals along with silent tread,
Found oft'nest in what least we dread.[56]

Have we not wrestled with the problem of almighty power and predestination, God's foreknowledge and man's free will? But we are not fatalists, and no more were the Greeks. Take the story of Pelops as Pindar tells it in the first Olympian ode. Enamored of the lovely Hippodamia, he resolves to enter the lists to win her, though failure will be certain death. Alone in the darkness he stands upon the seashore, and invokes the aid of Posidon, with whom in the past he has found favor. Knowing full well the peril— for thirteen suitors already have been slain—nevertheless, with undaunted courage he says: 'Forasmuch as men must die, wherefore should one sit vainly in the dark through a dull and nameless age, without lot in noble deeds? Not so, but I will dare this strife. Do thou give the issue I desire.'[57] The gods help those who help themselves: Posidon grants his aid, and Hippodamia is won. Where is the fatalism in this story? Pelops has determined to hazard his life for the prize he longs for, and only when thus resolved does he invoke the aid of the god. This is the true Greek spirit—daring in the face of peril, confidence in the ability to achieve success, and love of glory and honor and deeds that bring fame—and this the theme of poet and orator as well.

'But what of Oedipus?' a believer in the fatalism of the Greeks will ask. His destiny does seem to have been marked out for him, I grant; and yet Sophocles plainly shows even in his case that his own traits of character brought on and augmented the catastrophe. Further, this play is but one, and might be taken to illustrate the emphasis occasionally put upon that something which seems to defy forethought and calculation, in some lives bringing disaster upon disaster, which culminate in utter ruin in spite of every well-meant

---

[54] *3 Henry VI* 4. 3. 57.
[55] *Othello* 5. 2. 264.
[56] Cowper, *A Fable* 36-37.
[57] Pindar, *O.* 1. 82-85.

effort to avert the impending woe. But to the Athenian audience
this play had something to teach quite apart from the truth of
prophecy and oracular decree.   They saw in it the lesson that was
brought home to them again and again, how man cannot tread his
path with sure self-confidence, how it may happen that in his very
effort to save himself from peril, he will be rushing straight on to
the dreaded evil. The play is a wonderful exponent of the irony
of destiny, and abounds in dramatic satire.   In his loyal devotion
to the State, Oedipus pronounces an awful curse upon the man who
has murdered Laius and now pollutes the city by his presence; little
dreaming that he is the guilty man himself, and that it is upon his
own head that he is calling down the fearful imprecation.   This is
what wrought upon the souls of the Athenian audience, and thrilled
them with pity and fear—the consciousness of man's blindness and
ignorance, the possibility that the seeming good may be evil; for
it was precisely when Oedipus stood forth great and wise before
all men, on the very pinnacle of power and honor, that the crushing
blow came, to hurl him to the lowest depths of misery.   But though
the play is most dramatic in conception, and most dramatically
worked out from point to point, it is often misunderstood. Many
people see in it merely the fulfilment of the oracle, a man in the toils
of fate; and that, I repeat, is not what quickened the imagination
of the Greeks.   The play wrought upon their thought and feeling
because it so forcibly illustrated the painful truth that great power,
high station, riches, honor, rest on no secure basis, and the greater
the height attained, the greater may be the fall.   As Sophocles
expresses it in *Philoctetes:* 'Do thou save me, do thou show me
mercy—seeing how all human destiny is full of the fear and the
peril that good fortune may be followed by evil.   He who stands
clear of trouble should beware of dangers; and when a man lives
at ease, then it is that he should look most closely to his life, lest
ruin come on it by stealth.'[58]   Or as Shakespeare puts it:

> This is the state of man: to-day he puts forth
> The tender leaves of hopes; to-morrow blossoms,
> And bears his blushing honors thick upon him;
> The third day comes a frost, a killing frost;
> And, when he thinks, good easy man, full surely
> His greatness is a-ripening, nips his root,
> And then he falls, as I do.[59]

[58] Sophocles, *Philoctetes* 501-506.   Jebb's translation.
[59] Shakespeare, *Henry VIII* 3. 2. 353-359.

Moreover, in the case of Oedipus, we must not forget that we have a contrast of the opposite kind in the beautiful play of *Oedipus at Colonus*. There Oedipus is an outcast and wanderer, old and blind, to all men most pitiable; but it is then, when he has become chastened and humbled, that the gods lift him up, and give to him an ending of life glorious almost beyond belief.

A few years ago the changes were rung upon heredity and environment. What we were for weal or woe, for good or evil, was all marked out for us from the cradle to the grave, and we were the merest automata, with no more volition than marionettes. But in spite of all that was said, and learnedly confirmed, the sober sense of people rose in revolt; for we know that we can change our inheritance, that we can rise superior to circumstances, that there are currents and cross-currents in life, and that even in a wretched environment there may open a door of opportunity and success. Nevertheless, heredity and environment are things to reckon with, and on many they do lay a heavy hand. The family stained by a great crime, the family with evil upon evil charged to its account, does fasten a taint upon the offspring, and unless he be of heroic mould and purpose, he too will follow on in the same way, and add to the count of crime and wrong. Is not the life of the individual inextricably bound up with the life of the family? Does not the new-born child come into the world with the inherited blessing of the house bright upon him, or with the curse casting its dark shadow over him? This is the truth which the Greeks have embodied in those wonderful tales of illustrious but guilty families; but so graphically have they represented the inherited blessing and curse, that it has impressed itself upon men's minds to the exclusion of the rest of their teaching. And even so, to them the case is not hopeless, for Orestes stays the curse from the Atridae, and the upright Thersander is proof against the evil of the Labdacidae. But the Greeks also saw other aspects of life; and heredity, far from being the central, pivotal theme, made only one element in their poetry. Much more do they dwell upon this, that man is free; but while he ranges wide in thought and fancy, exulting in his freedom, Zeus and his laws he must hold in reverence. 'Insolence is the very "child" of impiety; but from healthfulness of soul cometh what all desire and pray for—happiness.'60

In dealing with the Greeks, we must remember that we have to do with a people of vivid imagination, to whom the created world not only was instinct with life and energy, but had in it something of the

60 Aeschylus, *Eumenides* 536-540. Verrall's translation.

divine as well.   And so the rippling, laughing streams had their naiads, and the forest glades and mountain hollows their nymphs, while dryads dwelt in the murmuring, swaying trees, and the fifty Nereids in radiant beauty danced amid ocean's dancing waves. So did thought and fancy play over all nature, weaving and interweaving those many-stranded myths of perennial freshness and charm.   And not simply the world of sensible realities, but abstract qualities as well, were quickened by their imagination; no longer cold abstractions, they were conceived of as having the imprint of the divine and the warmth and glow of life; as, for example, Reverence and Compassion (Αἰδώς), and Justice (Δίκη) enthroned with Zeus, and Oath (Ὅρκος), the servant of Zeus who witnesseth all things.

So perhaps Μοῖρα, the allotment of Zeus to mortals, becomes a deity; though only three times even in Homer do we find the Μοῖραι regarded as persons who at the birth of each man weave for him the lot of life and death.   What is the meaning of this word Μοῖρα? It comes from μείρεσθαι, *to divide,* and means *part* or *allotted portion.* Thus each god has his allotted portion or province—a certain department of nature or field of activity.   In the *Iliad,* Posidon, referring to Zeus, declares: 'We are three brothers . . . and in three lots are all things divided, and each *took his appointed domain* [or 'privilege,' 'status'] ; . . . masterful though he be, let him stay quiet in his own third *part* [μοίρῃ].'[61]   'We may be certain,' says Farnell, 'that they [μοῖρα and τύχη] did not arise owing to the force of the conception of an over-ruling fate, but more probably as unpretentious daimones of birth, who gave his luck or his lot to the infant. . . . As Democritus well said, "Men have feigned an image of Luck, a mask of their own folly." '[62]   So Euripides: 'From the beginning have the fates [Μοῖραι, the goddesses who presided at my birth] stretched out for me a cruel childhood.'[63]   And so Pindar: 'Now if there be enmity between kin, the fates [Μοῖραι] stand aloof, and would fain hide the shame.'[64]   According to Fairbanks: 'Moira (often translated *fate*) is not any power higher than the gods, and therefore the ultimate background of the universe; it would be truer to call it the *conscience* of the gods.   As men ought to uphold the moral order, ought not to act ὑπὲρ μόρον,

---

[61] *Iliad* 15. 187 ff.   Compare Bacchylides 4. 20; Sophocles, *Antigone* 170, 896; Euripides, *Medea* 860, 987, 995, 1281.

[62] Farnell, *Cults of the Greek States* 5. 447.

[63] Euripides, *Iphigenia among the Taurians* 203-207.

[64] Pindar, *P.* 4. 145-146.

so the gods feel under obligation to uphold the moral order of the universe. . . . The existence of natural law in the physical world, and of eternal principles in the moral world, early made a deep impression on the Greek mind. . . . The precepts in the *Works and Days* of Hesiod, or in the poetry of Theognis and Solon, embody the thought of generations on law and order in the physical world and in the moral world.' 'It is Zeus who dispenses good and evil to men, Zeus to whom the epic heroes commonly pray. . . . As an actor in the poem, however, Zeus cannot always follow his personal desires; when Sarpedon is hard-pressed by Patroclus, Zeus questions whether to let his friend die or snatch him away to his home in Lycia, till Hera reminds him that it is Sarpedon's lot to die at this time. "Neither men nor gods can ward it off, when the baleful lot of death overtakes a man." Is this lot or portion a fate higher than Zeus? or is it part of the "ancient decrees of the gods" which Zeus is bound to obey? The question is never asked in such form by the poet, who recognizes no power higher than that of Zeus. . . . If Zeus saved Sarpedon he would be acting ὑπὲρ μόρον, contrary to the "ought" which he felt binding on himself.'[65]

To the same effect writes F. M. Cornford: 'Further, as in the Ionian philosopher, so in Homer, the ordinance of fate is not a mere blind and senseless barrier of impossibility; it is a moral decree—the boundary of right and wrong. We may even say that the two notions of Destiny and Right are hardly distinguished. This comes out in the phrase "beyond what is ordained," "beyond fate" (ὑπὲρ μόρον, ὑπὲρ αἶσαν), which in Homer halts between the two meanings: "beyond what is destined, and so *must* be," and "beyond what is right, and so *ought* to be." Thus, when the first sense—destiny—is uppermost, it is denied that God or man can make anything happen "beyond fate."'[66] But elsewhere we find, on the contrary, that things do happen "beyond fate." In the *Iliad*[67] the Achaeans prevail for a time in battle ὑπὲρ αἶσαν.[68] . . . Here, it is evident, the moral sense is uppermost. The offenders went beyond, not their fate, but the bounds of morality. Hence in such cases the balance is redressed by swiftly following vengeance, which itself is "beyond what is ordained" in the sense that the sinners brought it upon themselves by their own wickedness, so

[65] Fairbanks, *A Handbook of Greek Religion,* pp. 310, 140, 141.
[66] *Iliad* 6.487.
[67] *Ibid.* 16.780.
[68] *Odyssey* 1.34 has 'beyond what is ordained.'

that they, and not fate, are responsible.'[69]   When Croesus blames the oracle for his defeat, Apollo throws the responsibility upon Croesus because he took the interpretation that pleased him, without further inquiry, and Croesus thereupon acknowledges 'that the fault was his, not the god's.'[70]   'The casting the lots of Hector and Achilles into the scale,' says Farnell,[71] 'cannot be interpreted as a questioning of the superior will of fate, for Zeus never does this elsewhere; the act might as naturally be explained as a divine method of drawing lots, or, as Welcker prefers, a symbol of his long and dubious reflection.'[72] . . .

After a careful study of all the passages in Sophocles bearing on the topic, Dr. Josef Kohn reaches this result: that the Μοῖραι do have a personal existence; that they are subordinated to Zeus; that their activity is more or less completely in the background, while Zeus appears as the sole ruler of the world and guide of the fate allotted by him with wisdom to each one.[73] . . .

A question of this kind, however, cannot be settled by citations and the statistical method; it is determined rather by the ideals and general trend of life, and especially by the delineation of heroes and heroines in literature.   Take Odysseus, a typical Greek, and what do we find?   A man resourceful, ready to meet emergencies, quick-witted, daring—an excellent hero for a tale in which we have a curious interplay between divine agencies and human strength and prowess.   Of himself, Odysseus gets the better of the Cyclops when his venturesomeness has nearly cost him his life; nor is there anything cleverer in the whole story than his cunning escape.   In his meeting with Circe, however, he is fortified against her magic arts by the antidote that he has received from Hermes; but, on the other hand, he has strength in himself alone to hold out against Calypso of the radiant hair, his deep longing for his native land and those he has left behind giving way not even to the lure of becoming an immortal.   And while his companions are fine examples of those who in spite of ample warning perish through their own folly, it is his own heart, and not the gods, that the hero chides, when he is trying to regain his own, upon his return to his native land.[74]   As Odysseus is portrayed, with a keen love of knowledge,

[69] Cornford, *From Religion to Philosophy*, pp. 13, 14.
[70] Herodotus 1. 91.
[71] Farnell, *Cults of the Greek States* 1. 79.
[72] For reasons of space, a small portion of the article by Miss Leach is here omitted.—EDITOR.]
[73] Kohn, *Zeus und sein Verhältnis zu den Moirai nach Sophokles.*
[74] *Odyssey* 20. 18.

energetic, hopeful; sometimes cast down and in fear, but soon
gathering together his forces for new endeavor; alert, active, with
mind quick to conceive, and with courage to execute; what has he
in common with the stolid fatalist who grimly says: 'If it must
come, it must, and there is nothing I can do to change it'?

Not man's impotence, but man's power, not his limitations, but
his achievements, are the favorite theme of the Greeks—as in the
chorus of the *Antigone:* 'Many wonders there are, but nothing is
more wonderful than man.'[75] 'He hath resource for all; without
resource he meets nothing that must come.'[76] The danger is that
he will be led astray by his very strength and power. 'Seek not
to become Zeus,' says Pindar; 'mortal things befit mortals.'[77] This
is the keynote of Greek teaching. No dark, sinister fate hovers over
them, chilling enterprise and benumbing their hearts. The gods
are not inflexible in purpose or inexorable. In the *Iliad* Glaucus
prays Apollo to heal him of his wound in order that he may rescue
the body of Sarpedon, and Apollo grants him his wish.[78] According to Euripides, there is a saying that 'Gifts persuade even the
gods.'[79]

The Greeks were wonderful interpreters of life. Clear-eyed, they
looked out upon the world, and they knew how to record what they
saw so that it lives again for those who read. And what did they
see? The same that any one sees who goes through life and reflects
upon it—that, calculate as we will, forecast events as we will, however fortunate and successful we may be, yet outside and beyond
the reach of any effort of ours, there is an incalculable element with
which we have to reckon. Before it we stand powerless; the unforeseen intervenes, our purposes are frustrated, our endeavors
baffled, our success changed to failure, our prosperity to ruin.

We say: 'Mysterious are the workings of Providence.' 'We
know not what a day will bring forth.' 'God's ways are inscrutable
and past finding out.' 'Verily thou art a God that hidest thyself.'—All of which means that there is some mysterious power
working its will in the world, in unaccountable ways, and with
tragic consequences at times.

'Count no man happy till his death,' said the wise Solon; and

75 Sophocles, *Antigone* 332.
76 *Ibid.* 360.
77 Pindar, *I.* 5.14; *I.* 5.16.
78 *Iliad* 16. 523 ff.
79 Euripides, *Medea* 964.

the Greeks repeat the sentiment again and again in their literature.
So, for example, Simonides:

> Mortal man that thou art, never say what will be on the morrow;
> Nor yet, when thou beholdest one prospering, shalt thou say how
>   long time he will continue;
> For swift comes the change,
> Yea, swifter than in the life of the long-winged fly.[80]

What do the Greeks say? They say: Man is a free agent, but
with an ancestral heritage for blessing or bane. Man is a free
agent, but subject to forces he cannot control. Man is a free agent,
but the area of his powers is hedged about with impassable limits.
Man is a free agent, but he is mortal. Do we not say the same?
Who has ever been able to set the bounds and to mark out where
free agency ends and divine intervention begins? But this does
not prevent us any more than the Greeks from trying to carve out
our fortunes, or from believing that, measurably at least, we are
masters of our fate.

Wherein lay the greatness of the Greeks? Was it not in that
creative genius, essentially free and untrammeled, which they possessed to such a high degree, and which found expression in their
matchless literature and art? Was it not in the free play of
thought and fancy, that delighted to range at will? Freedom of
thought, freedom of action, love of the beautiful, joy in living,
incessant activity, eager emulation in pursuit of honor and glory,
fertility of resource, and confidence in their own resolute daring—
all these are incontestably theirs; and all these are diametrically
opposed to any fatalistic doctrine, to anything bordering on patient
and unquestioning submission to the fixed and unalterable decrees
of fate. The Greeks merely did not deceive themselves. 'In a little
moment,' says Pindar, 'groweth up the delight of men; yea, and in
like sort falleth it to the ground, when a doom adverse hath shaken
it. Things of a day—what are we, and what not? Man is a dream
of shadows.' But then comes the other note: 'Nevertheless, when
a glory from God hath shined on them, a clear light abideth upon
men, and serene life.'[81]

80 Simonides 32 [46].
81 Pindar, P. 8. 92-97. Myers' translation.

XI

OEDIPUS REX: A TYPICAL GREEK TRAGEDY [1]

By Marjorie L. Barstow

In an ideal tragedy, says Aristotle, 'even without seeing the things take place, he who simply hears the account of them shall be filled with horror and pity at the incidents'; and he adds: 'So it is with the Oedipus.' But the modern reader, coming to the ancient classical drama not wholly for the purpose of enjoyment, will not always respond to the story with intense and purifying sympathy. He is preoccupied with what he has heard concerning the 'fatalism' of the Greek drama; he is repelled by what seems to be a cruel injustice in the downfall of Oedipus; and, finding no solution for these intellectual difficulties, he loses half the pleasure which the Oedipus Rex was intended to produce. Perhaps we trouble ourselves too much concerning Greek notions of fate in human life. We are inclined to regard them with a lively antiquarian interest, as if they were something remote and peculiar; yet in reality the essential difference between these conceptions and the more familiar ideas of a later time is so slight that it need hardly concern a naïve and sympathetic reader. If we substitute 'heredity' for 'fate,' and 'environment' for the series of external accidents which result in the downfall of Oedipus, we begin to perceive that the hero of the old Greek story was, as Aristotle says, 'a man like ourselves,' living and suffering under the same laws. But, after all, the fundamental aim of the poet is not to teach us specific laws, but to construct a tragedy which shall completely fulfil its artistic function. In this function there is a regenerative power infinitely more vital than any specific teaching.

But the student of literature cannot stop with naïve and sympathetic reading. It is his business, not only to feel, but to think. And whether he thinks of the Oedipus Rex as representing what the Greeks observed and thought concerning human life, or whether

[1 This paper was prepared by Miss Barstow when she was a Sophomore in Cornell University. It was first printed in the Classical Weekly for October 5, 1912, and is reprinted with slight alterations.—EDITOR.]

he is interested in the artistic structure of the tragedy, he encounters the same problem—the real relation of the character of the hero
to the external accidents which seem to determine his fate.   Although Aristotle seems to regard the *Oedipus* as well-nigh a perfect
tragedy, he also says that a tragic hero should be a man not 'pre-
eminently virtuous and just,' who meets disaster through some flaw
in his own nature.   But to the sympathetic reader Oedipus seems
almost as virtuous and just as a man may reasonably be expected
to be.   He does what is moral and expedient according to his lights;
and his ruin appears, at first, to result from a flaw in the universe,
an irrationally malignant fate, rather than from any flaw in his
own generous personality.   But if we consider what 'pre-eminently
virtuous and just' meant to a Greek, the difficulties vanish.   In
other words, when we seek the standard of a perfect tragedy in
Aristotle's *Poetics,* let us seek the standard of a perfect life in his
Ethics.

In the *Nicomachean Ethics,* Aristotle defines the end of human
endeavor as 'happiness.'   By this he means, not pleasure—for
pleasure is only a part of happiness,—but a harmonious and unhampered activity of the whole human personality throughout a
complete lifetime.   This happiness does not spring primarily from
the gifts of fortune—wealth, social position, personal beauty, and
the like.   A man may have all these and yet be wretched.   It results
from a steady and comprehensive vision by which he perceives the
relation of various experiences and choices of life to one another and
to the supreme goal.   By the light of this vision the wise man preserves a just balance among his own natural impulses, and firmly
and consistently directs his will and emotions in accordance with
'true reason.'   He will not sacrifice the health of a lifetime to the
satisfaction of a particular appetite, for instance, nor in a moment
of wild anger blind himself to all considerations of wisdom and
humanity.   Being at peace with himself, he has an inward happiness which cannot be shaken save by great and numerous outward
misfortunes; and, moreover, he attains to an adequate external
prosperity, since, other things being equal, the most sensible people
are the most successful, and misfortune is in large measure due to
lack of knowledge or of prudence.   Even if he is overwhelmed by
some great external disaster, the ideal character of the *Ethics* is not
an object of fear and pity; for the 'truly good and sensible man
bears all the chances of life with decorum, and always does what is
noblest in the circumstances, as a good general uses the forces at his
command to the best advantage in war.'   The spectacular self-

destruction with which a tragedy often ends would be impossible for a hero who 'bears all the chances of life with decorum.'

Such is the ideal character who is best fitted to achieve happiness in the world of men. On the other hand, the tragic hero is a man who fails to attain happiness, but fails in such a manner that his fall excites, not blame, but pity and fear in the highest degree. To arouse our pity, his misfortunes must seem, in a measure, undeserved; he must be a man whom we wish well, a lovable or admirable man. To arouse our fear, his case must seem typical. We must feel that he is a man like ourselves; that what he does we, under like circumstances, might also do. Yet, as Aristotle notices, the fall of a perfectly good man through no fault of his own is so shocking to our sense of justice that we are repelled by it rather than touched to pity. Therefore the tragic hero must be, not pre-eminently good—not wholly under the guidance of true reason; and he himself must be directly, though not always wittingly, responsible for what happens to him. Moreover, in order that his downfall may be as striking as possible, he must be 'of the number of those in the enjoyment of great reputation and prosperity.'

How does all this apply to Oedipus? According to our usual standards, Oedipus is a good man; there is even a certain vehemence in his wish to do right. In most of the crises in which he makes a choice that eventually brings misfortune, he is either impetuously trying to avoid what is wrong, or ardently striving to do what is right. He has the best intentions in the world. Moreover, he is not a fool. He has the quick wit and brilliance that all men especially admire and envy. The moment a problem is presented to his mind, he has a solution—a solution which his courage and enterprise lead him to test by immediate action. Clever, bold, and generous. he seems born to be a leader and a hero. Most popular heroes in literature and life are men like Oedipus. Yet his noble purposes end in the crimes whose very names filled him with horror; and his brilliant inspirations only blind him to the truth that a duller man might see. But this spectacular and ironical failure furnishes no greater contrast to the dignified harmony of the ideal life suggested in the Aristotelian *Ethics* than does the character of Oedipus to that of the perfect man whose wisdom bears fruit in happiness; for Oedipus lacks the one vital and essential element in this happiness—the power to see the relation of one thing to another and to maintain a due proportion in the expenditure of energy. Oedipus can see only one thing at a time, and it is his habit to act immediately on half-knowledge with the utmost intensity and abandon.

His lack of the 'intellectual virtues' of Aristotle is paralleled only by his inability to keep the mean in the 'moral virtues.' And so his fits and starts of noble action, being without purpose or design, nullify and contradict each other, and end in hopeless confusion and ruin. This is the flaw in the character of Oedipus—a weakness at the very centre of his being, from which all other weaknesses, such as his fatal tendency to anger, naturally arise. Perhaps this will be clearer if we consider how Oedipus acts in each crisis of his life.

When the drama opens, his thoughtless energy has already led him into the very crimes which he has striven to avoid. Once, at a feast in Corinth, a man had tauntingly said that Oedipus was not the true son of Polybus. These idle words of a man in his cups so affected the excitable nature of the hero that he shortly went to Delphi to learn the truth—to consult the most holy shrine in Greece, the sacred tribunal to which great national questions were submitted. The sole response of the oracle was the prophecy that Oedipus would kill his father and marry his mother. This, of course, should have given a real importance to what was originally only an idle suspicion; it was now necessary to know the truth. So, at least, a wise man who does what is best in the circumstances, 'as a good general uses the forces at his command to the best advantage in war,' would have thought. But Oedipus, wholly absorbed in another fear, completely forgot his former doubt. Supposing the prophecy to refer to Polybus, he determined never to return to Corinth, and hastened away in the direction of Thebes. Thus his disposition to act without thinking started him headlong on the road to destruction. At a place where three ways met, all unawares, he encountered his real father, King Laius of Thebes. When the old man insolently accosted him, Oedipus, with his usual misguided promptness, struck him from the chariot, and slew him and all but one of his attendants. Thus, by an unreasonable act of passion, Oedipus fulfilled the first part of his prophetic destiny. Yet, in these cases, as in most of the crimes of his life, either one of the two fundamental Greek virtues—either temperance or prudence—would have saved him. A temperate man, with the Greek sense of fitness and decorum, would never have permitted the chance words of a man in his cups to send him to Delphi, in the first place; and so he might have remained safe in his ignorance. A prudent man, having attached so much importance to the suspicion, would not have forgotten it so soon. Again, a temperate man would not be so ready to kill an old man who angered him; a prudent man, even one of violent emotions, after hearing the oracle, might have deemed it best to put some restraint upon himself in the future. But Oedipus possessed neither the unselfish wisdom of a good man, nor the selfish prudence of many a bad one.

Yet in the crisis in which Oedipus found the city of Thebes, his energy and directness served him well. By the flashing quickness of thought and imagination which, when blinded by egoistic passion, so often hurried him to wrong conclusions, he guessed the riddle of the Sphinx. Then he married the widowed queen, seized the reins of government, and generously did his best to bring peace and prosperity back to the troubled land. In this way, by the very qualities that ultimately wrought his ruin, he was raised to the height from which he fell. But here again he displayed the thoughtlessness that was his destruction; for he neglected to make the natural inquiries concerning the murder of Laius, and took as little care to avoid a rash marriage as he had taken to avoid killing a stranger. His failure to investigate the death of his predecessor is explicable only in the light of his natural violence and intensity of action. He was always completely absorbed in the one matter that happened to engage his attention. He could not be interested in an accident in the past when there was work to be done in the present. In this case also his mistake was due to a lack of both wisdom and temperance.

Between his accession to the throne of Thebes and the opening of the drama, there intervened a long period of time in which Oedipus had prospered, and, as it seemed to the Chorus, had been quite happy. The play of Sophocles is concerned with the last stage in his tragic career—the complication of mistakes which is suddenly untangled by the words of the old Herdsman. At the beginning the land is blasted by a great dearth. Old men, young men, and children have come as suppliants to the king, seeking deliverance from this great evil. Oedipus appears, generous, high-minded, and prompt to act, as ever. When Creon brings the message that the slayer of Laius must be cast out of the land, Oedipus immediately invokes a mighty curse upon the murderer, and we thrill with pity and fear as we hear the noble king calling down upon his own head a doom so terrible. His unthinking haste furnishes the first thread in the complication of misunderstanding which the dramatist has so closely woven. Tiresias enters. When Oedipus, with angry insistence, has forced from his unwilling lips the dreadful words, 'Thou art the accursed defiler of this land,' he forgets everything else in his wrath at what he deems a taunt of the old prophet, and entangles a second thread of misunderstanding with the first. Still a third is added a moment later, when he indignantly accuses Creon of bribing Tiresias to speak these words. In his conversation with Jocasta the tendency of Oedipus to jump at conclusions does for one moment show him half the truth. He is possessed with a fear that it was he who killed Laius, but here again he can think of but one thing at a time; and, again absorbed in a new thought, he forgets his wife's mention of a child of Laius, forgets the old question concerning his birth, and accordingly misses the truth.

Then comes the message from Corinth. After his first joy in learning that his supposed father did not die as the oracle had foretold, Oedipus loses all remembrance of the oracle, and all fear concerning the death of Laius, in a new interest and a new fear— the fear that he may be base-born. Eagerly following up this latest train of thought, he at last comes upon the truth in a form which even he can grasp at once. In his agony at the vision to which for the first time in his life he has now attained, he cries out: 'Oh!' Oh! All brought to pass—all true! Thou light, may I now look my last on thee—I who have been found accursed in birth, accursed in wedlock, accursed in the shedding of blood.' In a final act of mad energy, he puts out the eyes which could not see, and demands the execution upon himself of the doom which he alone had decreed. This is the end of the great-souled man, endowed with all the gifts of nature, but heedless alike of the wisdom and temperance by which the magnanimous man of the *Ethics* finds his way to perfect virtue and happiness.

Perhaps we are not entirely reconciled to the fate of Oedipus. Perhaps the downfall of a tragic hero can never satisfy the individual reader's sense of justice. If the doom is wholly just, why should we pity the sufferer? The poet, by the necessity of his art, is bound to make the particular representation of a universal truth as terrible and as pitiful as he can. Surely this result is accomplished in the *Oedipus Rex*. And in the production of this tragic effect, the apparent 'fatalism'—in the oracles, for instance, and in the performance of the prophesied crimes by Oedipus, in ignorance of the circumstances—is a powerful agent. Aristotle himself mentions crimes committed in ignorance of the particulars as deeds which especially arouse pity. The oracles have a threefold artistic function. They produce that sense of impending doom, that fearful consciousness of the ironical contrast between the actual facts and the opinions of the hero, which raises pity into awe. They serve as a stimulus to the hero's own nature, without determining the result of the stimulus—though it is noteworthy that the initial impulse is not derived from them. [And lastly, they point out in clear and impressive language the course of the story. Shakespeare, in *Macbeth* and *Hamlet*, introduces less noble and less probable forms of the supernatural for the same purpose. The oracles of Sophocles, like the ghosts and witches of Shakespeare, are but means to an artistic end. The representation of their effect upon the characters is not the end of the drama, and must not be so regarded. They embody the final teaching of the poet as little as the words of particular dramatic characters, in particular circumstances, express the poet's own unbiased thought and feeling.]

The central conception of the *Oedipus Rex* is plainly not more fatalistic than the philosophy of Aristotle. Oedipus is the architect of his own fortune as truly as the magnanimous man of the *Ethics* is the architect of his. If any reader finds the doctrine hard, he may remember that Sophocles himself completed it, somewhat as the Christian Church completed Aristotle, and in the death of Oedipus at Colonus crowned the law with grace. Nevertheless, for the understanding alike of Greek philosophy and Greek art, it seems necessary to recognize the relation between these two ideal conceptions—the magnanimous man of the *Nicomachean Ethics*, ideal for life and happiness, the tragic hero of the *Poetics*, ideal for misery and death. [According to Aristotle, the man who is truly happy in this world is the wise man who sees in all their aspects the facts or the forces with which he is dealing, and can balance and direct his own impulses in accordance with that vision. He is a general, victorious, not only because he is courageous, but because he has planned wisely; an artist who makes of his life something as perfect as a Greek temple or a Greek play. In the *Oedipus Rex*, Sophocles had already shown the reverse. The man who sees but one side of a matter, and straightway, driven on by his uncontrolled emotions, acts in accordance with that imperfect vision, meets a fate most terrible and pitiful, in accordance with the great laws established by the gods.]

This philosophy of Aristotle and Sophocles is clearly suggested in the drama itself. 'May destiny still find me,' sings the Chorus, 'winning the praise of reverent purity in all words and deeds sanctioned by those laws of range sublime, called into life throughout the high, clear heaven, whose father is Olympus alone; their parent was no race of mortal men, no, nor shall oblivion ever lay them to sleep; the god is mighty in them, and he grows not old.'

XII

THE CHARACTER AND EXTENT OF GREEK LITERATURE [1]

By Ulrich von Wilamowitz-Moellendorff

The literature of Greece is the only one in the civilized world that developed wholly out of itself. It brought forth in profusion not only perfect works of art but rigorously exclusive artistic types and styles, through which it became the basis and model of the European and of various extra-European literatures. Greek literature is the vessel that contains, or has contained, the fundamental works of all science; for it was the Greeks, and no others, that brought science as such into the world. These incomparable advantages—which nevertheless in the final analysis are relative—interfere with an absolute appraisal of Greek works and their authors; for when a work has served as a pattern during two thousand years, to see it as it appeared to the man who once created it is no easy matter; and to see in him an agonizing, striving, erring human being is even harder. Nothing more effectually obscures a human figure than to deify it, and nothing seems so far removed from the accidents of genesis as a classic work of art—in both cases exaltation occurs at the expense of life. But, in point of fact, Homer is classic at the date when he is first known to us; and at the birth of Christ Greek literature is already classic to the same extent and in the same sense as a hundred years ago when the historical study of it began; this last is not older. The relation of Goethe to the Greeks is not essentially different from that of Virgil and Horace, who, together with Cicero, produced the first classical literature in another tongue upon the Greek foundation. Through the mediation of this daughter, Greek literature dominated the Occident even

[1 This extract, by the leading classical scholar of to-day in Germany, and probably in the world, is translated from *Die Griechische und Lateinische Literatur und Sprache* (pp. 1-4). B. G. Teubner, Berlin and Leipzig, 1905. (*Die Kultur der Gegenwart, ihre Entwickelung und ihre Ziele*, herausgegeben von Paul Hinneberg, Teil I, Abteilung VIII.)—EDITOR.]

in the long interval when Western Europe was without knowledge of the original works; and when the original works became known after the fifteenth century, they were still primarily viewed with the eyes of the Romans, or of Greeks of the Roman era, who stand under the same spell of classicism. But when Winckelmann, with an energy conscious of its aim, made bold to return to the genuine Greeks, and undertook to draw for sculpture the line of its historical development, and when the next generation in turn carried this movement over to literature, it was only the absolute estimation of the classic originals that rose; for in regard to historical knowledge, no one as yet was expected to trace the process by which the Greek people came into being—the history and results of this process. And so the origin of Greek literature and its types was identified with the absolutely normal and natural, the gaps in historical knowledge were bridged with philosophical abstractions, and what had been effected by definite, concrete conditions, and by the individual power and will of important men, became the product of immanent natural laws. The types of Greek poetry and artistic prose—epic, elegy, ode, tragedy, comedy, epigram, history, dialogue, oration, epistle—appeared as natural forms in the arts of discourse. In all this the interpreters still stood under the spell of the ancient theory. An actual science of history the Greeks did not produce; their thought was bent upon abstracting rules from observation, and then working with these abstractions; and so they actually regarded those types, which had grown up among them historically, as conceptually pre-existent. The first man to compose a tragedy was not the inventor—he was 'the first one to find it,' as they said. Preliminary stages, of course, were recognized, but then they represented imperfect forms which had best be forgotten. The decisive moment is that in which the type 'attains to its own true nature.' From the moment when tragedy has reached this point—from that moment on for ever one can compose tragedies only after this pattern; and their success or failure is measured as they give better or worse expression to the idea of tragedy. Starting with this view, the moderns came to an extravagant overestimation of the finders or inventors—or better, of the classic works,—and to a depreciation of everything subsequent; precisely as scholars, following the ancient purists, regarded the entire evolution of the language after Demosthenes as decadent. In truth it often looked as though Greek literature had ended with Alexander. And yet more unjust was it when, from among the works of a later age, that was preferred which seemed to come nearest to the classic, that is, nothing more or less than pure imitation. Moreover, there was still another great want; for the philologists had recognized only in principle that historical understanding and historical evaluation must grasp each work and each author first of all in terms of his own age and his own intention, and hence independently of later estimates quite as much as of distorted historical tradition or secondary reconstructions of texts. As for schoolmasters who identify the literature with the authors employed in the service of education—where the standard is a fixed rule, preferably of the narrowest description— we need not consider them. It is naïve presumption when these ignoramuses put on the air of philologists.

But in reality the history of Greek literature is still in its beginnings, and indeed, considering its youth, this could not be otherwise. An account that should turn away from classicism simply on principle has in fact never been attempted. And indeed, such an account could not as yet by any possibility be written. First of all, the extant works must be understood; and therewith the artistic forms, and the principles in accordance with which they were composed, must be grasped, before they can be genetically explained and their history written. And the individual personalities of the authors must be seized before they can be arranged in historical connection, and hence before any judgment can be pronounced upon them. But for much the larger part of the extant literature this process has scarcely begun. Yet before one tries to understand the works in question one must possess them. But for whole masses of the literature we have only inadequate texts, while for other sections, as the Christian writers from the fourth century on, the texts are inaccessible. To secure these, Greek philology has striven with vigor and success. But not all the civilized nations have supplied large numbers of willing and able collaborators for the undertaking; and furthermore, precisely from the most important periods only too many works are lost; these it is necessary to restore so far as we have the power—so far as, with our best efforts, the task is not utterly hopeless. Much, indeed, has already been accomplished, yet the fact remains that not even the fragments have been completely assembled; and this is only the first step. For the history of literature the second step is to trace out subsequent influences, and it is almost more important than the other. Still further, Greek literature is all-embracing; it will not do to limit the term to belles-lettres (a conception for which the Greeks had no equivalent), and to exclude the special sciences. But now we must remember that the works on medicine, astronomy, and mechanics cannot be understood without a knowledge of these sciences. Here the collaboration of various specially trained investigators is demanded—something long needed, but now, thank Heaven! no longer wanting. The culture of the twenty-first century will look down with pity, let us hope, on the small extent of our present knowledge, and will rectify many of our judgments; but it unquestionably will hand on to its future more to do than, under the most favorable circumstances, its advantage will amount to in comparison with us. True it is, the feeling of one's own inadequacy in the face of such a task is not quieted by the thought that in any case the problem can at the moment obtain but an inadequate solution; yet to the man who reads as well as the man who writes we may apply the utterance of Hippolyte Taine—who knew what it was to read and write: 'The keenest pleasure of a toiling spirit lies in the thought of the toil hereafter to be accomplished by others.'

It could not be otherwise than that, in accordance with the extant materials, the treatment of them should be widely varied; for on the one hand it is impossible to set such works as we have constantly in the centre, so as to make the accidental circumstance of their preservation more or less determine the question of relative importance; and, on the other hand, investigation has not everywhere managed to survey the motive forces to such an extent that one may find an historical thread by which to order all the particulars. The single principle of following each literary type separately would, of course, preserve unity, but this very procedure would completely involve us again in the ancient schematism. Accordingly, what would on artistic grounds be the only satisfying method has here been renounced, and the attempt has been made to treat each period in accordance with the status of the materials and of our knowledge. If this procedure seems to subordinate the classical period as compared with what is subsequent thereto, let the reader recall not merely the sum total of the extant writings, and the length of the periods, but also the fact that the opposite injustice has only too long prevailed.

The periods are automatically divided according to the great sections of history. The first is the Hellenic, from about 700 B. C. to the Persian wars, to which is attached the Attic, delimited about the year 320 by the death of Alexander, Aristotle, and Demosthenes. If we speak of the fourth century, the age embraces but eighty years, and the same is true of the fifth. The glory of Athens was brief. Then come the three Hellenistic centuries, separated from one another by, say, the year 222 (beginning of Polybius), the year 133 (beginning of revolutionary times at Rome), and the year 30 (conquest of Alexandria). The differences between the centuries are easily felt; but precisely for this period the historical sequence has had to be abandoned. The fourth, or Roman, period, down to Constantine, is the one of which we have most knowledge. Following this must come the period of the Eastern Roman Empire, down to the invasion by Islam and the outbreak of iconoclasm (for from then on the continuity is quite interrupted), or at least down to the year 529 and the closing of the school of Plato (for the age of Justinian already has a rich, new life). Meanwhile the information of those who do the reporting, and the economy of our account, have permitted only a glance at the latter end of the Hellenic literary types. This procedure is in so far justified that antiquity in very truth passed away with the downfall of the Empire and the state religion.

XIII

THE 'TRADITION' OF GREEK LITERATURE [1]

By Gilbert Murray

The object of us Greek scholars is to find out all we can about
ancient Greece and—still more important—to understand what we
find. For the first part of this work we have various instruments.
The inscribed stones, immense in numbers, which happen to have
weathered the ages and come down to us in a legible condition.
The surface of the earth and sea in Greek regions, which naturally
has changed far less than the human institutions. The inscribed
coins, which, by all kinds of strange fates, have been neither decom-
posed nor melted, but have turned up still more or less decipherable
and charged with history. The fragments of papyri, preserved by
the accident of the Egyptian climate and other chances, which give
us bits of letters and of books which may have been handled, if not
by Plato, at least by Callimachus or Didymus or Mark Antony.
Lastly, the customs and rites and ways of life of various races of
mankind still existing in a savage or primitive state, which throw
light on the condition from which the Greeks emerged as they became Greeks, and which enable us to understand vast masses of
ancient myth and custom which seemed meaningless before. One
could enumerate other instruments too. But the fact remains that
by far the greatest part of our knowledge of the ancient Greeks
comes from the books which they wrote, and which have come down
to us by a long process of handing-on from generation to generation: *traditio* is the Latin word, *paradosis* the Greek. That is to
say: The books which we now possess are those which, for one reason
or another, have been constantly copied and re-copied, and never
allowed quietly to pass on to the natural end of books and men.
It is not only that they were always considered worth reading by
somebody; it is that somebody was always willing to take the great

[1 From the *Yale Review* 2. 215-233. The author of the article is Regius
Professor of Greek in the University of Oxford. In this country he is best
known for his gifts as a translator of Euripides.—EDITOR.]

trouble of writing them out again. That process is the literary 'tradition,' and it is that that I propose to discuss in the present paper.

I will first make some general comments on the characteristics of the literary tradition, as compared with our other sources of knowledge. I will then consider the main defects in the tradition as a process: I mean, the question how far the things that are preserved are preserved accurately; and lastly, the defects in the content of the tradition, that is: what important classes of books are not preserved at all, and for what reason.

First, then, the general characteristics. Obviously the literary tradition, where it exists, is much fuller, more intelligible, more explanatory, than our other sources of knowledge. This is almost too obvious to dwell upon. At the very beginning of Hicks' inscriptions you find the bases of the pillars of the temple at Ephesus inscribed: Βασιλεὺς Κροῖσος ἀνέθηκεν'—and how interesting it is! But, without Herodotus, not only could the inscription never have been read; without Herodotus, it would not have been in the least interesting if it had been read. Βασιλεὺς Κροῖσος would have been nothing to us. Think again of the condition of our Cretan remains unaccompanied by literature. How rich they are, and how enigmatical! A story is there waiting to be told, but there is—so far at least—no literature to tell it. Think how all our knowledge would be trebled if Dr. Evans unearthed for us the feeblest fragment of a Minoan historian.

It is as a rule literature that explains; consequently it is to a large extent literature that gives interest. This, however, is not a question of literature as against archaeology; it is merely a question of art against that which is not art. The Hermes of Praxiteles does not wait for a literary text to explain or illuminate him. It is he who explains and illuminates an otherwise quite uninteresting text in Pausanias. But, in the main, as compared with the great mass of archaeological evidence, the literary remains are what we call art—that indescribable thing which aims at stirring our interest and sense of beauty. And this brings me to the second characteristic of literary tradition.

It is what we, in our rather stupid phraseology, call 'idealized.' In Greek it is occupied with the *kalon* rather more than the *anankaion*, with what you aspire to do rather than what you have got to do. Of course there are degrees. In the higher poetry, as in the higher art, *to kalon* has things all its own way. And the same in most philosophy. Whatever historical conclusions can be drawn from the *Agamemnon* or the *Symposium*, it is quite clear that Aeschylus and Plato were not chiefly concerned in depicting contemporary facts. They were chiefly concerned with thinking and expressing the highest thoughts in their power; whereas the man who inscribed the Erechtheum accounts was mainly concerned with getting the figures right—and did not bother about *to kalon* except for cutting his letters well.

What of history? According to some conceptions of history, *to anankaion* would be absolutely paramount. 'The task of history is to investigate how things happened,' according to Ranke's dictum. But, as a matter of fact, I do not see how there can be any doubt that the works of all ancient historians—Thucydides as much as any—are works of art. *To kalon* has an enormous sway over their minds. I do not wish to raise the question whether the search for beauty and the search for truth are irreconcilable, either ultimately or in ordinary practice. Thucydides, the most accurate and scientific of ancient historians, probably possesses also the most terrible emotional and artistic power. But I do suggest strongly that in all ancient literary history there is a great deal of selection and idealization, a striving for *to kalon,* which removes it from the sphere of mere recorded fact. Do you want an example—a gross example? Take the fact that almost all ancient historians, in their finished work, refuse to give documents and speeches in the authentic words, but re-write them deliberately in a way that will harmonize with the style and tenor of their own work.

Our ancient literature, then, gives on the whole far more of the *kalon* than the *anankaion.* That makes the record a little one-sided, and explains the extraordinary interest which we tend to take in those few books that belong to the other tendency, which are not lofty, not idealized, and have the touch of common life in them. That is why we are interested in the tract of the Old Oligarch on *The Constitution of Athens* and his remarks about the lodginghouse-keeper's vote and the cabman's vote. It is why we revel in the fragments of familiar history that can be extracted from Aristophanes (though Aristophanes cared little enough for *to anankaion;* he pursued *to kalon* like any other artist, only his *kalon* took the comic form). It is why we accept with gratitude even such a child of the mud as Herondas. These things help to complete our historical knowledge, and to make it alive. On the other hand, the fact always remains that they are valuable, not for themselves, but only *allou heneka,* for the sake of something else; for the sake, ultimately, of that very selected and idealized literature against which they are in conscious revolt.

These two qualities, the full and explanatory character of the literary tradition and its pursuit of *to kalon,* must be set against one clear inferiority which belongs to it as compared with archaeological evidence. It is richer, but it is less trustworthy. Coins, and even inscriptions, can be forged; but where you do get a contemporary inscription or coin, the information which it gives you is final. Even in points of language it is the same. Most of our knowledge of Attic forms comes from the manuscripts and the grammarians; but they are not final authorities. If they tell us to write *Troizên,* and all the contemporary stones write *Trozên,* we know that the matter is settled. *Trozên* must be right.

So much for the general characteristics of the literature as against the other evidence. Let us now consider how far the *paradosis,* or *traditio,* of the literature, has been an accurate process. We can consider first the comparative soundness or corruptness of our manuscript texts in the matter of mere wording, and secondly the larger changes of form which belong to what is called the higher criticism.

As to the corruption of manuscripts, one important fact has come out clearly during the last twenty years. It is that on the whole the handing-on of our classical texts from Alexandrian times to the present has been astonishingly exact. I am referring here to verbal accuracy, to accuracy in transmitting the actual *grammata* or written signs from manuscript to manuscript down to the twelfth or thirteenth century. The evidence is in the papyri and ostraka and a few fragments of very ancient manuscripts or palimpsests. Let us take instances. Our oldest regular manuscript of Plato was written in the year 895 A. D., say 1250 years after Plato's death. In 1891 Flinders Petrie discovered a large papyrus fragment of the *Phaedo,* which was written in the third century B. C.—very likely in the lifetime of people who had seen Plato. Here was a test case for the accuracy of the *paradosis.* The papyrus might well have shown that our text of the *Phaedo* was a mass of mistakes or interpolations. As a matter of fact, the differences between the traditional text and the papyrus were almost negligible—in that particular case they affected chiefly the order of the words—and where they occurred, the papyrus seemed most often to be in the wrong.

Again, there are many fragments of Euripides preserved on

papyri or ostraka. In the preface to my first volume, I mentioned
fourteen, to which one or two more must now be added. Of course
the passages so preserved are mostly short. But the total of lines
covered is very considerable. Now, how many places are there
where the papyri or ostraka give an absolutely new right reading?
I mean, one which is preserved in no manuscript, and has not been
reached by conjecture? It seems extraordinary, but I believe there
are only two places—*Phoenissae* 1036 and 1101. And even those
two cases of failure are almost a testimony to the general accuracy
of the tradition. In the latter a papyrus gives us ξυνῆψαν, 'they
joined,' instead of ξυνῆψεν, 'he joined'; and no one happened to
have made that conjecture, although they easily might, if they had
studied the scholia, which evidently imply a plural. In the former,
1036, there are two short lines, ἰήιον βοάν, ἰήιον μέλος, where for metrical reasons we need an iambus more in each line. They are ordinary
iambic dimeters. They mean, you see, 'the cry of *iê*, the music of
iê'—*iê* being one of the regular cries of wailing. People emended
by doubling the words βοάν and μέλος. The scholiast observed that
'It is found in the poets that way, *iê iê*, just like *iô iô*.' Yet by
some accident we never thought of emending the line to ἰηιήιον βοάν,
ἰηιήιον μέλος—'the cry of *ie-ie*, the music of *ie-ie*.' Clearly that is
what the scholiast meant. And it so happens that one of the
Oxyrhynchus papyri gives it so. Of course that is right.

Let me take two more instances to show how steady the tradition
has been. From the study of our fourteenth century manuscript
L, Wilamowitz came to the conclusion that L's group of manuscripts was descended from an archetype which contained all the
plays of Euripides, not merely those selected for educational purposes, without any notes, but with variant readings written above
the line. When Grenfell and Hunt discovered the *Hypsipyle*
papyrus, it proved to be a manuscript without notes but with
variant readings written above the line, and of course the *Hypsipyle*
is one of the unselected plays.

A last instance of the same steadiness. In *Phoenissae* 131—

τὸν δ' ἐξαμείβοντ' οὐχ ὁρᾷς Δίρκης ὕδωρ;
See you not him crossing Dirce's water?—

a Byzantine group of manuscripts add at the end of the line a
gloss, 'λοχαγόν'—'see you not that captain?' A late Byzantine gloss,
critics used to say. But on a certain very ill-written ostrakon in
the British Museum, dating from the second century, you have the

word λοχαγόν already there. It is a mistake. A mere gloss. But it was in the text by about 150 A. D., and has been religiously copied by a whole chain of scribes.

Of course *humanum est errare.* All manuscripts have lots of mistakes in them. What I am here comparing with the papyri is not the text of any particular manuscript, but the text that results from the critical examination of all the manuscripts by a good scholar using his knowledge as best he can. When by criticism you succeed in finding out what the 'tradition' really is, that tradition proves to be surprisingly accurate.

But here comes an important qualification. This evidence of the papyri only takes us back, at earliest, to the Alexandrian age. From the second century B. C. onwards, the tradition has been careful; but before that thousand years of care, there had been some two hundred of carelessness. The great Alexandrian scholars were probably almost the first people in the world to understand the meaning of exactness in preserving an ordinary secular text. Some of the papyri themselves show us how careless a pre-Alexandrian text could be. Our scholia to the tragedians show that the greatest of our difficulties and corruptions were mostly already there when the commentaries were made. Again and again the critical editor has to make his footnote: '*corruptela iam Didymo antiquior.*' And if it comes to that, general considerations of the history of Greek literature would have led us to the same conclusion. It is late in the day that a man turns from the natural conception that his book ought to be as good and full as possible, to the scholarly and self-denying conception that it ought to be exactly what the writer left it.

By the time of the Alexandrians, when our tradition began, manuscripts were often already badly corrupted. An instance of what I mean can be found in some of the latest plays of Euripides. Our text of the *Phoenissae* is probably nearly as good as the text that was edited by Aristophanes of Byzantium. Yet the play that we have is, in the opinion of most critics, a perfect mass of interpolation. It was acted, no doubt, again and again, in Athens and in less cultured places, during the fourth and third centuries, and the only copy the Alexandrians could get was one that had been exposed—like most plays that have life in them—to the improvements and additions of the stage-manager. The same is hardly less true of the *Orestes.* The *Iphigenia in Aulis* happens to have some of its history recorded, so we can speak of it with more certainty. True, the archetype of our two manuscripts was defective at the end; the manuscripts themselves say so; and the end that we now have is apparently work of the early Renaissance. In that respect the Alexandrians were better off. But for the rest of the play how does it stand? We know that the *Iphigenia in Aulis* was produced and prepared for the stage by Euripides the younger after his father's death. An inscription tells us that 'The Iphigenia of Euripides'—very probably this play—was acted again in 341 B. C., and that the actor Neoptolemus received a prize for it. Doubtless it was acted more often than that. And the version that has come down to us bears the natural traces of this history. It has two distinct and scarcely compatible prologues. It makes the impression, upon practically all scholars who have studied it, of containing masses of work by different hands. Unfortunately we have no scholia to the *Iphigenia in Aulis*. But we may be fairly sure that, when the Alexandrian scholars set to work to collect the works of Euripides, the only copy they could get of this famous play was one already badly knocked about by the actors. As a matter of fact, both the extant prologues are quoted by writers of the generation after Aristotle. The mischief had begun as early as that. In the case of the *Rhesus*, there were actually three prologues going in Alexandrian times. The *Rhesus* question is too complicated to discuss at length. But it is clear that the Alexandrians could not get hold of a copy that satisfied them.

Again, what are we to make of such a fact as the comparative condition of the several Homeric hymns? The *Hymn to Aphrodite* is excellently preserved; the *Hymn to Apollo* is in a state of desperate confusion. But the confusion is not such as comes from faulty manuscript tradition. It does not yield to criticism and emendation. It goes back to the time when the old epic literature was but newly dead, and its fragments were collected and formed into such wholes or attempts at wholes as circumstances allowed, probably by people who had as yet no particular sense of scholarship.

To sum up: In the cases where ancient books or parts of books have been preserved to us entire, and where our manuscripts are of good average quality, we find that the tradition, from Alexandrian times on, has been to a surprising degree careful and trustworthy. I leave aside, of course, special cases of bad or mutilated manuscripts; anthologies in which the quotations were modified in order to stand without their context; and the handbooks which have been systematically interpolated and improved by their owners.

Let us next consider the content of the tradition. That is, how much of what it tried to preserve has it actually preserved? Here we have a very different story.

Take first the kinds of literature of which we seem to have a large stock: epos, drama, oratory, and history. Epic perhaps belonged to very early times, so that it is not surprising that we have only two poems remaining out of a whole wide literature, and those in a very late recension. Of lyric poetry, too, we may say that it flourished chiefly in non-Attic regions, whereas our tradition has its roots in Athens. So we ought not to complain if out of a large number of lyric poets the tradition has preserved complete poems by only one, and of him only about a fifth part of his whole writings. The papyri give us a few complete poems by another. As for tragedy, there must have been, as far as we can calculate, well over nine hundred tragedies produced in Athens; we feel ourselves rich with thirty-three out of that number. But that is a vague way of considering the question. Let us take two periods to compare with our own, and to make out how the great losses took place.

We have a fair amount of evidence about the books in the Alexandrian library: that should be one point. For another we may take the interesting *Bibliotheca* or Μυριόβιβλον of Photius. Photius was Patriarch of Constantinople from 857 to 879 A. D., and the *Bibliotheca* is a list, with notes and epitomes, of three hundred books which he had had read to him. It is dedicated to 'his beloved brother Tarasius.' Apparently Photius was in the habit of having books read aloud in his learned circle, where Tarasius was usually present. This is a list of books which Tarasius somehow missed, and is sent to him on that account, and also to console him for the absence of Photius himself on an embassy to the Assyrians—that is, as Gibbon said, to the Caliph of Bagdad.

To take some definite figures, comparing first merely the Alexandrians and ourselves, and omitting Photius for the moment. Aeschylus wrote ninety plays; the Alexandrians possessed seventy-two of them; we have seven. Sophocles wrote one hundred and twenty-three; we do not know the Alexandrian number, but it must have been very large; we have seven. Euripides wrote ninety-two; Alexandria possessed seventy-eight; we have nineteen. Of Pindar, the Alexandrians possessed seventeen books; we have four, not complete. Of Simonides they had a considerably larger number of books, though we cannot be sure of the figure; we have none. Of Alcman they had six, of Alcaeus at least ten, of Sappho nine; we have none. They had twenty-six books of Stesichorus; we have none. They had the books of Heraclitus, Empedocles, Parmenides,

Anaxagoras. They had the splendid mass of Chrysippus. They had Dicaearchus' *Life of Hellas;* they had the great scientific and imaginative works of Eratosthenes; they had the thirty books of Ephorus' universal history, the twelve books of Theopompus' *Hellenica,* and the fifty-six of his *Philippica.* Of all which the tradition has brought us nothing. They had great masses of Old and New Comedy, of elegy and romance, of which we possess only fragments.

I have been considering only authors of the first rank of genius or importance. Even in that region our loss is overwhelming.

Now let us turn to Photius. It so happens that Photius, in the three hundred books of the *Bibliotheca,* describes no poetry. It was not that, as a bishop, he disapproved of it. He speaks with respect of various poets, and he epitomizes novels and romances with a fulness that suggests enthusiasm. Of course we must remember that the pronunciation of Greek had completely changed, and that the Byzantines, having lost the sense of quantity, and scanning only by accent, had lost all that gives melody and meaning to the forms of ancient verse. But I think we shall see later the real reason for Photius' neglect of poetry.

Of the writers we have just mentioned, the only one that comes in Photius' list is Theopompus. It is one hundred and seventy-sixth in the list: 'Read, the historical books of Theopompus. Those preserved amount to fifty-three. Even some of the ancients said that the sixth and seventh and twenty-ninth and thirtieth had perished. And these I have not seen, either. But a certain Mênophanes—an ancient and not contemptible person—in giving an account of Theopompus says that the twelfth had perished also. Yet we read it together with the others. The contents of the twelfth are as follows . . .' That is one big loss that has come to us since the time of Photius.

And there are others. We must remember that Photius mostly read Christian Fathers, and that the writers of the Roman period were for him among the ancients. He had several of them in a more complete state than we have, Diodorus for instance; but those do not affect our present question. Of classical Greek writers he had read Herodotus—without much appreciation. Also Ctesias, in twenty-four books, twenty-three of *Persica* and one of *Indica.* These are known to us only by Photius' epitome. His Ctesias seems to have been a rare book, since he took special pains with it, just as he did with that twelfth book of Theopompus. He had also the *History of the Diadochi* and the celebrated account of the Red

Sea by the geographer Agatharchides: he devotes forty columns to
it. He had apparently the history of the Alexandrian Cephalion.
But much the greater bulk of his ancient literature consists in the
Attic orators. He had the sixty speeches of Antiphon, twenty-five
of them considered spurious, where we have fifteen. Of Andocides,
like us, he had only four. Of Lysias, where we are perhaps almost
content with an imperfect thirty-four, he had apparently four hundred and twenty-five, of which two hundred and thirty-three were
considered spurious. (If that corpus were ever rediscovered, what
opportunities it would give to our historians!) Of Isaeus he had
sixty-four, fifty of them genuine; we have ten and a half. Of
Isocrates he had sixty, twenty-eight of them genuine; of Hyperides
he had seventy-seven, fifty-two of them genuine. And so on. We
have twenty-one speeches of Isocrates, and know Hyperides only
from the papyri.

Masses of prose oratory! A great part of it not especially eloquent in its form, most of it—to Photius at least—unintelligible as
to its matter. That is the chief treasure that he finds in classical
literature. If you count the columns that he devotes to his abstracts
of the various writers, they tell the same tale. Herodotus is dis-
missed in about half a column. Himerius' *Meletai*, or studies in
the art of rhetoric, are epitomized in sixty-eight columns. It is the
usual phenomenon of late Greek literature, the absorption of all
other literary subjects in the all-engrossing study of rhetoric. It
is the same tendency that has enriched us with the vast unreadable
mass of the *Rhetores Graeci*.

What is the meaning and the historical cause of that tendency?
For what reason did sane human beings preserve sixty-four speeches
of Isaeus, and let Sappho and Alcaeus and even nearly all Aeschylus perish? People talk about certain alleged peculiarities and
abnormal sensitivenesses of these late Greeks. But it is a pity to
assume that human beings were very unlike ourselves merely because they did strange things. So often the strange things they
did are just what we should have done under the same circumstances.

Greek antiquity from Alexander onward had before it a great
duty, and a duty which it consciously realized. It had first to
spread, and then to conserve, the highest civilization that mankind
had yet reached. The task, as we all know, was too hard for it.
From about the second century A. D., ancient learning and civilization are conducting, not a triumphant progress, but a stubbornly

defended retreat. The very feeling of defeat perhaps sharpened men's devotion to the cause.

Hellenism was based on culture; and the great emblem and instrument of that culture was the Attic Greek language. We often sneer at the late Atticists for writing in an idiom which they did not speak. But they were doing the right thing. The spoken idiom of a Spartan peasant still differed from that of an Athenian; both would have difficulty in making themselves understood in Macedonia. But the language of Plato was studied and understood by cultured men from Gades to Cappadocia; and those who could write it had a common ideal and a common birthright. In Plutarch's dialogues men from the remotest places meet together at Delphi, a professor from Britain, a sophist from Sardis, a Roman official, a Boeotian country gentleman; all can speak the same language and respond to the same ideas.

You will say that such an artificial state of things could not last? But it did last. It provided the world with that extraordinary chain of historians writing all in practically the same language and each with a consciousness of his predecessors, down to Photius himself, down even to Eustathius and to people well on this side of the Norman Conquest.

On the other hand, to keep this instrument going, a slow and constant sacrifice had to be made. Part of the cargo was constantly thrown overboard in order to save the rest. Plutarch knew his ancient poets well. He knew Pindar in his full condition, before the selection that we possess came into existence. But a century or so after Plutarch nobody read these difficult poets. Julian, enthusiast for Hellas as he was, had read hardly any more ancient poetry than we ourselves. The men who were practically fighting for Hellenism during those centuries of tough decline, had enough to do to keep alive the bare necessaries of culture. Knowledge of course was still spread chiefly by lectures and speeches, and by reading aloud. Civilization depended on the art of speech— not on what we call rhetoric, but on what the ancients called *rhêtorikê;* the art of speaking clearly, persuasively, intelligibly, and of course correctly, so that you should in the first place expound your culture well to such auditors as would listen, and in the second place let them draw in from your lips the best possible imitation of the pure Attic spirit.

The thing that a man can use in his own life is, as a rule, the thing that attracts and interests him. That is why the late Greeks read Hyperides and Isaeus and the private speeches of Demosthenes in preference to Aeschylus and Alcman. It is why, when they did read tragedy, they vastly preferred Euripides to Aeschylus, though, as a matter of fact, having no sense of drama left, they preferred to read him in extracts in an anthology. That is why our tradition has so ruthlessly left most of the old poets to perish.

But the retreat took another form also. Let me quote as typical some sentences from the preface of the physician Oribasius to his *Epitome of Galen:* 'Your command, Most Divine Emperor, that I should reduce to a smaller compass the medical works of the admirable Galen, has found in me enthusiastic obedience. For people undertake this profession, as Galen himself says, who have neither the proper talents nor the proper age; often they have not even begun the simplest education (*ta prota mathemata*), and consequently cannot understand properly a systematic treatise (*tous kata diexodon logous*). What I am now about to write will suffice for them; it will take a shorter time to learn, and it will be easier to understand, for I undertake that my reduction of the style to conciseness will never result in obscurity.'

Oribasius addressed his book to Julian (362 A. D.). That is a typical date, though many literary subjects had been epitomized long before. The seven plays of Aeschylus were apparently selected about then; with the result that afterwards nobody read anything beyond the seven. The same with the seven of Sophocles, and the ten (or nine) of Euripides, though in the last case a large fragment of an old uncommented and unselected *Euripidis Opera Omnia* happens to have survived also. Afterwards these selections were reduced to three plays out of each tragedian. Four books out of the seventeen books of Pindar had been selected and fitted with a commentary rather earlier. The old elegiac poets seem to have been treated in a different and less satisfactory way. A miscellaneous expurgated collection seems to have been made, and passed current under the name of Theognis. There is no need to multiply instances. The principle is always the same. The text is selected from one of the old complete text editions; the commentary is abridged from the *sungrammata* and *hupomnemata* of scholars of the great Roman period, from Didymus to Herodian.

The clue to the matter is education. The task of keeping up the culture of the world has become a hard burden. Few men are reading the classics freely, for the mere joy of the thing. The classics are for youths to learn in the schools and universities, not because they like it, but because it is good for them. What the cultured world really cares for—apart from the maintenance of orthodoxy—is the maintenance of Attic.

The predominance of education explains another fact about late Greek literature. The educational profession is one possessed of extraordinary virtues, compared with most other professions; but it has its weaknesses too. And one of the chief of them is a tendency to pretend to knowledge which it does not possess. Late Greek literature is full of books which—though no doubt written innocently enough—obtained long life and popularity because they enabled teachers to make a great show of erudition. First of all, the anthologies. Many excellent fourth-century writers throw about with a free hand their quotations from ancient literature; but we find on examination that nearly all their quotations occur also in the anthologies of Stobaeus and Orion. Again, think what a display could be made by any one with a good memory who had read Athenaeus. He would be equipped with anecdotes and quotations from all the most abstruse and curious parts of ancient literature. One strange book which Photius read with much interest seems almost to have been specially written for this particular fraudulent purpose. It is the *Kainê Historiê* of a certain Ptolemaios, *Ptolemaiou tou Hephaistiônos*—whatever exactly that genitive means. For some people think he was the father, not the son, of Hephaestion; and Tzetzes thinks he was Hephaestion himself. Ptolemaios was a writer belonging to a very good period, the second half of the first century A. D. The book, known to us only from Photius, consisted of anecdotes from extraordinarily abstruse sources, generally professing either to give information about things no one could know or else to contradict the ordinary received tradition. He may really have been an eccentric man of amazing erudition, but Hercher, who has studied him critically, prefers the alternative of regarding him as an *'unverschämter Schwindler.'* The important point for us is that such a book should have lived on and been popular.

Education and the needs of education in a world where intellect is decaying and knowledge gradually growing less—these are the guiding conditions of the *paradosis*. And if we reflect for a few minutes on that fact, we shall reach a rather important and interesting conclusion.

Of what sort are the books that education specially produces and selects? We ought to know, though we must remember that we live in an age when education is enlightened and progressive and daring; in the centuries we are now considering, from the second to the ninth, education was in a state of slow decay, it was frightened, conservative, and unhopeful.

First, education selects the undoubted classics; not specially because anybody likes them, but because everybody approves of them. They read Shakespeare at Amelia Sedley's school, because it was right, though they doubtless left out a great part of him, and did not much like what remained. Our Greek *paradosis* has duly preserved Homer and Plato, Demosthenes and a good deal of the canonical Attic writers. It has preserved a certain selection of Aeschylus, Sophocles, and Euripides. Doubtless it was actuated more by a sense of duty than by genuine taste; but in any case it clearly did right, and we ought to be thankful that it had a sense of duty. Secondly, education selects and produces handbooks and aids to knowledge. I need not dwell on the extent to which these bulk in our tradition. Thirdly, if it goes further, if it goes beyond the indubitable classic and the mere text-book, it tends to choose what is correct, obvious, and sober. (When I say correct, I do not necessarily mean correct in morals. A work may be considerably improper provided that it is sanctioned by antiquity; Aristophanes held his place in Constantinople as the Elizabethans do with us.) It avoids the kind of writing about which there tend to be very different opinions, which seems to one man inspired, and to another utterly silly. It avoids literature that has a special personal quality, it avoids the intensely imaginative, the enthusiastic, the rebellious. It is guided by the respectable man; it shuns the saint and the bohemian.

The importance of this consideration is, I think, very great. When one reads accounts in text-books of the characteristics of the Greek mind—its statuesque quality, its love of proportion and order and common sense, its correct rhetoric and correct taste, its anthropomorphism and care for form, and all those other virtues which sometimes seem, when added together, to approach so dangerously near the total of dull correctness and spiritual vacuity,—it is well to remember that the description applies, not to what the ancient Greeks wrote, but to what the late Roman and Byzantine scholars preserved.

Suppose it had been a little otherwise. Suppose that as well as Aristotle's defense of slavery we had the writings of his opponents, the philosophers who maintained that slavery was contrary to nature. Suppose that, to compare with Plato's contemptuous references to the Orphics, we had some of that 'crowd of books' which he speaks of. Suppose instead of Philodemus we had all Heraclitus

and Empedocles and the early Pythagoreans. Suppose we had
Antisthenes and the first Cynics, the barefooted denouncers of sin
and rejectors of civilization. Suppose we had that great monu-
ment of bitter eloquence and scorn of human greatness applied to
history, the *Philippica* of Theopompus. Suppose we had the great
democracy of the fifth century represented, not by its opponents,
but by the philosophers who believed in it—by Protagoras, say,
and Thrasymachus. Suppose that we had more of the women
writers, Sappho above all and Corinna and Nossis and Leontion.
Suppose we even had more literature like that startling realistic
lyric, Grenfell's Alexandrian Erotic fragment, in which the tragedy is, that between a man and a woman *Cypris* has taken the place
of *philia:* 'It has been free choice in both. Friendship came before
passion. Anguish seizes me when I remember.' (It is explained by
Wilamowitz in the *Goettinger Nachrichten* for 1896.)

Had the conditions of the *paradosis* been different, all that might
easily have happened. And how different then would have been
our conception of the supposed limitations of Greek literature. Let
us remember the facts. Let us be sceptical a priori towards most
statements of limitation and negation—all generalizations which
state that 'The Greeks had no conception of this, no understanding of our elevated sentiments with regard to that.' As a rule the
only truth in such statements is that those Greeks who had, were
not canonical in Byzantine schools. And, what is of more practical
significance to ourselves, let us remember that the literature which
we do possess has been filtered through the same limiting and
cramping medium which rejected the rest, and that the traditional
interpretation of our texts, especially the poetical texts, has been
mainly the work of those generations whose activity I have been
describing, and suffers still from the need of a freer air and a wider
imagination.

XIV

THE CLASSICS IN EUROPEAN EDUCATION [1]

By Edward Kennard Rand

The ancient classics, the literature of Greece and Rome, were regarded as a vital constituent of education from the moment when they were produced. Studied with devotion as the immortal memorials of a great past, they have led, when rightly followed, to new and high achievement in the present. With this consideration as a clue, let us travel on as briskly as the moments at our disposal require down the centuries of European history.

I know not what Homer studied when he went to school—for may we not, encouraged by recent discussions, not only think of Homer in personal terms, but even boldly picture him as a schoolboy once upon a time?—I know not what Homer studied; but everybody knows that Homer was part and parcel of the education of a great age that came after him, the age of Periclean Greece. In that age, moreover, we see that twofold impulse of the human spirit which the study of classical literature normally inspires—reverence for the past, and the passionate desire to act worthily in the present. Aeschylus, who described his dramas as mere slices from the Homeric feast, prepared for his own times, as Herder remarked, another kind of banquet. The Alexandrian age, which created canonical lists of the best authors, among whom Aeschylus now took his place, was also an age of startling innovations in philosophy and politics; in literature, much pondering of Homer led, not to remote and archaistic fancies, but to the translation of heroic types into

[1 Dr. Edward Kennard Rand, Professor of Latin in Harvard University, produced this article as a contribution to the volume entitled *Latin and Greek in American Education, with Symposia on the Value of Humanistic Studies,* edited by Francis W. Kelsey. New York, 1911. The article is now reprinted with the consent of its author and Professor Kelsey. It is the first of three articles in Symposium VI, The New Education (pp. 260 ff.), the other two being *The Classics and the Elective System,* by R. M. Wenley, and *The Case for the Classics,* a notable study, with a wealth of references in the footnotes, by Paul Shorey.—Editor.]

contemporary terms. Then came the Romans, not an alien race with a hybrid culture, save in the sense that all culture is hybrid, but creators of another great period in the development of antiquity, a period less novel in the invention of literary forms, but fertile and to the highest degree original in the adaptation of the old. Rome's innovations in human history are conspicuous enough; they followed naturally from a loyal consecration to the past. Beginning with a devotion to their own heroic past, they connected this past deliberately with the glories of Greek literature and history, when once that potent influence had made its presence felt. Think for a moment of these typical Romans, and the double outlook on the past and on the present, conspicuous in their lives and works: Ennius, who refashioned Latin verse in the new Grecian measure, that in this verse he might immortalize the history of his country; Cicero, reverent student of the ancient poetry of Ennius, and leader of his times in the year 63; Horace, who bids the learner

Thumb Greek classics night and day,

and, thanks to such a training, arraigns the age in a splendid series of Alcaean odes. Poets who know their own day only are the 'singers of Euphorion,' in Cicero's contemptuous phrase. Young Virgil, perhaps included in that phrase, has so little fame from his early poems, which bear the mark of Euphorion, that until recently nobody believed he could have written them. Virgil's great message to his generation, and to ours, came in a poem which reveals an intense study of his country's past and an intense study of Homer and Greek tragedy.

I have tarried a moment with the ancients, instead of beginning much later in the history of Europe, expressly to suggest that the best things in ancient literature were not written solely from the artistic but often from the social motive as well. Letters, and, originally, men of letters, were not sundered from public life, but actively contributed to it. If the classics have moulded later history, it is not merely because of their great qualities as literature, but because they are involved in the history of their own times, and because they enshrine the ideals of a liberal and four-square education, such as their authors possessed. This is a matter that will become obvious, in a moment, when we consider the educational program of Italian humanism.

But first we must quickly traverse the intervening ages—Middle Ages, but not wholly dark—which a new system of education controlled. It is a mistake to suppose that the Christian Church was hostile to pagan culture; on the contrary, after a brief season of combat and readjustment, the old learning was appropriated for a new purpose. But the purpose was new. Whereas to Cicero and Quintilian the goal of education was *eloquentia*, the art of expression and its application to the business of state, the Christian monastery removed from the world and prescribed hours of silence. Ill would the sophist Polemo have fared there, who was buried before the breath left his body, that he might not be seen above ground with mouth shut. The Christian Church maintained both systems of education for some time, but monasticism gained the day, and was the main strength of education till later, in the Middle Ages, when the university came. Now the classics did not perish under the new régime; in fact, we can thank the monastery for preserving them for us. They constituted the first step in education, the 'Human Readings,' as Cassiodorus called them, to be succeeded by 'Divine Readings' later. More than that, in the revival of learning under Charlemagne, and later at the school of Chartres, the ancient idea came again to the front. John of Salisbury in the twelfth century had a great deal to say about *eloquentia,* while Hildebert of Tours wrote epigrams delightfully antique, which could deceive the very elect; for they are included in certaifi modern editions of the *Anthologia Latina.* Church, State, and learning were more intimately associated than before. The university, too, though its tendencies were philosophical rather than humanistic, created a new interest in Greek by finding the real Aristotle again, and thus led the way for the humanists' quest of all Greek literature. Men of the Middle Ages did not differ radically from those of succeeding centuries in their attitude toward the classics. Humanism and philosophy had their battles in that period as in every period, but the importance of classical culture for education was in general unquestioned. The great and striking difference lay in the amount of classical culture available. The division of the empire into an East and a West effected curious results in civilization. Byzantium, after dark ages of its own, settled down to an eminently respectable scholarship which created little in literature or thought. It treasured the Greek authors, but forgot the Roman. When the monk Maximus Planudes at the end of the thirteenth century translated various Latin authors into Greek, he selected those most in vogue in the West at that time, such as Ovid, Boethius, Augustine, Donatus, Dionysius Cato; there was evidently no separate tradition of Latin literature at Byzantium. In the West, similarly, the stream of Greek was trickling feebly; the knowledge of the language had not completely disappeared, and technical writers like Aristotle and the author of the *Celestial Hierarchy* were directly introduced, but the writers typical to us of the Hellenic genius were none of them known. Now a world without Homer, the Attic drama, Thucydides, Herodotus, Demosthenes, Theocritus, a world without the real Plato, is bound to be a very different world from our own. Not that this loss which befell the Occident was ultimately a calamity. The very isolation of the Roman spirit permitted its most triumphant expression in Dante, for whose poetry we should willingly forego whatever a combined East and West might have achieved.

To see how the mediaeval imagination was still fixed faithfully upon antiquity, though less able than before to understand its meaning, we turn to Dante, who mirrors truly the vital sentiments of his times. Many a reader has felt the beauty of that scene in the *Purgatorio*, where Dante and Beatrice come upon a troop who sing:

> *Benedictus qui venis,*
> E fior gittando di sopra e dintorno,
> *Manibus o date lilia plenis.*

Christian liturgy and pagan poetry, which to some could sound only a discord, blend harmoniously here. But for a more striking instance still I turn to Dante's seventh letter, addressed to Henry VII of Germany in 1311. In this letter Dante speaks of 'the new hope of a better age' which 'flashed upon Latium' when that monarch came down into Italy. 'Then many a one, anticipating in his joy the wishes of his heart, sang with Maro of the kingdom of Saturn and of the returning Virgin.' But since this sun of their hopes seems to tarry, as though bidden to stand by a second Joshua, Italy is tempted to cry: 'Art thou he that should come, or do we look for another?' Dante himself has firm faith in the 'minister of God' and 'the promoter of Roman glory,' but wonders still why he can delay, apparently believing that the boundaries of Rome end at Liguria. But the real Rome 'scarce deigneth to be bounded by the barren wave of ocean; for it is written for us:

> Nascetur pulchra Troianus origine Caesar
> Imperium Oceano, famam qui terminet astris.'

Had not the edict 'that all the world should be taxed' issued from the 'council chamber of the most righteous princedom,' the Son of God would not have 'chosen that time to be born of a Virgin.' So let the emperor not delay, but 'let that word of Curio to Caesar ring forth once more:

> Dum trepidant nullo firmatae robore partes,
> Tolle moras; semper nocuit differre paratis;
> Par labor atque metus pretio maiore petuntur.

Let that voice of the chider ring forth from the clouds once more against Aeneas:

> Si te nulla movet tantarum gloria rerum, . . .
> Ascanium surgentem et spes heredis Iuli
> Respice; . . .

for John, thy royal first-born . . . is for us a second Ascanius who, following in the footprints of his great sire, shall rage like a lion all around against every Turnus, and shall be gentle as a lamb toward the Latins.' Dante then warns the emperor by the example of David, whom Samuel rebuked for sparing 'the sinners of Amalek.' He warns him by the example of Hercules, for there are many heads of the Italian hydra, and if Cremona is lopped off Brescia and Pavia will remain. He must strike at the viper itself, even Florence, who is that 'foul and impious Myrrha that burns for the embraces of her father Cinyras,' 'that passionate Amata who rejected the wedlock decreed by fate,' thus resisting 'the ordinance of God' and worshiping 'the idol of her proper will.' So come, 'thou lofty scion of Jesse. Take to thee confidence from the eyes of the Lord God of Sabaoth . . . and lay this Golias low with the sling of thy wisdom and the stone of thy strength.'

Surely for this act of public service—the greatest, Dante doubtless thought, that he could render his country—the authority of Virgil and Lucan and Ovid seems well-nigh as efficient as that of Scripture itself. May we not say that for Dante, as truly as for any later humanist, the study of the ancients had an immediate bearing upon the problems of the day?

When Dante had finished his work it was time for a new epoch. Scholasticism had run its course. After so minute and comprehensive a vision of the kingdom of this world and the next as St. Thomas records, some sort of protest and readjustment is inevitable if the human sense of wonder is to persist; in a universe where nothing escapes the observer, the observer, as Lucretius knew, will find at last:

> eadem sunt omnia semper.

So scholasticism declined and a new age came, in which education returned to the methods of antiquity. We need not pause to examine the causes of this event; but its most significant concomitant is the return of Greek literature to the Western World. There is a humorous aspect to the triumphs of the humanists, who 'discovered' Latin authors long treasured on monastic shelves. Quintilian, welcomed back with such a furor, had been the patron saint of the school of Chartres. The humanists could rediscover because in the thirteenth century the classical interests of the twelfth had yielded to philosophy, and in the fourteenth, monastic discipline and the monastic library had lapsed into decay. But I would not belittle the importance of what to the contemporaries of Poggio were certainly discoveries. For the thirst for discoveries led also to the more careful study of the authors existing. Petrarch initiated the movement; though curiously mediaeval in some respects, he deserves his title of the first modern man, and this because of his passion for antiquity. His great service is not so much the discovery of Cicero's letters as the exaltation of Ciceronian ideas, which were from that time on the guiding principle of humanistic education. Petrarch's craving for Homer, too, ill satisfied by the wretched translation which his teacher made, gave impetus to the general demand for the Greek authors. Work after work was won back; practically all the authors that we have to-day were recovered before the fall of Constantinople in 1453, which date surely does not mark the beginning of the Renaissance. What wonder if the age, intoxicated by the new draught, indulged itself in various excesses? What wonder, too, if at first the habits of centuries prevented men from rightly valuing their new treasures, so that throughout the Renaissance the doctrine prevailed that the greater literature was the Latin? The Greek authors had at any rate returned, and civilization could not remain as before.

For a glimpse into the new school of the humanists after Greek had its sure place there, we can do no better than open a little book by Battista Guarino, *De Ordine Docendi et Studendi*, published in 1459. Battista Guarino is less celebrated than his father, and distinctly less celebrated than Vittorino da Feltre, the greatest teacher of the Renaissance. The curriculum at this school is narrower than that of Vergerio or Aeneas Silvius; for this reason it is a safer guide to the average practice of the day. Guarino restricts the disciplines to ancient literature and history, Greek and Latin; logic and ethics, for instance, are introduced, not as independent studies, but because they are necessary for the explanation of

Cicero. The program sounds rather barren, but we must study it
more deeply to see what it means. Literature involves grammar,
of course, and prosody, and likewise composition in both prose and
verse. The works of Virgil should be learned by heart, for 'in this
way the flow of the hexameter, not less than the quantity of individual syllables, is impressed on the ear, and insensibly moulds the
taste.' Nor should the contents of poetry be neglected. Its fictions
have moral as well as artistic value. They exhibit the realities of
our own life under the form of imaginary persons and situations;
Cicero's authority is quoted for this sentiment, and St. Jerome is
cited to good purpose. The lessons of history, too, are of great
value. By it, Guarino states, the student will learn 'to understand
the manners, laws, and institutions of different types of nations,
and will examine the varying fortunes of individuals and states,
the sources of their success and failure, their strength and their
weakness. Not only is such knowledge of interest in daily intercourse, but it is of practical value in the ordering of affairs.' Now
though logic and ethics may have been an aside, they involved the
direct study of Aristotle and Plato. We find other asides, too—
astronomy, and geography, and Roman Law, and the writers on
those subjects. Moreover, independent reading is a vital part of
the plan, and among authors suggested as appropriate for such
reading are St. Augustine, Aulus Gellius, Macrobius, the elder
Pliny, 'whose *Natural History* is indeed as wide as nature herself.'
The pupil is bidden to practise his memory by going over at the
end of each day what he has just learned; he is told to do much
reading aloud, since this will give him the confidence which the
public speaker needs. Throughout these instructions there is constant reference to the moral goal of education. 'In purity of grace
and style,' Guarino affirms, 'in worthy deeds worthily presented, in
noble thoughts nobly said, in all these, and not in one alone, the
learner finds the nourishment of his mind and spirit.' But literature
is not merely moral; it trains the dramatic imagination. 'In this
way,' he continues, 'we are not disturbed by the impieties, cruelties,
horrors, which we find there; we judge these things simply by their
congruity to the characters and situations described. We criticize
the artist, not the moralist.' The ultimate secret of this method
is its foundation in personality, and humanity. 'Finally,' he declares, 'through books and books alone, will your converse be with
the best and greatest, nay even with the mighty dead themselves. . . . To man only is given the desire to learn. Hence what

the Greeks called παιδεία we call *studia humanitatis;* for learning and virtue are peculiar to man; therefore our forefathers called them *"humanitas,"* the pursuits, the activities, proper to mankind. And no branch of knowledge embraces so wide a range of subjects as that learning which I have now attempted to describe.'

Nothing but Greek and Latin. Under Guarino's cultivation, these ancient roots branch out as widely as the flower in the crannied wall. These studies of antiquity educate the whole man— moral, aesthetic, intellectual; they train him to independent thinking, for the authors are but the starting-point; they inculcate reverence for the past; they teach its application to the present. Now two historical facts are plain with reference to this program. First, it is simply the ancient method of Cicero and Quintilian all over again. Both authors are constantly cited for principles as well as facts; *'virtutis laus omnis in actione consistit,'* said Cicero, and Vittorino echoes the words. Second, it is the basis of every truly humanistic program established from that day to this. Its principles appear in some dozen treatises of the day, and from Italy spread to the North. What I have quoted does not touch all the elements in humanistic education. Science and mathematics received more consideration than one might suppose. Religious training was not neglected, as it is with us; polite demeanor, dress, physical exercise, all were matters for attention. And let me emphasize again the point I would specially make: the twofold character of their education, its reverence for the past and its interest in the present, derives clearly from the ancient prototype.

It is not necessary to quote *in extenso* the leading humanists of the North for proof that the new educational ideals are eagerly appropriated and applied. Rudolphus Agricola in Germany, Vivès in Holland, but originally from Spain, Dorat and the learned Budé in France, diverge in no essential particular from Vittorino. Let Erasmus, the most cosmopolitan man of his day, speak for them all. 'The first object of education,' he declares, 'is to teach the young mind to foster the seeds of piety, the next to love and learn the liberal arts, the third to prepare itself for the duties of life, the fourth, from its earliest years to cultivate civil manners.' Erasmus truly represents England, as well as his own land, but a native voice was also heard from our mother-country at that time. I mean, not Roger Ascham, who comes later in the sixteenth century, and whose system is a bit ladylike in its painful propriety, but Thomas Elyot, who, in his *Book of the Governour* (1531), interpreted Erasmus and Budé to England. The idea that the study of the classics was merely the study of two foreign and ancient tongues would find no favor with him. 'Only to possess language,' he declared, 'is to be a popinjay.' Homer holds for him far more than that. 'If by reading the sage counsel of Nestor, the subtle persuasions of Ulysses, the compendious gravity of Menelaus, the imperial majesty of Agamemnon, the prowess of Achilles, the valiant courage of Hector, we may apprehend anything whereby our wits may be amended and our personages more apt to serve our public weal and our prince, what forceth it us though Homer writes leasings?' As with Guarino, the poetic lie has its moral function. Elyot concludes: 'I think verily if children were brought up as I have written, and continually were retained in the right study of every philosophy until they passed the age of twenty-one years and then set to the laws of this realm . . . undoubtedly they should become men of so excellent wisdom that, throughout the world, men should be found in no commonweal more noble counselors.'

These words have the ring of a familiar passage in Bacon's *Advancement of Learning,* concerning the learned governor. 'Nay, let a man look into the government of the Bishops of Rome,' he remarks, 'as by name, into the government of Pius Quintus, and Sextus Quintus, in our times, who were both at their entrance esteemed but as pedantical friars, and he shall find that such Popes do greater things, and proceed upon truer principles of estate, than those which have ascended to the papacy from an education and breeding in affairs of estate and courts of princes.' Or, to translate this into modern terms, let future lawyers take Classics in college, and not confine themselves to Economics.

Need I say that all Bacon's thinking was seasoned through and through with the classics? He was no pedantic advocate, surely no advocate of the Ciceronianist, whom he berates as soundly as he does the scholastic. 'Then did Car of Cambridge and Ascham, with their lectures and writings, almost deify Cicero and Demosthenes, and allure young men that were studious, into that delicate and polished kind of learning. Then did Erasmus take the occasion to make the scoffing echo: "*Decem annos consumpsi in legendo Cicerone*"; and the echo answered in Greek "Ὄνε," (= "*Asine*").'

Bacon brings us naturally to Milton, a Puritan and a rebel, who also, thanks to the ancients, could temper his virtue with Epicureanism, and show in his poetry that liturgic reverence for the past which is ingrained in classic literature. Milton writes a brief treatise *Of Education* to his friend Samuel Hartlib, and in it he says: 'I call, therefore, a complete and generous education. that which fits a man to perform justly, skilfully, and magnanimously all the offices, both private and public, of peace and war. And how all this may be done between twelve and one-and-twenty, less time than is now bestowed in pure trifling at grammar and sophistry, is to be thus ordered.' Then, outlining his main topics, as studies, exercise, and diet, he treats of the first: 'First, they should begin with the chief and necessary rules of some good grammar . . . and . . . their speech is to be fashioned to a distinct and clear pronunciation, as near as may be to the Italian, especially in the vowels.' He is speaking, of course, of Latin grammar. He proceeds with a lengthy list of readings in Greek and Latin literature, which soon runs into mathematics and many natural sciences, politics, philosophy, and religion. 'And either now or before this,' he interposes, 'they may have easily learned at any odd hour the Italian tongue.' As with Guarino, education was not all done by courses.

Thus far our examination of the history of classical education in Europe has been pleasant enough, at least for those who are favorably disposed toward the classics. We have seen the ancient ideal reintroduced in the Italian Renaissance, disseminated in the northern countries, and established once for all, we should imagine, by mighty thinkers like Bacon and Milton. But no human institution is permanent, and, even in the times with which we have been dealing, forces were at work which tended to discredit an educational program based on the classics.

One such force was the decay of the method itself. All movements tend eventually to a period of formalism and petrifaction. Petrifaction seized the classical program when the limits of good Latin style were restricted to Cicero, and taste in general became puristic. Politian had read sympathetically in the authors of silver latinity, and appropriated their phrases at will, because, he said, he was expressing, not them, or Cicero, or anybody but himself. Bembo shrank from calling Deity anything but *dii immortales,* and warned a young friend against too much reading of the New Testament, lest it spoil his Latin style. That was the age, too, when handbooks of imaginative etiquette were compiled to save the poets from mistakes. Lists were furnished of proper epithets for frequent nouns; thus *aer* could be *liquidus* and *igneus* and a few other things, but under no circumstances anything else. Clearly a system which engendered such absurdities was not destined to long life. Two events came to the rescue of humanism. One was its transfer to the other countries, where its vital elements were bound to take hold, and where the absence of patriotic interest left the judgment more free and critical; though France was somewhat bitten with Ciceronianism, though the delicate Ascham approved it, the sturdy sense of the greatest men of the period, like Erasmus and Bacon, dealt it crushing blows.

The other event was the Protestant Reformation. The relation of the Reformation to humanism is somewhat complex. In its wilder and iconoclastic manifestations it was the foe of all culture, but the national element in protest against Rome should not be forgotten. Nationality is allied to secularism, and both are allied to humanism. Further, the method of the schoolmen had a stronger hold in the North, especially in France, the land of its birth, than it had in Italy. There the normal antagonist of humanism was the Sorbonne, and the Sorbonne stood for Catholic theology and the Roman Church. Thus George Buchanan, in temperament much like Erasmus, at any rate untouched by the evangelical fervor of Protestantism, found it natural, not, like Erasmus, to remain in the Roman fold, but with many of his French associates to go over to Protestantism. In Italy this *via media* did not exist. It was humanism and the Church, or, for the humanist who did not care for the Church, it was humanism and neo-paganism. Now, while we must appreciate the great service performed by the Reformation for the humanistic ideal, and admire characters like Melanchthon and Zwingli, and not form hasty generalizations on the barrenness of Puritanism when it includes a Milton, we must also recognize the other half of the truth which I have just suggested, namely, that the exaggerations of the spirit of the Reformation were a blow to culture, and that they must be reckoned as a second force operative against the classics.

From France there proceeded another disturbing influence toward the close of the seventeenth century, the famous *querelle des anciens et des modernes*. The moderns, whose sentiments first found effective expression in Charles Perrault and his poem on *Le Siècle de Louis le Grand* (published 1687), represented a wholesome national and Christian feeling, but committed absurdities both in the defense of their own position and in their attacks on the ancients. The chronological argument loomed large. With centuries of high achievement behind them, why should not the present, profiting by experience, do still greater things? This reasoning seemed convincing, so long as the modern illustrations of superiority were not mentioned; when Chapelain and Desmarets were adduced as such, the proof fell rather flat; for the literary works of the moderns, so far from representing anything of the spirit of romantic revolt, were pseudo-classic in character, and their literary criticism was distinctly pseudo-classic. Virgil came off fairly well at their hands; it was because he stood several centuries nearer modernity than Homer did, and because he was comparatively free from glaring inelegancies. On Homer fell the brunt of their attack; the vulgar characters admitted into his poems, and the indecorous behavior of his nobilities, made him an obvious target for the well-mannered critic of the seventeenth century. The reply of the beleaguered classicists is not particularly significant. Most of them were ready to acknowledge the superiority of Virgil over Homer; in fact, it had been accepted ever since Vida and the Renaissance, and most vituperatively proclaimed by the elder Scaliger. Fénelon, it is true, refused to decide between the poets, and Madame Dacier even gave the palm to Homer. But her declaration that nature had exhausted its resources in Homer, and had not the power to produce another like him, is of the excessive, pseudo-classic sort of criticism that makes appreciation stagnant.

At all events, the close of the seventeenth century was not an auspicious epoch for the classics, especially for Greek. Indeed, it would seem that nobody had really entered into the spirit of Greek literature, save possibly the members of the Pléiade in the sixteenth century, since its recovery in the Renaissance. The interrelation of Greek and Latin, the dependency of Latin literature, was recognized; 'Latin is a rivulet, Greek a mighty river,' said Erasmus, in the words of Cicero. Ascham laughs at the good bishop who thought the need of the Greek tongue was fulfilled now that everything had been translated into Latin, and compares the Latin scholar without Greek to a bird of one wing. At the same time a remark of his own betrays an intelligence hardly finer than the Bishop's: 'And surely,' he says, 'if Varro's books had remained to posterity, as by God's providence the most part of Tully did, then truly the Latin tongue might have made good comparison with the Greek.'

Are we distressed, sometimes, that we live no more in the ages of accepted humanism, and that Greek is going to the wall? We have only to remember that it has seen gloomy days, days of misappreciation, before. Even in the sixteenth century Casaubon could write: 'I am deep in Athenaeus, and I hope my labor will not be in vain. But one's industry is sadly damped by the reflection how Greek is now neglected and despised. Looking to posterity or the next generation, what motive has one for devotion to study?'

We should take heart of grace, likewise, in recalling that educa-

tional follies are not exclusively the product of the nineteenth and
twentieth centuries: Montaigne's father brought him up by the
latest pedagogy. 'As to Greek,' he remarks, 'of which I have but
a mere smattering, my father also designed to have it taught me
by a trick; but a new one, and by way of sport; tossing our declen-
sions to and fro, after the manner of those who, by certain games at
tables and chess, learn geometry and arithmetic; for he, amongst
other rules, had been advised to make me relish science and duty
by an unforced will and of my own voluntary motion.' We see
that the method of 'not teaching but informally introducing' is
not the last word of the latest philosophy. In such fear was this
good father that he might disturb the brain of his child that in the
morning he did not rudely wake him by a shake, but had gentle
music played to him that the waking might be gradual. This educational scheme did not last very long; the boy was so heavy, idle,
and indisposed that, he declares, 'they could not rouse me from
my sloth, not even to get me out to play.' He therefore was sent
to school, where the discipline was so strict that he enjoyed reading
Ovid on the sly; even so the poet Lowell cut conic sections for a
private hour with Aeschylus.

To pass on now to the eighteenth century, we may note pseudo-
classic influences in all the countries as a preservative of the humanistic scheme—they preserved by embalming it, but contributed nothing to its growth. In France, especially, Roman Catholic education
was closely identified with the Jesuits; from the end of the sixteenth
century they had shown, by basing their own instruction upon the
classics, particularly the Latin classics, that humanism was not
the exclusive property of the Reformers. The famous Delphin editions, published toward the close of the seventeenth century for a
very indifferent young Dauphin, proved acceptable in many other
schools besides those of the Jesuits. The order maintained its
prominence in education in the eighteenth century, and has not
ceased its activities to-day. Whatever else may be said of this
illustrious company, it is interesting to note that its tremendous
missionary undertakings have been the product, or the concomitant,
of an educational system that is classical, if not pseudo-classical, in
character. England was not influenced vitally by the Jesuits in the
eighteenth century, but in its own way maintained the supremacy
of the classics. 'All the faculties of the mind,' remarked Gibbon,
'may be exercised by the study of ancient literature.' A classical
training was firmly believed to be an admirable preparation for
political life. Statesmen like Chatham and Fox and Pitt and

Burke did not fail to recognize its bearing upon modern problems, or to point an argument with a classical quotation. They were simply continuing the tradition that we have seen before in Bacon, and before him in Vittorino, and before him in Dante.

To England, too, is due a fresh appreciation of ancient literature for the reason that the meaning of Homer was at last beginning to grow clear. Pope, whatever his offenses, deserves, with Bentley, whom he abused, no small share of the credit, and Blackwell and Wood made further advance. This is a quiet little movement, the approach to romanticism in eighteenth-century England, and a gain for classical education. But the doctrines of Rousseau and the impetus of the French Revolution broke in a romantic storm which in principle carried with it little reverence for antiquity. At the same time it benefited the classics by clearing away false notions of their immaculateness, and by revealing Greek afresh. For the latter event we must be grateful, not only to England, but to the German school of criticism, inaugurated before the days of Romanticism by Winckelmann, and completed by Lessing, Herder, Schiller, and Goethe. True, in this Teutonic Hellenism there are exaggerations, strange lights that never shone on sea or land, and it led to a dearth in the appreciation of Latin literature in Germany, down till only a few years ago. England took the movement more soberly. Wordsworth, the high priest of nature, could look back to Horace and sigh for

The humblest note of those sad strains.

No change in the humanistic ideal was made in the nineteenth century, wherever that ideal was truly interpreted. Arnold of Rugby, who typifies English education at its best, founded his system on the classics. 'The study of language,' he said, 'seems to me as if given for the very purpose of forming the human mind in youth; and the Greek and Latin languages . . . seem the very instruments by which this is to be effected.' Arnold was also deeply impressed with the moral inspiration that comes from association with the past—not only with the literature of the past, but with the very buildings in which education has made its home. 'There is, or there ought to be,' he declares, 'something very ennobling in being connected with an establishment at once ancient and magnificent, where . . . all the associations belonging to the objects around us should be great, splendid, and elevating. What an individual ought and often does derive from the feeling that he is born of an old and illustrious race, from being familiar from his childhood with the walls and trees which speak of the past no less than the present, and make both full of images of greatness, this, in an inferior degree, belongs to every member of an ancient and celebrated place of education.' Finally, Arnold directed the enthusiasm thus gained from the past upon the immediate present. He writes to a friend: 'I cannot deny that you have an anxious duty— a duty which some might suppose was too heavy for your years. But it seems to me the nobler as well as the truer way of stating the case to say that it is the great privilege of this and other institutions to anticipate the common time of manhood; that by their whole training they fit the character for manly duties at an age when, under another system, such duties would be impracticable.' The classics, he thought, then, so far from abstracting the learner from the present, prepare him more speedily than any other system does for its service.

As we go farther in the nineteenth century, and especially as we come to our own times, we are forced to acknowledge that to many thinkers the classics are no longer an indispensable part of education. The causes of this attitude are not far to seek—romanticism, naturalism, and the breaking-down of authority of all kinds. Germany has contributed largely. Germany rediscovered Greek literature, and exterminated Latin. Germany has led the way to the scientific study of the classics, and garnered more results than any other nation. It contributed the philosophy of relativity which, joining forces with the doctrine of evolution, the product of English science, led to new methods and manifold results in the study of history. But an excessive scrutiny of origins has impaired the efficacy of the classics. The tendency of the historical spirit is to compel illustrious characters of the past to know their place, whereas the Middle Ages and the Renaissance summoned the ancients to transgress their periods—yes, to walk down the centuries and shake hands. A late mediaeval tapestry at Langeais sets forth a goodly troop of knights, all caparisoned cap-à-pie in the same manner; they are Godfrey of Bouillon, Julius Caesar, Samson, and some others. We shudder when we find the Byzantine chronicler Malalas putting Polybius before Herodotus, or John the Scot setting Martianus Capella in the times of Cicero, but are ourselves inclined to forget that, though history has its periods, the imagination has none. We should encourage it to glorious anachronisms, or rather *hyperchronisms,* for if it is chronologically fettered the classics become demodernized. A further tendency of historical analysis is to resolve great personalities and traditions into causes and effects. An author is not regarded as an entity unless he is influencing somebody else; when the critics look at him, he disappears in a mist of sources. Let me not be misunderstood. I regard the critical method of the historian as indispensable; but this very method is imperfect if it does not reckon with ethical and imaginative values as well.

But to proceed no further with this arraignment of the age, let me conclude by referring to the hardest problem of all, which has been gradually accumulating for our generation, namely, the presence of various modern literatures of great power and beauty, which were only beginning to exist when the humanists based all teaching on the classics. May not the literature of any of the great nations of Europe serve the purpose as effectively? How can we neglect any of them, and how can we elect? Further, I would inquire, how have we teachers of the classics fulfilled our tasks? Have we always kept before us the true ideal of humanism? Have we made the sacred past living and contemporary, or have we banished our subject to a timeless district, illumined, not by the dry light of reason, which is a wholesome effluence, but by the dry darkness of the unprofitable? I raise these issues contentedly, and bequeath them to the other speakers at this meeting. With many startling leaps down the centuries, and, I fear, with many hasty generalizations, I have at least made clear that the true program of humanism, which is nothing but the ancient program revived, has always pointed men to the treasured ideals of the past, and inspired them to action in the present.

XV

MILTON'S USE OF CLASSICAL MYTHOLOGY [1]

By Charles Grosvenor Osgood

The importance of Greek and Roman mythology is proved by
its unfailing vitality. After the visible forms of states and empires
had passed away, the myths of the ancients survived with their
politics and philosophy and poetry as a part of the heritage which
the new peoples received from the old. This power of classical
myths to survive is explained principally by two facts: first, they
were the embodiment of the moral, religious, and artistic ideals of
the Greeks and Romans; secondly, morality, religion, and art were
serious and fundamental realities in ancient life.

These two facts explain also the kind of vitality by which the
myths have survived. It consists not merely in the repetition of
a tale through centuries, but also in the variation of its quality, and
in its susceptibility to employment for various uses. The old
mythology was a kind of plastic material which received through
individuals a national impress. As the life of the Greeks became
modified from century to century, so Greek mythology was similarly
modified by the poets, teachers, philosophers, and artists who were
the master-workmen of this people. The stories and conceptions of
gods and heroes are strong, aspiring, or weak, as the people who
invented and cherished them manifested the corresponding qualities. And when the Roman civilization adopted Greek culture,
Greek mythology suffered modification, and became in some degree
a reflex of the Roman life into which it had entered.

The poet who was religious, and hence peculiarly and continually
sensitive to moral truth, found in existing mythology a partial
expression of the truths dear to him, and in his poetic treatment
added to the moral, religious, or imaginative value of the myth

[1 From *The Classical Mythology of Milton's English Poems* (pp. x-xxxii).
Professor Osgood's excellent dissertation appeared as No. 8 in *Yale Studies in
English*, edited by Albert S. Cook. The present extract is reprinted with the
author's consent, slightly abridged both in the text and the footnotes. References from this to other parts of the dissertation have been omitted.—Editor.]

which he employed. Reverence as well as imagination characterizes such treatment. We feel it in the mythology of poets like Homer, Plato, and Virgil. Thus in the first book of the *Iliad,* where Chryses prayed for revenge upon Agamemnon, 'Phoebus Apollo heard him, and came down from the peaks of Olympus wroth at heart, bearing on his shoulders his bow and covered quiver. And the arrows clanged upon his shoulders in his wrath, as the god moved; and he descended like to night.'[2] This passage not only shows Homer's imagination in its vividness and dramatic power, but contains moral enthusiasm for divine justice, and reverence for the superior and majestic power of the god. But Homer's reverence had a lower object than that of either Plato or the Christian. His ideal of conduct, as represented by his heroes, and magnified in his divinities, was nourished by a smaller life and a lower conception of the universe than the Platonic or the Christian ideal. His greatest men and women are brave, dignified, and generous, sometimes even tender. Yet they treat their enemies with horrible cruelty, they violate our ideas of moral purity, and they exhibit lack of self-control and fear of death. Already in the palmy days of Greek civilization Plato criticizes them for such shortcomings.[3]

The reverence of this poet-philosopher for mythology was not based upon a literal belief in the old religion. He appreciated the beauty of some of its myths, and saw that they were sufficiently plastic to receive his teaching. In his adaptation he has impressed them with the imagination, and with the enthusiasm and reverence for truth which are exhibited in his philosophy. Under the influence of his higher and larger ideals and conceptions, mythology underwent a sort of expansion. It was sublimated, rarefied, and projected into larger space. It received a nobler form than that which it possessed in Homer. At the same time, however, it assumed a new function; it became symbolic and almost allegorical. Thus in the *Phaedrus,* where Plato is discussing the upward flight of the perfect soul, he says: 'Now the divine is beauty, wisdom, goodness, and the like; and by these the wing of the soul is nourished, and grows apace; . . . Zeus, the mighty lord holding the reins of a winged chariot, leads the way in heaven, ordering all and caring for all; and there follows him the heavenly array of gods and demi-gods, divided into eleven bands; for only Hestia is left at home in the house of heaven; but the rest of the twelve greater deities march in their appointed order. And they see in

2 *Iliad* 1. 45.
3 *Republic* 3. 386.

the interior of heaven many blessed sights; and there are ways to and fro, along which the happy gods are passing, each one fulfilling his own work; and any one may follow who pleases, for jealousy has no place in the heavenly choir. This is within the heaven. But when they go to feast and festival, then they move right up the steep ascent, and mount the top of the dome of heaven.'[4] To appreciate more fully the difference between Homer and Plato, this passage should be compared with the famous feast of the gods in the first book of the *Iliad*,[5] where jealous Hera stirs a quarrel with Zeus; but at his threats 'the ox-eyed queen was afraid, and sat in silence, curbing her heart; but throughout Zeus' palace the gods of heaven were troubled.' Then the drollery of Hephaestus made a truce, and 'laughter unquenchable arose amid the blessed gods to see Hephaestus bustling through the palace.'

An allegorical and naturalistic application of mythology was made by Plutarch. The attempt was afterwards made to identify many myths with early or sacred history through euhemeristic interpretation, or to discover in them an allegorical form of Christian and moral truth. Such uses of mythology find early precedent in a euhemerist like Diodorus, or a moralist like Plutarch. They were later practised by certain of the Fathers, such as Eusebius, and were resumed with great enthusiasm by scientific writers of the Renaissance, such as Bacon and Bochart.

In the times of Greek and Roman decadence, when faith in the old religion had died, leaving empty the hearts of men, and when morality was by many regarded as inconvenient and unnecessary, the treatment of a myth in art became correspondingly irreligious and non-moral. As a diverting tale it admitted of imaginative treatment only. A Horace or a Claudian made it serve as a dainty and effective ornament. Ovid clothed the old stories in new apparel and ornament, and, thus renovated, they gave the world fresh amusement; his importance to us as a mythologist consists much less in any moral or artistic excellence of his treatment than in his great accumulation of mythological material from sources many of which have long since disappeared.

Having thus considered the vitality of ancient myths as illustrated by their varying quality and the various ways in which they were applied, we may ask whether this vitality has failed at last, or whether it is so great that the myths may live with us a life in

[4] *Phaedrus* 246, 247. Compare also the use of mythology in the story of the journey of Er, *Republic* 10. 614-621.

[5] *Iliad* 1. 493-600.

some degree as intimate as that which they lived with the ancients. When Christian civilization supplanted that of Greece and Rome, it seemed likely that pagan mythology would perish with the old order of things. It was too closely interwoven with earlier belief to survive the antagonism of the new faith, which first dreaded the ancient world, and then triumphed over it. Within the last five hundred years classical mythology has been partially revived, generally as a relic or a plaything. But whether it can again receive the inspiring power of revelation which it possessed for many of the ancients remains a question. The answer to such a question we may hope to find by a study of this element in the art of Milton. . . .

Let us now consider some of the principal facts revealed by an examination of the classical mythology in Milton's poems. His methods of introducing such allusions are principally three. First, they may be introduced in simile or comparison. Thus in the Second Book of *Paradise Lost* he describes the turmoil of the fiends who

> Rend up both rocks and hills, and ride the air
> In whirlwind; Hell scarce holds the wild uproar—
> As when Alcides from Oechalia crowned
> With conquest, felt the envenomed robe, and tore
> Through pain up by the roots Thessalian pines,
> And Lichas from the top of Oeta threw
> Into the Euboic Sea.[6]

At times the comparison may be very brief, as when the beasts are represented more obedient to the call of Eve

> Than at Circean call the herd disguised.[7]

Or it may even not exceed the mere mention of 'Typhoean rage'[8] or 'Atlantean shoulders.'[9]

Milton often masses classical allusions of this kind, piling them sometimes four or five deep, and obtaining by means of this accumulation an effect of great richness. Thus of the tempter disguised as a serpent he says:

6 *Paradise Lost* 2. 540-546.
7 *Ibid.* 9. 522; cf. 4. 250; 5. 16, 378; 10. 559; *Vacation Exercise* 93.
8 *Paradise Lost* 2. 539.
9 *Ibid.* 2. 306; cf. 655; 3. 359; 10. 444; *Sonnets* 15. 7.

> Pleasing was his shape
> And lovely; never since of serpent kind
> Lovelier—not those that in Illyria changed
> Hermione and Cadmus, or the god
> In Epidaurus; nor to which transformed
> Ammonian Jove, or Capitoline, was seen,
> He with Olympias, this with her who bore
> Scipio the highth of Rome.[10]

Even supposing that the reader is not familiar with all the allusions of this passage, the very succession of sonorous vowels and liquids, which Milton so often effected by his choice and arrangement of proper names, enhances the splendor of this massed comparison. In some cases such comparisons are reinforced or extended by allusions which are not mythological or even classical. Or mythological allusions introduced for another purpose than comparison may occur in close connection with these passages. It is by such treatment that the description of Eden, in the Fourth Book of *Paradise Lost*,[11] expresses through its own rich luxuriance the luxuriance of the garden. We hear first the sound of clear water running over beds of pearl and gold, now sparkling in the sun, now lost in the green twilight of deep woods. Against the dark foliage is the gleam of fruits with golden rind, 'Hesperian fables true.' The air is filled with the fragrance of gorgeous flowers and with the soft call of unseen birds. Where the leafy branches part little vistas invite exploration.

> Airs, vernal airs,
> Breathing the smell of field and grove, attune
> The trembling leaves, while universal Pan,
> Knit with the Graces and the Hours in dance,
> Led on the eternal Spring. Not that fair field
> Of Enna, where Proserpin gathering flowers,
> Herself a fairer flower, by gloomy Dis
> Was gathered—which cost Ceres all that pain
> To seek her through the world—nor that sweet grove
> Of Daphne, by Orontes and the inspired
> Castalian spring, might with this Paradise
> Of Eden strive; nor that Nyseian isle,
> Girt with the river Triton, where old Cham,
> Whom Gentiles Ammon call and Libyan Jove,

10 *Paradise Lost* 9. 503-510.
11 *Ibid.* 4. 205-287.

Hid Amalthea, and her florid son,
Young Bacchus, from his stepdame Rhea's eye;
Nor where Abassin kings their issue guard,
Mount Amara, though this by some supposed
True Paradise, under the Ethiop line
By Nilus' head, enclosed with shining rock,
A whole day's journey high, but wide remote
From this Assyrian garden, where the Fiend
Saw undelighted all delight, all kind
Of living creatures, new to sight and strange.

It will be noticed that Eden has been compared to three mythical gardens, and then to a garden of Abyssinia, and that besides these allusions, reference is also made to the Hesperides, to Pan, the Graces, and the Hours. This method of accumulation or massing of mythology is not confined to similes, but is also practised in other connections, as we shall see later.

Here we may pause to consider a characteristic of all great art which attempts to interpret the beauty of the natural world to men. Every work of art which maintains a strong and permanent influence over men contains some element which brings it in touch with humanity. However divine the truth which the artist feels, however radiant the beauty of nature is to him, his art is incomplete if his thoughts of these things are not brought home to men in terms of human life. It is for this reason that a painting or a description of a landscape which reproduces simply the landscape itself is imperfect. The best art therefore personifies the forces of nature, or perhaps is content with suggesting types or phases of human life which seem to correspond in spirit to the particular type or phase of nature. It is thus that in Corot's pictures of the glad morning, figures are seen dancing, or blithe and tuneful Orpheus appears, giving utterance to the joyful harmony around him. In Milton's description of Eden the same principle applies to the mention of Pan and the Hours. Furthermore, in the comparisons occurring here Milton has not stopped with mere allusions to myths, as in his description of the serpent-fiend, but has outlined in his concise and significant way the stories of Proserpina and Amalthea, and has suggested the voice heard in the Castalian spring sacred to the Apollo and Daphne of the Orient, thus furnishing appropriate personal types to reflect the natural beauty previously described.

Of all the allusions to mythology in simile by far the greatest

strength and finest balance are found in a certain double mythological simile in the Fourth Book of *Paradise Regained,* in which each
member is firmly and concisely outlined. It is where Satan, in the
last temptation, commands Christ to leap from a pinnacle of the
temple:

> To whom thus Jesus: 'Also it is written
> "Tempt not the Lord thy God." ' ' He said, and stood.
> But Satan, smitten with amazement, fell.
> As when Earth's son, Antaeus (to compare
> Small things with greatest), in Irassa strove
> With Jove's Alcides, and, oft foiled, still rose,
> Receiving from his mother Earth new strength,
> Fresh from his fall, and fiercer grapple joined,
> Throttled at length in the air expired and fell;
> So, after many a foil, the Tempter proud,
> Renewing fresh assaults, amidst his pride
> Fell whence he stood to see his victor fall.
> And, as that Theban monster that proposed
> Her riddle, and him who solved it not devoured,
> That once found out and solved, for grief and spite
> Cast herself headlong from the Ismenian steep,
> So, strook with dread and anguish, fell the Fiend.[12]

It may be observed that the similes and comparisons which have
been cited are all from *Paradise Lost* and *Paradise Regained.* We
may say that with few exceptions, principally in *Comus,* this
manner of introducing mythological allusion is peculiar to these
two longer and later poems;[13] but it is not just to infer from this

---

[12] *Paradise Regained* 4. 560-576. The strength of this passage is not due alone
to the balance of these two similes, nor to the fact that not more than two are
used. It lies partly in the grandeur of diction, but most of all in the deeper
meaning common to the three solemn events here described. Each is the victory
of a hero; each is the triumph of right over wrong, of light over darkness; and
in each struggle is involved the fate of generations. The comparison of Christ
to Heracles is implied in *Passion* 13. The idea may have been suggested to
Milton by some writer of the Renaissance, or more likely by one of the Fathers.
Cf. *Paradise Lost* 2. 1017-1020; 4. 713-719.

[13] In *Samson Agonistes,* the nature of the subject and the form in which it
was cast naturally prevented almost entirely the use of Greek mythology.
Neither Samson nor his friends and enemies could very appropriately be made
to talk of things so far removed from them as classical myths, and in the drama
the poet may not appear in person, as in the epic, to make these allusions in his
own name. Strictly, only one such allusion occurs in this dramatic poem, and

that Milton ultimately came to prefer such a form of allusion. It seems more likely that the subjects of the two epics offered so little opportunity for the incorporation of classical mythology within the story itself that, if the poems were to be enriched to any extent by means of pagan lore, it must be accomplished by the somewhat more remote method of simile and comparison.

A second method of introducing allusions to classical mythology is illustrated in nearly all the poems, though the earlier and so-called minor poems supply the best examples. It consists in the incorporation of a myth or the ancient conception of a divinity into a poetical setting of Milton's own creation.

This is accomplished in two distinct ways. First, the myth or conception, of which the several details may come from several different sources, may be removed, for example, from the peculiar setting of Homer, Apollonius, or Ovid, and placed in the different setting of *Comus, Il Penseroso,* or the First and Second Books of *Paradise Lost.* Thus the indefinite and shadowy classical idea of Chaos, as either a place or a divinity, or merely an unordered condition of things, has been elaborated under Milton's treatment, and separated into two distinct meanings in the cosmography of *Paradise Lost.* On the one hand, the word is applied to the deep and confused region between heaven and hell. On the other, it names the divinity who rules in this region. The principal source of the latter conception is in Hesiod, though his representation is much less definite than Milton's, and amounts to little more than a personification of a condition in the order of nature's earliest development. In *Paradise Lost* the consort of Chaos, and his co-ruler, is Night. The Miltonic conception of Night is based upon that of the Orphic cosmogony, which makes her eldest and first of all things. Thus the two early Greek cosmogonies are combined, and introduced into the Second Book of Milton's great epic. By the same method, Saturn and Jove and the other Greek gods are made to appear among the devils, the most conspicuous of them all being

that a very remote one. It is where Samson accuses himself of revealing God's secrets,

> a sin
> That Gentiles in their parables condemn
> To their abyss and horrid pains confined.
> (499-501.)

He evidently means Tantalus and Prometheus. But in addition to this one instance I have also discussed in their respective places the references to the Chalybeans (133), to 'dire Necessity' (1666), and to the phoenix (1699), as being mythological and having their probable sources among classical writers.

Hephaestus, or Mulciber, the skilful craftsman and architect of Pandemonium.[14] In *Paradise Regained,* naiads, wood-nymphs, and the 'ladies of the Hesperides' figure in the temptation of Christ, and harpies snatch away the feast which has been spread by Satan.[15] Much of the mythology of the earlier poems is introduced in this manner. Thus in *Arcades* the Arcadian background is suggested by the presence of silver-buskined nymphs and gentle swains, these latter being the descendants

> Of that renownèd flood, so often sung,
> Divine Alpheus, who, by secret sluice,
> Stole under seas to meet his Arethuse.

And the last song of the poem is musical with the sweetness of such names as Ladon, Cyllene, Erymanth, and Lycaeus, places dear to Pan and the nymphs. In *Comus* the element of enchantment and sensuality is largely composed of references to Bacchus and Circe. It also includes the mention of dark-veiled Cotytto, who rides with Hecate through the night, concealing the wicked excesses of her worshipers. The magic song of Circe and the sirens quiets the rage of Scylla and Charybdis, and Comus is consigned to be girt with harpies and hydras, and

> With all the griesly legions that troop
> Under the sooty flag of Acheron.

This element of sensuality in *Comus* is offset, on the other hand, by an element of purity and benignity. The latter is composed of references to the high air of Jove's court, to the propitious aid of Neptune and all sea-gods, to the glory of Iris, the sweetness of Echo, the virgin majesty of Diana and Minerva. It is sustained at the end by a description of the paradise of Virtue, where the Hesperides sing, and whither the Graces and Hours bring abundance. Here the air is cooled with Elysian dew, and here sleeps the translated Adonis. Here Love is reunited with Psyche, and to them are born Youth and Joy.[16] *L'Allegro* and *Il Penseroso* should be

---

[14] *Paradise Lost* 1. 732-751.

[15] *Paradise Regained* 2. 353-357, 403.

[16] It is worthy of notice in passing, that Milton, in making Youth and Joy the children of Psyche and the celestial Cupid, has transcended the grosser treatment of Apuleius, who makes Voluptas their daughter. Spenser is content with this version, and calls her Pleasure. Cf. Spenser *Faerie Queene* 3. 6. 50; *Hymne of Love* 288. A comparison of these passages in Spenser with the closing speech of *Comus* reveals the principal difference between Milton's method of treatment

mentioned as important examples of this manner of treatment. In these poems Milton has selected certain conceptions of the ancient divinities, and expressed them through the scenes and activities occurring in the life of a refined man. It is the light spirit of Zephyr and Aurora which predominates in the one poem, and the sombre spirit of Vesta and Saturn which predominates in the other. . . .

Occasionally, instead of removing the whole myth from its classical setting and inserting it in his own, Milton adapts certain mythological events or features by removing from them the persons and localities with which they are connected in his sources, and substituting his own persons and localities. This is the second way in which mythology is incorporated or inwoven with his story. One instance is Eve's story of discovering her own beauty.[17] It is Ovid's story of Narcissus and his love for the face that he saw reflected in the water of a spring, except that Eve is put for Narcissus. Milton, as usual, follows many of the details of his original, but by a process of selection and exclusion renders them more delicate. The same sort of adaptation occurs when Milton derives incidents from the visit of Odysseus to Circe in the *Odyssey*,[18] and inserts them in his story of Comus and the lady. As Circe by means of her drug and wand changes all strangers to swine, so Comus with his orient liquor and wand changes travelers into brutish forms. As Odysseus was protected against these charms by the moly, so the good spirit checks the magic of Comus with a plant called haemony. Again, in the battle between the rebel angels and

and Spenser's. The latter poet is nearly always the more diffuse. Though the amount of mythology in his considerably larger body of poetry appears to be much greater than in Milton, yet it represents less extensive reading in the classics, and covers a range of allusion no wider, if as wide. Milton's wonderful conciseness is of great artistic import, as one of the necessary elements of his classicism. Without the composure, reticence, and finish which this implies, no work of art is truly Hellenic. We feel that Milton has gained these traits, or at least has developed them, through direct contact with pure Greek culture. We feel, on the other hand, that, however much Latin and Greek Spenser read, he was in some degree perverted by the restless and unsettled spirit of the early Renaissance from a deep and just sense of true classicism. He is therefore less faithful to originals. His mythology has more the nature of external ornament rather profusely applied. There is evidence that, like the Italians, he was more charmed with its sensuous and even sometimes fleshly aspect than with the deeper spiritual significance—which indeed he may have perceived. It is in this way that his treatment becomes more lavish of epithet, color, and circumstance than Milton's.

[17] *Paradise Lost* 4. 453-469.
[18] *Odyssey* 10. 135-574.

the army of God, many incidents are transferred from Hesiod's battle of the Titans and the gods. Since the occasion and general character of these two struggles, as well as certain details, are similar, a comparison of the two descriptions as a whole would be profitable. We have space, however, only to point out a few details in the *Theogony* which are adapted by Milton. Hesiod tells us that the gods, taking great masses of rock in their hands, hurled them upon the Titans. Zeus, without exerting his full strength, smote the Titans with his thunderbolt, and drove them into the depths of Tartarus, whither an anvil could not fall in nine days. Here they are confined for ever. Nearly the same incidents are repeated in Hesiod's story of the fight between Zeus and Typhoeus. In Milton these details all appear with slight modification. As the Son of God advanced to battle, the steadfast empyrean shook beneath the wheels of his chariot, 'yet half his strength he put not forth.' His warriors

> plucked the seated hills, with all their load,
> Rocks, waters, woods, and, by the shaggy tops
> Uplifting, bore them in their hands.[19]

He himself hurled his thunders upon the host of Satan, who fell headlong from Heaven:

> Nine days they fell; confounded Chaos roared,
> And felt tenfold confusion in their fall
> Through his wild anarchy; so huge a rout
> Encumbered him with ruin. Hell at last,
> Yawning, received them whole, and on them closed.[20]

[19] *Paradise Lost* 6. 644-646.

[20] *Ibid.* 6. 871-875. Many instances of this treatment exist in Milton. The descent of Raphael in 5. 277-287 is derived in part from similar descriptions of Hermes in Virgil and Homer (*Aeneid* 4. 222 ff.; *Iliad* 24. 341). When in *Paradise Lost* 8. 59 the poet says, speaking of Eve,

> With goddess-like demeanor forth she went,
> Not unattended; for on her as Queen
> A pomp of winning Graces waited still,

he is thinking of a conception of Venus, or Aphrodite, which is very common in the classics, and is illustrated in *Odyssey* 8. 364, where the Graces bathe and anoint the goddess. Cf. the Homeric *Hymn to Aphrodite* 3. 61; Horace, *Carm.* 1. 4; 1. 30; 3. 21. In *Paradise Lost* 8. 510, where Adam leads Eve to the nuptial bower, Earth and the powers of nature 'gave sign of gratulation.' The situation is similar to one in *Aeneid* 4. 165, where Earth and the storm show approval of the union of Dido and Aeneas in a cave. The amorous words addressed by guilty Adam to Eve (*Paradise Lost* 9. 1029-1033) are much like those spoken

We may now consider the third method by which Milton introduces allusions to classical mythology. His descriptions of nature are generally either mythological or touched with mythology. Especially is this true in descriptions of the dawn, of night, and of the progress of the sun and moon.[21]

We have already noticed how Milton can enliven and illuminate a description of natural beauty by throwing into it a touch of human life which reflects the spirit of that which he is describing. This is what Shakespeare does in peopling the forest of Arden with blithe spirits who make us forget that trees are not always green, and brooks merry; and in Milton the same result is produced by reflecting the spirit of nature from the personalities of the old gods, often slightly modified by the poet's art. It is thus that he tells of the beginning of another day:

> Now Morn, her rosy steps in the eastern clime
> Advancing, sowed the earth with orient pearl.[22]

And again he speaks of the Sun,

> who, scarce uprisen,
> With wheels yet hovering o'er the ocean-brim,
> Shot parallel to the earth his dewy ray,
> Discovering in wide landskip all the east.[23]

While it is true that Milton humanizes nature by means of mythology, we may go further, or perhaps reverse the statement,

by Paris to Helen in *Iliad* 3. 442, or by Zeus to Hera in *Iliad* 14. 315. In *Paradise Lost* 11. 184-203, the eagle appears as a bird of omen in the manner of *Aeneid* 1. 393-397; 12. 247-256. The description of the bounds of Hell in *Paradise Lost* 2. 645 ff. bears traces of similar descriptions in Homer, Hesiod, and Virgil. The sound of Hell's gates in *Paradise Lost* 2. 879-882 suggests as an original *Aeneid* 6. 573-574. In *Paradise Lost* 2. 752-758, Sin is represented as springing from the head of Satan, as Athena sprang from the head of Zeus. When Satan was wounded (*Paradise Lost* 6. 320 ff.),

> A stream of nectarous humor issuing flowed
> Sanguine, such as celestial Spirits may bleed.

So Homer speaks of the wounded Aphrodite (*Iliad* 5. 339): 'Then flowed the immortal blood of the goddess, such ichor as floweth in the blessed gods.'

[21] Strictly speaking, the use of mythology in descriptions of nature is only another application of the second method by which myths are incorporated into Milton's poetry. Yet in a consideration of its artistic excellence it falls more conveniently under a separate head.

[22] *Paradise Lost* 5. 1-2.

[23] *Ibid.* 5. 139-142.

and say that in general, whatever the occasion of introducing the myth, if its persons or incidents connote even in the slightest degree the beauty or the power of nature, Milton makes us feel it. Thus broad meadows and shady places are made visible when he speaks in *Comus* of

> such court guise
> As Mercury did first devise
> With the mincing Dryades
> On the lawns, and on the leas.[24]

The sound of the sea is suggested in the following lines:

> Scylla wept,
> And chid her barking waves into attention,
> And fell Charybdis murmured soft applause.[25]

The luxuriance of spring is felt in a reference to the love of Zeus and Hera:

> As Jupiter
> On Juno smiles when he impregns the clouds
> That shed May flowers.[26]

The name of Jove seems often to suggest the upper air and the broad sky.[27]

This consideration of the mythology in Milton's descriptions of nature is the most important of any thus far, since it opens the way to more thorough appreciation of his independence and originality, and of the true nature of his classicism and his artistic temperament.

As we approach these questions, the first thing for us to consider is that the part assigned to mythology in such descriptions varies widely in extent. One description may be entirely made up from mythology; another may reveal only a slight touch of it; in a third the mythical element may be wholly lacking, the personification employed being derived from another source. An analysis of several passages will clearly reveal the variation. In *Lycidas* the line,

> While the still morn went out with sandals gray,[28]

24 *Comus* 962-965.

25 *Ibid.* 257-259.

26 *Paradise Lost* 4. 499-501.

27 This is evident in *Comus*, especially in the beginning, and in the lines *On the Death of a Fair Infant* 43-46.

28 *Lycidas* 187. The ancients did not speak of the morning as 'gray.'

contains no mythological allusion. In the same poem occur the lines:

> Oft till the star that rose at evening bright
> Toward heaven's descent had sloped his westering wheel.[29]

This last passage contains only a slight mythical coloring. It consists in the allusion to the star's chariot, an idea which is more commonly associated with the sun, or moon, or night.[30] The mythological element is slightly increased in the following passage of *Paradise Regained:*

> Thus passed the night so foul, till Morning fair
> Came forth with pilgrim steps, in amice gray,
> Who with her radiant finger stilled the roar
> Of thunder, chased the clouds, and laid the winds.[31]

The mention of the Morning's 'radiant finger' appears to be an adaptation of the Homeric epithet 'rosy-fingered,' and her action in driving away the clouds may be partly suggested by the common idea that she puts the Night to rout, and partly by an expression which Virgil uses of Neptune.[32] The rest of the passage is peculiar to Milton. Again in the Fifth Book of *Paradise Lost* the Morning Star is addressed as

> Fairest of Stars, last in the train of Night,
> If better thou belong not to the Dawn,
> Sure pledge of day, that crown'st the smiling Morn
> With thy bright circlet.[33]

Of this passage the words 'last in the train of Night' are all that suggest the classical idea that the stars are attendant upon Night.

Let us now examine a passage in which the mythological element is increased, even though it is not more conspicuous than the actual

---

Milton, however, seems to have delighted in this color as applied to the morning. See *Paradise Lost* 7. 373; *Paradise Regained* 4. 427; cf. the use in *Paradise Lost* 5. 186; *L'Allegro* 71.

[29] *Lycidas* 30-31.

[30] Milton often used the chariot or moving throne as an accessory in myths. It occurs frequently in his reference to the sun, or moon, or night, and is often transferred to other connections. Examples are found in *Paradise Lost* 1. 786; 2. 930; 3. 522.

[31] *Paradise Regained* 4. 426-429.

[32] *Aeneid* 1. 143: 'Collectasque fugat nubes.'

[33] *Paradise Lost* 5. 166-169.

phenomenon of nature itself. Referring to sunset and sunrise,
Milton says in *Lycidas:*

> So sinks the day-star in the ocean bed,
> And yet anon repairs his drooping head,
> And tricks his beams, and with new-spangled ore
> Flames in the forehead of the morning sky.[34]

In the beginning of this passage we have the old figure of the god
Helios sinking to rest in his bed at the end of a long day's journey.
But as the passage proceeds this mythological idea fades, and in its
place shines the brightness of the sun itself, like a flaming jewel in
the forehead of the morning. Still more pronounced is the mythological character of the following lines:

> First in his east the glorious Lamp was seen,
> Regent of day, and all the horizon round
> Invested with bright rays, jocund to run
> His longitude through heaven's high road; the gray
> Dawn and the Pleiades before him danced,
> Shedding sweet influence.[35]

Though this passage is founded principally upon the Bible, yet
Milton, in combining the different parts, has given it a decided
classical coloring, slightly modified by characterizing the Dawn as
'gray'; and so nicely are the parts fitted together that a seam is
imperceptible, nor is it easy to tell where classical mythology ends
and any other element begins.

The majority of natural descriptions in Milton resemble the last
four examples in that they contain a more or less prominent sug-
gestion of the mythical conception, together with a large element
of Milton's elaboration.

We may now consider what is more rare, namely, a description

[34] *Lycidas* 168-171.

[35] *Paradise Lost* 7. 370-375. At least two Biblical passages are represented
by these lines. The more important one is Ps. 19. 4-6: 'Their line is gone out
through all the earth, and their words to the end of the world. In them hath
he set a tabernacle for the sun, which is as a bridegroom coming out of his
chamber, and rejoiceth as a strong man to run a race. His going forth is from
the end of the heaven, and his circuit unto the ends of it: and there is nothing
hid from the heat thereof.' The second passage is Job 38. 31, where is mentioned
'the sweet influence of the Pleiades.' The resemblance of the dance of the
Pleiades to the dance of seven figures, who may represent Pleiades, in Guido's
picture of Aurora, has been remarked by Todd. Apparently this is the only
classical antecedent of these lines.

composed almost entirely of mythology. It occurs at the opening of
the Sixth Book of *Paradise Lost:*

> All night the dreadless Angel, unpursued,
> Though Heaven's wide champaign held his way, till Morn,
> Waked by the circling Hours, with rosy hand
> Unbarred the gates of Light. There is a cave
> Within the Mount of God, fast by his throne,
> Where Light and Darkness in perpetual round
> Lodge and dislodge by turns, which makes through Heaven
> Grateful vicissitude, like day and night;
> Light issues forth, and at the other door
> Obsequious Darkness enters, till her hour
> To veil the Heaven, though darkness there might well
> Seem twilight here. And now went forth the Morn,
> Such as in highest Heaven, arrayed in gold
> Empyreal; from before her vanished Night,
> Shot through with orient beams.

In this passage there is an almost literal adaptation of at least
four classical poets or poetic conceptions. The general idea of
Dawn's opening the gates is from Ovid; the action of the Hours is
from Homer; the cave of Light and Darkness is Hesiod's house of
Day and Night; the final rout of Night before the beams of the
sun is a common conception in Greek poetry, though perhaps in this
case referable to Dante.

We may notice that in this passage Milton intends to describe, not
the earthly dawn, but the grateful vicissitude of light and darkness
in heaven. There is, however, in his description a beautiful reflection of the dayspring as it has appeared to many men, and this
reveals to us a most important quality in Milton's treatment of
mythology and nature. He appreciates the values of two things,
nature and the myth, but to him the value of nature outweighs
that of the myth. This accounts for the vividness and reality and
enthusiasm, which, if the proportion of values were reversed, would
tend to become pedantry and dry conventionality. With a view to
this statement, let us take the first lines of the preceding passage:

> Morn,
> Waked by the circling Hours, with rosy hand
> Unbarred the gates of Light.

Let us analyze this passage in comparison with its originals. As
already suggested, there are two passages in the classics which are

here represented. The first is in the Fifth Book of the *Iliad,* where Hera drives forth her chariot from Olympus: 'Self-moving groaned upon their hinges the gates of Heaven, whereof the Hours are warders, to whom is committed great Heaven and Olympus, whether to throw open the thick cloud or set it to.'[36] The other passage is in the Second Book of Ovid's *Metamorphoses:*

> Ecce vigil rutilo patefecit ab ortu
> Purpureas Aurora fores et plena rosarum
> Atria.[37]

We may first inquire what help Ovid has given Milton. He suggests the idea that the Dawn at her rising throws open certain gates, but further than this his influence can hardly be said to extend. As usual he has made a tableau, overloading it with gay color. Milton, however, in speaking of Aurora's rosy hand, lends color enough, and stops before he smears. He is speaking of dawn in Heaven, and the thought of gates naturally leads him to think of the Hours, who are the warders of Heaven's gates. They are therefore adapted from Homer, with the addition of a beautiful epithet, 'circling,' from the common tradition of Greek poetry. But the mere juxtaposition of these things is not enough. Milton, like a true artist, realizes that though color is lovely, something else is still lovelier, more important, and more vital. He loves the morning for its freshness, its action, its grace, its dignity, its progress toward glorious climax, and all these qualities are present in his description. There is action in the words 'waked' and 'circling' and 'unbarred,' and in the intervening or accompanying movement which they suggest. There is freshness and grace in the swift Hours, in the modest but effective touch of color, and in the fact that we do not hear the harsh groan of the gates upon their hinges. There is dignity, because the movement, though rapid, is not hurried, and stays slightly at the words 'with rosy hand.' Lastly, there is progress toward a climax. Morn is waked by the Hours; she rises, throws back the bolt; the gates swing open without effort, and Light leaps forth and overspreads the sky. This action is suggested, if not expressed, and to feel the full effect of progress and climax the passage should be read aloud slowly with perfect enunciation. Much of its movement and progress is expressed in the effect of light consonants and liquids, and in the fine succession of

[36] *Iliad* 5. 749-751.

[37] *Metamorphoses* 2. 112-114. 'Lo, the watchful Aurora opened her purple doors in the ruddy east, and her halls filled with roses.'

vowels which seems to accompany the meaning and open out at the end.

It would be a mistake to assume that Milton deliberately and consciously went about arranging his description in this way. He rather felt deeply and keenly the glories of a new day at first hand, so deeply and keenly that his poetic sense of these things rushes in and informs his description, with a result such as this before us. Thus the myth does not remain or become, in his hands, a lifeless convention; nor is it a sort of mythological veil, through which we faintly see the loveliness of nature. Rather, on the one hand, he understands the spirit of nature, and is in harmony with it; on the other, he has sympathized with the Greek imagination until he imagines in part as a Greek. When, therefore, he hears from the Greek lyre, though echoed never so faintly, a note first stirred by the great harp of nature, he recognizes it, and sounds it again, loud and clear, inseparably mingling the qualities of the two instruments in one tone.

It follows from this as a sort of converse statement that Milton was also independent in his use of the myth. It never threatens to get the better of him, for his use of it is governed by an unfailing sense of things more serious and important to the human heart and mind. However extensive the mythological element in a given passage, the result is no less vivid and imaginative. The myth never encumbers the poet and gets in his way. It does not have the appearance of something in the wrong place, which makes itself the excuse for being there. Rather it is properly related to the more important thing, and falls into the place where it belongs.

After this somewhat detailed analysis and consideration of the more apparent facts in connection with Milton's treatment of nature, let us endeavor to weigh the value of the mythological element in Milton's art, and discover, if possible, the true benefit of its influence upon him.

As we have already seen, mythology is not the product of one man, possessing the marks of his peculiarities, but is the reflection of national character and ideas. It is only in part subject to the personal variation of the individual who treats it. Its nature is therefore chiefly universal, containing qualities and truths which appeal, not to men of a certain narrow class, but to nearly all men. For this reason classical myths, when presented in an artistic and appreciative manner, exert a strong and refining influence, and many have therefore insisted upon a study of them as an element in the best culture; for culture is not an exaggeration and devel-

opment of the oddities and idiosyncrasies of the individual, but is
rather the result of assimilating in one soul, so far as may be, the
best part of the past and contemporary life of men, that is, the part
which is most permanent and universal. It is according to such
a principle that mythology possesses artistic value. The best and
most permanent qualities of the Greek people are to be found
there; and the artist who selects his material from it, and who treats
it lovingly and with understanding, may be sure of a certain steadiness and universality in his art, while at the same time the material is of such a pliant nature that he may express with it much
of the best that he has within himself. Take, for example, the
passage which we have already discussed:

Morn,
Waked by the circling Hours, with rosy hand
Unbarred the gates of Light.

We have seen already the extent and importance of the classical
element in this passage. The pure and beautiful imagery is wholly
classical. It possesses Greek dignity and repose. It contains the
elements of expectancy, action, progress, and climax, and these
qualities are the essential and universal ones by which the beauty
of the dawn appeals to men. But thoroughly mingled with the
universal elements of these lines are some of the best personal
qualities of Milton himself. They are not introduced in the form
of a curious and outlandish conceit; by his selection of certain
qualities from the Greek, and his emphasis of them, he reflects the
same qualities in his own nature. Such are his delicacy, dignity,
and repose. Then we feel also his purity of thought and emotion,
and his high reserve, which is felt elsewhere, in nearly every line, as
a distinguishing trait of the poet.

Milton lived in a time when the importance and development of
individuality had become the importance and development of personal peculiarity. Much of the poetry of his time suffered from
this fact, and as a result is full of conceits and curious figures,
while generally it no longer appeals strongly to men, and is now
read only at the promptings of an idle interest in its quaintness.
Milton himself did not always escape this tendency to conceit and
oddity. Whether he was aware of it or not, the fact remains that
mythology often served in his case as a sort of safeguard against
such mistakes, for while it suffered some modification under the
influence of his individuality, it kept his poetry within the bounds
of universal appeal.

XVI

THE GREEK GIFT TO CIVILIZATION [1]

By Samuel Lee Wolff

The Greeks meant one thing to men of the early Renaissance, another thing to Pope and Addison, another thing to Germans of the nineteenth century. Every generation has taken its Greek in its own way. And the present generation, heir of all the ages, is taking its Greek in nearly every way—except one. It is *not* taking its Greek for granted. An expositor of Hellenism to-day is almost obliged to become an apologist. He must 'show us.' Even as seasoned a Grecian as Professor Mahaffy, who surely is entitled, if any one is, to be at his ease in Hellas, does not resist this compulsion. The quiet and still air of his delightful studies is stirred with argument, about Greek in the college curriculum, about the neglect of Aristotelian logic by American youth, about, on the one hand, Greek versus 'Science,' and, on the other hand, the truly 'scientific' temper of Greek thought. Throughout he seems to feel that the Greeks need to be vindicated; and their vindication, throughout, is that they are 'modern.'

This seems to mean that they are free from mysticism and obscurantism, those sins of the Middle Ages; and Professor Mahaffy is the more inclined to praise Greek clear-sightedness in virtue of his own long-standing feud with mediaevalism. There is a fine old-fashioned flavor, as of some clergyman in Thomas Love Peacock—a Ffolliott, a Portpipe, an Opimian—in the valiant no-Popery flings of our author against the Church and against the theological prepossessions of mediaeval science and philosophy. The modern contentiousness about Greek here receives a temperamental reinforcement.

[1 This article, of which four-fifths are now reprinted, first appeared in the *Nation* (New York) for April 7, 1910, as a review of Mahaffy's *What Have the Greeks Done for Modern Civilization?* Section IV, dealing with the plan and scope of the particular book rather than the subject, has been omitted. The parts included are published with the consent of Dr. Wolff and the editor of the *Nation*.—EDITOR.]

All good things being Greek, and all bad things non-Greek, the Middle Ages were non-Greek; and the Renaissance, which put an end to them, was Greek. Such seems to be the latent reasoning at the bottom of Professor Mahaffy's view—and we admit it to be the popular view—that by means of a resurgence of Greek art, literature, and philosophy, the Renaissance superseded the Middle Ages, and that the Renaissance was in spirit and accomplishment truly Greek, truly classical. The naïve assumption of the humanists that they had emerged from a 'thick Gothic night,' Professor Mahaffy would modify by substituting 'Latin' for 'Gothic'; and, having thus given a bad name to the Scholastic Philosophy, to Romanesque and Gothic architecture, to the *Dies Irae* and to the *chansons de geste,* he would contentedly hang them all. Now, he believes, upon the thick Latin night up rose Greek, and up rose the sun: the classical Renaissance and the 'modern spirit' were a twin birth of the revival of Greek studies.[2] This view seems to us erroneous; and, as the conceptions underlying it determine Professor Mahaffy's treatment of his subject, we shall examine it at some length. Waiving all questions of chronology, disregarding therefore all mediaeval anticipations of the Renaissance or of the 'modern spirit,' granting that the light did not dawn till Greek began to reappear, and then dawned decisively, we believe it would not be difficult to show that the Renaissance itself was not essentially Hellenic.

The literature of the Renaissance, both in and out of Italy, is four-fifths of it Latinistic—Virgilian, Ciceronian, Senecan, occasionally Horatian, very heavily Ovidian. It springs not immediately, often not mediately, from Homer, Demosthenes, Pindar, Aeschylus, Sophocles, or even Euripides. The other fifth, which does draw nourishment from Greek literature, draws it from the Greek literature, not of the golden, but of the silver and the pinchbeck ages. Boccaccio, Professor Mahaffy points out,[3] is indebted to Greek prose fiction; but what he does not point out is that Boccaccio's debt runs mostly to very late Byzantine romances now lost. Lyly draws from Plutarch *On Education.* Sannazaro breaks from the Virgilian pastoral tradition to return to Theocritus. Tasso's *Aminta,* as is well known, gets what is probably its most famous passage from the late prose romance of Achilles Tatius. As is not so well known, the *Jerusalem Delivered,* too, professedly

2 Mahaffy, pp. 18, 19.
3 *Ibid.,* p. 95 n.

a restoration of the classical—that is, the Virgilian—epic, in repro-
bation of the composite romance-epic of Pulci, Boiardo, and
Ariosto, is itself full of the conceits of late Greek rhetoric.   The
Pastor Fido is based upon a story in Pausanias.   It seems well
within the truth to say that where Renaissance literature is Greek
at all, it is almost certain to be in the Alexandrianized, Romanized,
Byzantinized, and Orientalized vein that we call Greek only because
we have no better name for it.

The art and the philosophy of the Renaissance, like its literature,
do not draw from pure Hellenic fountains.   Botticelli, Raphael, and
Titian are not inspired by Greek statuary of the best period, very
little of which had been unearthed; Greek painting was probably
unknown to them, and, at any rate, Greek painting, as far as it has
survived at all, is of the Campanian, the Alexandrian style—distinctly post-classical.   The *putti* of the Renaissance may, indeed,
it is thought, be traced to the 'Egyptian plague of Loves'—those
Cupids, which, whether attendant upon the amorous adventures of
the gods, or nesting in trees, or wreathing garlands, or exposed in
cages for sale, 'flutter through the Pompeian pictures.'   And where
the great painters of the Renaissance thought of themselves as illus-
trators of 'literary' themes (we are just rediscovering how decid-
edly they did so think of themselves—to the confusion of 'art for
art's sake'), they looked for their themes, not in Homer, or the tragedians, or the myths of Plato, but in Ovid, or Apuleius, or Philostratus, or Lucian.   Raphael's frescoes in the Farnesina got their
Olympians, not from Hesiod, but from Apuleius.   Botticelli's
Calunnia, as Professor Mahaffy mentions elsewhere, is derived from
Lucian's description of the Diabolé of Apelles.   Mantegna, Titian,
Raphael, Giulio Romano, and others deliberately retranslated into
color and visual form the verbal descriptions by Philostratus of
paintings in a supposed picture-gallery.

As for the Platonism of the Renaissance, that too was composite,
with its leaning toward pseudo-Dionysian hierarchies and toward
elaborate theories of love.   It was the Platonism of Plotinus, rather,
after the school of Alexandria; for, in spite of Ficino's translation,
the Platonism of Athens was to them unknown—or, when known,
too purely Attic to be assimilated.   There was, indeed, an echo of
pre-Socratic Greek thought in the animistic philosophies of Southern Italy; but these Professor Mahaffy does not mention, despite
their influence upon Bacon by way of Telesio and Campanella.

In general, Renaissance taste is distinctly unclassical.   It runs to
digression and irrelevancy; to inserted descriptions and episodes;

to huge verbosity.   It revels in the 'word-paintings' (ἐκφράσεις) which were a specialty of the late sophists and rhetoricians; it never tires of their speechmaking.   It favors whole bookfuls of orations invented as patterns of the kind of thing that might be said upon a given occasion by persons imaginary, mythological, or historical. These ἠθοποιῖαι and μελέται bulk large in the Anthology, and reappear in collections like 'Silvayn's' *Orator*—to mention, perhaps, the most familiar name among many.   The prose of the Renaissance, again, like late Greek prose, tends, without resistance, to the most exaggerated conceits and antitheses, each country in Europe developing its own particular brands of bad taste—Euphuism, Gongorism, Marinism, and the rest—upon a common basis of Ciceronian and late Greek rhetoric.   In imitation, too, of the *tours de force* of degenerate Greek and Roman rhetoricians, the versifiers of the Renaissance often chose the most trivial themes, and embellished them with all the graces of *double entendre*.   To match the antique disquisitions 'Of Long Hair,' and 'In Praise of Baldness,' we have the *capitoli* of Berni and his school on 'Figs,' 'Beans,' 'Sausages,' 'Bakers' Ovens,' 'Hard-Boiled Eggs,' 'Chestnuts,' 'Paint-Brushes,' 'Bells,' 'Needles,' 'Going without Hats,' and 'Lying late Abed.' It is a far cry from this sort of thing to Homer or to the Periclean age.   Indeed, if by Greek we mean 'classic,' the Renaissance was not Greek.   Not until the late eighteenth century, after the way had been cleared by those 'pedants,' German and other, to whom this work alludes so slightingly, was the true Renaissance of classic Greek accomplished; only then may the modern world be said to have entered fully upon its Greek heritage.   What the Renaissance of the fourteenth and fifteenth centuries achieved was rather a pan-Latinistic revival, which attended especially to the process of recasting and enriching the vernacular tongues, mostly by means of Latin or post-classical Greek models, into vehicles of a modern *eloquentia* that might rival the antique.   Its degenerate models, together with its own taste in choosing them, made it, not pure, reposeful, imaginative, but composite, unquiet, fantastic, rhetorical, loquacious—all that is suggested when we say 'Alexandrian.'

One cannot help feeling that Professor Mahaffy's taste in these matters has been 'subdued to what it works in' by his extensive studies of post-classical Greek.   This bias appears in the estimate of Aristotle's *Poetics* and the dicta about Wordsworth, Tennyson, and others.   The *Poetics* is treated as if it were merely a collection of judgments upon individual works in Greek literature: if these judgments are erroneous, the work is a failure, of course.   It is not perceived, apparently, that the *Poetics* is an exposition of basic principles, the principles of poetry and of art in general; and that, in its justification of poetry as an imaginative embodiment of the *universal* (a view which Plato, for all his poetry, completely missed), and in its promulgation of the law of unity, it laid sure foundations for the criticism of all time, and established an unassailable canon of classic or ideal art. All this apart from the historical importance of the *Poetics* misunderstood—apart from the pseudo-classic of the sixteenth, seventeenth, and eighteenth centuries, apart from the controversies about 'imitation,' *catharsis,* and the 'three unities.' Of this really fundamental book Professor Mahaffy says:[4] 'I know of no poorer and more jejune exposition of a great subject'; and on the next page he cavalierly dismisses it upon the plea of lack of time. The same want of appreciation of the universal in Hellenism is responsible for some of the opinions here expressed upon the Greek in modern English poetry. Of the 'galaxy that illumined the early nineteenth century,' Wordsworth is considered to be 'the least Greek';[5] and this because of his failure to distinguish prose diction from poetical, and because of the inordinate length of the *Excursion.* Keats, however, had caught the Greek spirit, though at second or third hand;[6] in Shelley, 'we have that perfect combination of romantic imagination with Greek culture' which makes him the greatest of this group;[7] and Tennyson is 'the most classical of our modern lyric poets.'[8]

Read in view of the critic's Alexandrian bias and of the quotations which illustrate his criticism, these dicta become plain. Keats is Greek in being a master of isolated sensuous images, chaste or voluptuous—not in virtue of his delicacy in selection or his passion for beauty; certainly not in virtue of that architectonic which he never possessed. Shelley's 'clouds and sunsets' and spirits and flower-bells and pavilions—the imagery of romanticism—are at the service of his revolt and of his love of Greece and liberty. What matter that Shelley hardly touched human experience, hardly touched the general life of man? The case is still clearer when we come to Wordsworth and Tennyson. Of Wordsworth's purity and wisdom—of his *universality,* and of his 'plain and noble' style—of all that makes him a true classic, a true Greek despite his re-

4 Mahaffy, p. 62.
5 *Ibid.*, pp. 56-57.
6 *Ibid.*, p. 46.
7 *Ibid.*, p. 56.
8 *Ibid.*, p. 59.

current prosiness—there is not a word; though, of course, the specific Platonism in Wordsworth's wonderful Ode is recognized. But
what of *Laodamia?*—

> for the gods approve
> The depth, and not the tumult, of the soul.

What of *Dion?*—

> So were the hopeless troubles, that involved
> The soul of Dion, instantly dissolved.
>
> .   .   .   .   .
>
> Him, only him, the shield of Jove defends,
> Whose means are fair and spotless as his ends.

Or—to take Wordsworth not on classical ground, and in a vein not
sententious—what can be more Greek than those autochthonous
figures of the Leech-Gatherer, and of Michael at the unfinished
sheepfold?—

> . . . 'Tis believed by all
> That many and many a day he thither went,
> And never lifted up a single stone;

or this about Michael's wife?—

> Whose heart was in her house: two wheels she had
> Of antique form, this large for spinning wool,
> That small for flax; and if one wheel had rest,
> It was because the other was at work;—

lines of which Homer would not need to be ashamed. One might
as well say that Millet's Sower is not Greek, or that Lincoln's
speech at Gettysburg is not Greek—Greek as Simonides! Finally,
the Hellenism of Tennyson is here supposed to be shown by the
Lotos-Eaters and the Theocritean 'Come down, O maid,' and that
well-nigh intolerable piece of oxymoron and antithesis:

> His honor rooted in dishonor stood,
> And faith unfaithful kept him falsely true.

So much of Tennyson's work is Greek in a very pure sense that
it seems a pity to try to prove him Hellenic by what at best can
prove him only Alexandrian. . . .

The Greeks, more than all other peoples before or since, believed

in the power of mind, and practised their belief. Applying mind
to the raw material of sensation, they turned experience into wisdom, fact into truth, the Many into the One, chaos into law, the
particular and provincial into the ideal and the universal. But
they were not content to rest in this supersensible region: they
re-embodied their ideals in noble sensuous and intellectual forms,
which they chose from amid a welter of forms possible but ignoble
or insignificant, and which therefore have appealed to mankind
semper, ubique. So that, whether in the subtle curves of a building, or in the proportions of a statue, or in the shape of a vase, or
in the notes of the musical scale, or in finding how the human mind,
out of an infinite number of ways in which it can work, actually
does work towards truth; whether in art, or letters, or logic, or
science, or a hundred other departments of human activity, we
still perceive that they have performed for mankind, once for all,
the labor of selection. It is impossible to overestimate this accomplishment in the racial economy, just as it is impossible to overestimate the specific nobility and loftiness of the ideal heritage they
have left to the race.

Those who follow the Greek ways, and, without limiting themselves to old experience, fearlessly, and with confidence in the power
of mind, push into the new data of modern life along the path that
has proved possible—these are the pioneers; these are subduing
chaos and bringing it province by province under the rule of spirit.
Those who, refusing to profit by the Greek economy, try old failures again in ignorance or from choice, throw away their heritage.
It is only by accident that they may happen upon some worthy
thing. Their aberration, generally speaking, takes either or both
of two forms, according as they fail to value one or another phase of
the Greek accomplishment. Either they deny the validity of the
results achieved by selection, and still fancy that 'the world is all
before them where to choose'; or they deny the right of mind to
work selectively at all upon the data of experience, insist that all
things are of equal value except as weeded out by *natural* selection,
and enslave themselves to the crude fact. The first error is the
error of modern art, the second that of modern politics—at least,
so far as both have been evolved under democratic institutions.
The art of democracy is supposed to demand that no forms be
rejected as ignoble. The politics of democracy, theoretically allow-
ing free play to the conflicting wills of individuals, each striving
for the ends indicated by his 'enlightened self-interest,' fails to provide for right leadership, for a chosen mind to control the welter,

and so falls into the gripe of wrong leadership—for a mind of some sort is sure to gain control, soon or late. Modern science has escaped the second error, by selecting from the method of Bacon that part which is Greek in spirit. The Baconian induction, just in so far as it enslaved itself to fact, and disallowed hypothesis, and denied the rights of mind—just in so far as it was un-Greek—was a failure; and just in so far as it 'married mind with matter'—to use Bacon's own similitude—was, and is, a success. We are not to be, says Bacon again, like the ant, which gathers and stores up her hoard untransformed by aught that she does; nor yet like the spider, which spins her subtle thread all from within; but rather like the bee, which both gathers from without and transforms from within that which she gathers. Only thus shall we get 'sweetness and light.'

The Hellenist still believes that, things being given, ideas shall prevail. And so, instead of *fighting* things out, or letting the stress of competing forces among things work out its wasteful end, as nature does, at dreadful expense of pain, at dire expense of spirit and of life, he endeavors to *think* things out. He may, by international arbitration, substitute the sanction of ideas for the sanction of arms. Or, upon a broad basis of facts, he may build a luminous hypothesis or rise to a law. He may be designing a subway or a city, and planning it so that the work will not have to be done over after the lapse of years. He may raise wages or share his profits, not under the compulsion of a strike, but again under the compulsion of an idea—his own idea of equitable distribution. In many ways his mind, dealing with fact, will draw wisdom out of life; in many ways he will re-embody that wisdom in chosen forms of beauty, and with whatever materials life gives him will make of himself a poet, and of life an art. We leave the subject with a question for those of an inquiring mind: Is our 'modern' way of life favorable to tempers of this kind? Do *we* believe in the supremacy of spirit? And would it have been a merit in the Greeks had they been like us?

XVII

OUR DEBT TO ANTIQUITY [1]

By Thaddaeus Zielinski

The task before me is to interpret to my hearers, as far as the time at our disposal and my powers permit, the importance of the special department of knowledge of which I am the accredited representative at the St. Petersburg University—a department which I may briefly indicate by the title 'Antiquity.' Our end may be gained by three different ways, corresponding to the threefold aspect of the subject itself. Antiquity forms, in the first place, the subject-matter of that science which is commonly, though in some respects erroneously, called 'classical philology'; in the second place, it contributes an element to the intellectual and moral culture of modern European society; in the third place—and here its significance especially touches you, my hearers—it forms one of the subjects taught in the 'privileged' secondary schools of Russia—the so-called Classical Gymnasia.

Each of these points of view reveals to us a new aspect of antiquity; each compels the trained scholar to range himself in direct opposition to the opinion prevalent to-day among the educated in every country, and particularly in Russia. Men, indeed, have made up their minds that what is called 'classical philology' is a science which, however zealously cultivated, yet affords no longer any interesting problems for our solution. Our expert, however, will tell you that never has it had such interest for us as to-day; that the entire work of previous generations was merely preparatory—in fact, was merely the foundation on which we are

[1 This selection consists of the first 29 pages of the first lecture (pp. 1-30) out of eight in Professor Zielinski's *Our Debt to Antiquity*, translated by H. A. Strong and Hugh Stewart. London, 1909. The lectures were delivered in the spring of the year 1903 to the highest classes in the secondary schools of Petrograd, and were immediately published. The translators made use of the second edition. The selection is here reprinted under an agreement with the publishers of the translation, Messrs. George Routledge and Sons, Ltd., London.—EDITOR.]

only now beginning to raise the actual structure of our knowledge; that problems ever new, challenging research and demanding solution, meet us at every step in the field of our progress.

Again, in regard to the element contributed by antiquity to modern culture, a belief rules abroad that antiquity plays a meaningless part in the world of to-day; that it has no significance for modern culture; and that it has long since been superseded by the achievements of modern thought. But our expert, again, will assure us that our modern culture, both intellectual and moral, has never been so closely bound up with antiquity as to-day, and has never stood in such pressing need of its contributions. He will tell us, further, that we have never been so well equipped for understanding and assimilating it as to-day. Finally, in regard to antiquity as an element of education, people are disposed to deem it merely a singular survival, which has maintained its footing in our modern school curriculum in some unintelligible way and for some unintelligible reason, but which is destined to make a speedy and final disappearance. But the man who understands the true position of affairs will rejoin that antiquity, from its very nature and essence, owing to both historical and psychological causes, is and must be considered an organic element of education in European schools, and that if it be destined to disappear entirely, its end will coincide with the end of modern European culture.

We have, then, these three antitheses; and you will agree that sharper cannot easily be formulated. I am afraid that the very statement of these antitheses may trouble you and dispose you to look with suspicion on what I have to say. And as such an a priori prejudice may conceivably weaken the effect of the lecturer's words on the minds of his audience, pray allow me to dispel it, as far as prejudice can be dispelled by the operation of reason. Indeed, I can imagine your objection to be stated thus broadly:

'Does not the mere composition of the two parties to the dispute show who is right and who is wrong? Is it possible that the vast majority of men should be wrong, and that the expert of whom you speak, and with whom you probably identify yourself, Professor, should be right? Let us leave "classical philology" out of account for the moment; it has no interest for the world at large, so the world at large has the right to ignore it. But antiquity as an element in culture, antiquity as a vital factor in education—can we really admit that men have gone so far astray in settling questions which touch them so nearly? *Vox populi, vox Dei*, is no mere idle saying.'

Here I could make a reservation, and a fairly important one, with respect to this majority of which we hear so much; but let that pass. Let it be even as you say. Still, I cannot admit the applicability of the proverb about the *vox populi* to this majority, whether it be found to exist in reality or in imagination only—the history of all ages protests loudly against such an application. Only reflect how Rome drove the early Christians into the arena; think how Spain raged against the heretics, or Germany against the witches; think of the unanimous support long afforded to institutions like negro slavery in America, or serfdom in Russia, and you will agree that the *vox populi* is in truth only too often the *vox Diaboli,* and not the *vox Dei.* To-day we not only condemn such manifestations of the popular will, we explain them dispassionately; that is no bad thing. We show the reasons which in all the cases I have indicated have forced men to conclusions so adverse to their true interests. And in the present case also we can adopt the same attitude; in the present case also we can . . . analyze the cause of the adverse position taken up by modern critics against antiquity. We can distinguish the part played therein by well-intentioned and involuntary delusion from that which we must ascribe to intentional deception. For the moment my purpose is different: I am anxious only to shatter your simple faith—if you have a faith—in the infallibility of public opinion, and to protest against the misapplication of the proverb, *Vox populi, vox Dei.*

The proper meaning of this saying I will proceed to explain to you. Where must we look to hear the voice of GOD? Not in the deafening clamor which is so often the expression of mere passionate excitement, but in the calm, dispassionate command of that mysterious will which points out to humanity the path of development in civilization. In remote ages, before mankind had any inkling of the physiology of digestion or of organic chemistry, that voice warned mankind that if it would attain the highest possible degree of perfection, it should select as its main article of diet— *bread.* The Greeks, who could feel wonder for what really merited that emotion, recognized rightly enough the divine nature of this voice; they believed it to be the voice of their goddess Demeter. The biology of the present day, which does not recognize metaphysics, or which, to speak more correctly, has introduced, instead of the honored theological metaphysics of former times, its own special scheme of biological metaphysics, sees in that voice the effect of 'the law of natural selection' which it itself discovered, a law entirely analogous to that which has assigned its own proper diet to every living animal. Yes, gentlemen, this law of natural selection which, in cases where human society is its subject, bears the title of 'sociological selection'—that is the real *vox populi* and *vox Dei.*

Let us now ask, in what relation does this law stand to our present question? the question as to the part played by antiquity in the education imparted to the youth of our day, or, more briefly, to classical education. This, then, is the relation: now, nearly fifteen hundred years after the fall of Rome, and more than two thousand years after the fall of Greece, we find ourselves disputing as to whether the languages spoken by the two classical nations of antiquity shall, or shall not, occupy the central place in the teaching of our schools. You must needs concede to me, gentlemen, that the unanimous testimony of centuries is a far more impressive fact than the ephemeral verdict of modern society, even were its unanimity less fictitious than in fact it is. Think of the picture which the Neva presents when the fatal southwest wind is blowing! The set of its waves is plainly to the east. The river seems running up-stream into the Lake of Ladoga. And yet you know that every drop of that lake, thanks to an invisible but very real fall in the earth's surface, is making its way into the Gulf of Finland; and that the only result of this up-stream current produced by the wind is a temporary overflow of the Galeerenhafen. The same phenomenon is to be witnessed in a community and in public opinion. In them, as in our Neva, there are not one, but two currents. There is one which is for show—noisy, tumultuous, and capricious, and followed by inundations and misfortunes of every kind; the other, whose very existence is hardly suspected by the former, is quiet, soundless, and irresistible. Two currents, or, if you like, two souls, two 'I's.' You may adopt for society as a whole the sharp division which Nietzsche has wittily proposed for the individual members which compose it. He contrasts the 'little I,' which is self-conscious and carries, relatively speaking, but small weight, with the 'great I,' which, though subconscious, still prescribes with sovereign power the course of public progress. Well, this unfavorable view entertained by the contemporary world as to a training in the classics, a view which you may be inclined to oppose to my apparently isolated opinion, is the product, not of the modern world in its entirety, but merely of its 'little I.' Of course, this 'little I' can, and actually does, inflict on me as an individual a certain amount of annoyance; but it has no weight with me as a thinking man and a historian. As such I am in duty

bound to attend, not to its voice, but to the voice of the mysterious
'great I' which directs its destiny. And there I hear something
quite different; the 'little I' of the modern world repeats in all
the notes of the scale: 'Down with classical training!' The 'greater
I,' however, says to us: 'Cherish it as the apple of your eye!' Or,
to speak more correctly, it does not actually say this to us; it has
itself cherished classical education for some fifteen or twenty centuries, disregarding the repeated protests of its own 'little I'; and
you may be sure that it will cherish it in the future as in the past.

However, we have arrived at this result in favor of antiquity
only incidentally. In our next remarks we must seek to establish
our claims with more detailed arguments. Do not attach, for the
meantime, any importance to our present result, and merely bear
in mind what I have said about the two currents of public opinion
and their relative value. And now let us approach the subject.

At the beginning of my lecture I insisted on the threefold significance of antiquity for us: purely scientific, cultural, and educational. We will, however, adopt another order in our course; we
will begin with what concerns you all, and conclude with what
directly affects, or rather will affect, but a few among you.

And so, wherein lies the educational importance of a study of
antiquity?

Assuming, first of all, that my answer to this question must be
a confession of ignorance, or that it prove in any other way unsatisfactory, what would follow? When I explained to you just now
the purport of the law of sociological selection, I referred you, as
an illustration of my meaning, to one remarkable result of such
selection, whereby bread has come to be the principal article of
diet of civilized man. Permit me now to use this illustration for
a picture or allegory, which, indeed, has served me once before in
a similar case. Suppose that in the times when men were inclined
to regard the human organism as a mechanism, in the days of
Helvetius and Lamettrie, a commission had been appointed to
reform the diet of mankind. The speeches of the opponents of
the traditional methods of diet would have first and foremost
drawn a gloomy picture of the physical condition of mankind at
that period. Man lives some sixty or seventy years at most,
though nature intended him to live two hundred years—this was
precisely the opinion, later on, of Hufeland; and pray what sort
of a life has he during the brief space of his existence? He is
feeble and clumsy; he ages rapidly; and think of all the failures
of physical life! And so on.

Whence all this misery? Simply because his diet is irrational. Diet ought to renew the human body; but our diet consists mainly of materials which the human body does not require, and, indeed, rids itself of anew, as entirely useless. Our bodies need flesh, blood, muscles, marrow, etc. In spite of this demand, we supply them almost entirely with a vegetarian diet, of which bread forms the main factor. The mischief caused by bread is that it stands completely in the way of other articles of diet which are really useful; to prove its worthlessness you need only consider the human body. Are our arms, legs, hands, and lungs composed of dough? Certainly not. Of what, then? Of blood, flesh, muscle, bones, and so on. Well, then, pray give us a genuinely satisfying diet, answering to the composition of our bodies; give us a uniform diet to nourish the body generally, containing in one harmonious, evenly-proportioned compound every element needed by us for the renovation of our physical nature—flesh, blood, bones, muscles, and so on. Then, and not till then, will the failures of physical life disappear; then a man will live a couple of centuries, and his youth will endure longer than his life to-day, and so on. Now, what might a supporter of the traditional diet have urged by way of rejoinder? What might have been his reply when challenged to prove the value of bread as nourishment?

At the present day, of course, an answer suggests itself as possible which explains quite satisfactorily all the difficulties; on the one hand, physiology has thrown a light on the process of digestion in all its details; on the other, organic chemistry has analyzed our diet to its component parts. Chemistry warrants us in asserting that bread contains all, or nearly all, the constituents of food necessary for the human body; physiology helps us to trace the way by which our organism assimilates these materials. But we were supposing ourselves in a period when the process of digestion was but very imperfectly understood, while organic chemistry was quite unknown; and so, I repeat, what could the supporters of the traditional methods of diet reply to the champions of empirical dietetics of those days? I fancy their reply might have been as follows: 'You ask in what the dietetic value of bread, and, generally speaking, of a vegetable diet, consists. That I cannot tell you. But the fact remains that the nations which have adopted our food system are therewith the bearers of civilization, while those which diet themselves according to your theories are only the very rudest of barbarians. It is also true that the civilized nations multiply and spread, while the savages who feed on a meat diet are decreasing in number, and are being pushed ever further into the background. Further, it is a fact that civilized man, when he is by the force of circumstances constrained to deny himself the use of bread and fruit, and to adopt exclusively a meat diet, becomes enfeebled and dies out. Finally, it is a fact that you yourselves, while you have correctly pointed out the shortcomings of our physical life, have still failed to prove that those shortcomings are the natural result of our system of diet; nor have you deigned to bestow any notice on the circumstance that those who follow your system are neither longer lived, nor stronger, nor handsomer, nor healthier than we; which seems a mere mockery of the empirical method.'

Such, I fancy, would have been the answer of a supporter of the traditional dietetic system, and his inference would have been unassailable. Now I pass on to our present question. You ask me to show you wherein lies the educational value of 'antiquity.' I preface my answer by a question, namely: 'Has psychology clearly defined and explained the process of intellectual digestion in all its details? Does there exist a system of organic chemistry applicable to intellectual diet, and capable of providing a qualitative and quantitative analysis of this diet?' Should you then admit that the sciences which I have in view are sciences of the future, known to us at present only in their beginnings, you authorize me thereby to make this rejoinder: 'What is the educational value of the study of antiquity? That I do not, indeed, know; but it is a fact that the system of classical education dates from time out of mind; that it has at the present day spread to all the nations who enjoy the benefit of so-called European civilization, and who, indeed, could not be called civilized till they adopted this system. It is, further, true that if we were to follow the methods of the meteorologists and express the vicissitudes which the system of classical education has experienced in the different countries where it has been adopted throughout all the period of their existence by the figure of a curve, this curve would be found to express at the same time the variations in the intellectual culture of these same nations. It would thus demonstrate the close dependence of the general culture of any given country on the degree of importance attached to classical education. Thirdly, it is a fact that in the present day also the intellectual influence of any given nation asserts itself in proportion as classical education prevails in its schools; whereas nations who discard this system—the Spaniards, for instance—play no great part in the world of ideas, in spite of their large population and glorious past. It is also true that in Russia the blow inflicted on classical education by the reform of the gymnasia in the year 1890 has entailed a general depression of the level of education on the young men who leave our gymnasia, as is admitted even by our opponents. And, lastly, it is true that those who depict the short-comings of our gymnasia in such sombre colors have failed to show that these shortcomings are the result of classical education; they obstinately refuse to consider the fact that the same shortcomings are manifest in the pupils of the secondary schools in which classi-cal education plays no part.'

The inference is unassailable. In the interests of the mental cul-ture of the Russian people we are bound to aim at the highest possi-ble level of classical training in our gymnasia, regardless as to whether we succeed or not in giving a satisfactory answer to the question respecting the educational value of a study of antiquity.

And now, before proceeding further, let us look back a little. A consideration of the history of culture led us to the conclusion that the study of the classics offers in itself the standard of intel-lectual diet of the rising generation. I asserted that this conclu-sion was unassailable; and, in truth, every one who is accustomed to weigh his words and subordinate his feelings to his reason in matters of science—and it is with such that we have now to deal— is bound to agree with me. But, unfortunately, such persons are rare. Ordinary people subordinate their reason to their feelings; when any proposition which they dislike is proved to them to be true, they try to find in what you say some handle for contradic-tion; and if they succeed in hitting on any rejoinder which has but an external resemblance to a logical argument, they then allege, and often themselves actually believe, that they have refuted you. Of course, it is quite impossible to foresee refutations of this nature. One way, and one alone, leads to truth; whereas the paths to error are manifold. But as I am acquainted with much of what has been written on the question of the secondary schools, I can imagine that my adversaries will find two 'handles' in my statements.

This is the first one. I have just said, 'in the interests of the mental culture of the Russian people.' I took it for granted that any conclusions which might be drawn from the fluctuations of culture in Europe generally must be equally applicable to Russia. Is this assumption correct? In the ranks of my opponents there are not a few who will refuse to recognize this connection. 'No,' say they, 'the claims of a classical education are not supported by the history of Russia.' On this plea they discard classical education, and then proceed to launch projects of a special school curriculum

of their own, forgetting, however, to inquire whether its claims are
supported by the history of Russia or not. Matters, in truth, stand
thus: however scanty the support given to the claims of a classical
education by the facts of Russian history, any other type of education, existing or proposed, finds in them absolutely no support.
But for us this is not by any means the principal consideration.
The main point is this: Russia for a long time possessed no system
of classical education; the result was that during all that period it
was not an educated nation; nor did it become so till the introduction of classics as an educational medium. That is a fact, and,
moreover, one which fully confirms my conclusions.

The second objection runs parallel to the first, and stands in the
same relation to it as time to space. Our opponents in this camp
endeavor to assume for modern times just such another exceptional
position as their allies assumed for Russia. 'In old times,' say
they, 'the study of antiquity really formed an important branch
of learning, for it had lessons to teach; but at the present day we
have traveled far beyond it, and we have nothing more to learn
from it.' These opponents are very easily refuted; we have merely
to confront them with the question: 'When do they believe that we
outstripped antiquity?' That question they cannot answer. The
matter really stands thus: The question of classical education, as
we have seen, is subject to the law of sociological selection. The
operation of this law is determined by what is known as the
'heterogeneity of purposes'; that is to say, the non-correspondence
of the real and unconscious purpose with the apparent and conscious purpose. Thus the apparent purpose of which the bee is
conscious when it is enticed into the recesses of a flower is that the
creature may enjoy the sweet juice; the real purpose, on the other
hand, of which the bee is unconscious, is that the stamina of the
flower should be pulled about, and thereby produce its fructifica-
tion.

Precisely the same thing happens in this case also. The real
purpose of sociological selection (it will be understood, of course,
that I employ the word 'purpose' here in the relative sense in which
it is generally used in modern biology), in its maintenance of classical education, has been at all times one and the same—namely, the
intellectual and moral improvement of humanity. But the apparent purposes of which the world was conscious were different. They
varied at different times; and this leads us to make two interesting
observations. In the first place, scarcely has one of these apparent
purposes served its time, so to say, when another steps forward to

take its place. Secondly, those nations which mistook the ostensible apparent purpose for the real one, and which endeavored to achieve it, not by the path which the law of selection indicated to them, but by a shorter and more convenient path, have had a hard judgment pronounced on them for their would-be omniscience by the tribunal of history. This is precisely what we see in biology and biological laws.

Originally, in the early Middle Ages, the apparent purpose of classical education was the understanding of Holy Scripture and of the Liturgy, the works of the Church Fathers, the lives of the saints, and so on. Of course, there was another method, more simple and convenient for attaining this end, namely, the translation of all these writings into the mother tongue. This method was adopted by the nations of the Christian East, and the consequence was that the advance of culture left those nations hopelessly behind. At a later period, in the second half of the Middle Ages, this purpose retired to the background in favor of another—a knowledge of ancient science, as expounded, of course, in the classical languages. Here, also, another shorter and more convenient road was at the service of those who wished it—namely, the translation of the scientific works of the ancients into the mother tongue. This was the course adopted by the Arabs, and it brought Mohammedan civilization, after a brief period of prosperity, to a speedy and irretrievable ruin; as, indeed, was quite natural, since the Arabs transplanted on to their own ground merely the flowers of antiquity severed from their roots, the ancient languages.

But this plan, too, was discarded at the end of the Middle Ages; modern Europe had no sooner assimilated the science of the ancients than it passed beyond it.

To the question, then, propounded above—namely, When did we outstrip antiquity in the sphere of science? our reply must be: To some extent as early as the Middle Ages. That period discovered sciences that were unknown or almost unknown to the ancients, as, for example, algebra, trigonometry, chemistry, and so on, and raised the sciences already known to a higher degree. It now seemed that antiquity might really be dispensed with, and classical culture did indeed begin to decline in the fourteenth century. But precisely in this century this same culture bloomed afresh, rapidly and brilliantly; the Renaissance has begun. Ancient art, not merely figurative, such as architecture, sculpture, painting, but oratorical also, was discovered anew. Men began to study the Latin language for the sake of its beauties in respect to form, and to reproduce them both in prose and verse. This is what is known as the 'old humanistic movement.' The Latin language became once again the educator, so to say, of the languages of modern Europe. The result of this influence of Latin is seen in the elasticity and strength, in the artistic technique, of modern prose and poetry. The result, then, was attained, and it seemed that antiquity might now be relegated to archaeological shelves. But no! Scarcely had this purpose begun to recede into the background, when a fresh plan, the fourth of these transitory purposes, appeared to take its place. The intellectual value of ancient literature was discovered, philosophy being its crown and consummation. Before that time men had learnt Latin to be able to speak well and write well; now they learnt it to be able to think well and judge well, *pour bien raisonner.*

Such was the *mot d'ordre* of the so-called 'enlightened views' which started in England during the seventeenth century, and which continued in France during the eighteenth century, and were reflected in the culture of the rest of the Europe of that time— the time of Newton, Voltaire, Frederick the Great, and Catherine. But already, in the eighteenth century, this one-sided intellectualism called forth a reaction which began in England and in France (as instanced by Rousseau), but attained special force in the Germany of Winckelmann and Goethe. The watchword was now the harmonious development of mankind in the way pointed out by nature, and the true method of attaining this ideal was seen to be once again—the study of antiquity.

Accordingly, the Gymnasia set about their new task with extreme energy. This is the so-called 'new humanistic movement.' Then, for the first time, the Greek language and literature claimed equal rights with the Latin; for the leaders of thought of that day believed quite rightly that the life of Greece approached their ideal nearer than the life of Rome. At the present moment we are again in a period of transition, and we see already clearly traced the new point of view from which the coming century will regard antiquity. The development of the natural sciences has given prominence to the principle of evolution; antiquity has become doubly precious to us as the cradle of every one of the ideas which we have hitherto cherished. And we see how humanism finds itself at variance with the so-called 'historic movement' in the very questions connected with classical education. It seems, moreover, that the latter school is gaining the day. Of course, we shall have to return to this extremely important consideration. For the present, however, it will be sufficient to assure you that this is already the sixth con-

scious attitude in regard to the importance of the study of antiquity. It has made its appearance just in the nick of time to
relieve the 'new humanistic' attitude.

It is curious, too, to trace the changes which have passed over
the methods of instruction in classical education according to the
different points of view from which the purpose of this study was
apprehended. I am unable to dwell on this at length. I must
rest content with indicating the most obvious and palpable changes
which are expressed in the choice of authors at each different epoch.
During the first period, when Latin was studied for the salvation of
the soul, we find, as is natural, that religious works form the central point of the curriculum. During the second, which we may
call the scientific period, the main subjects of study were the handbooks of the respective sciences, such as the Latin Aristotle and
the so-called *Artes*—that is to say, treatises on mathematics and
astronomy, and also on medicine and law, and so on. In the third,
or 'old humanistic' epoch, it was Cicero as the master of Latin
oratory. In the fourth, the epoch of 'enlightenment,' it was Cicero
again, but this time as the philosopher. In the fifth, the 'new
humanistic' period, it was Homer, the tragic poets, and Horace.
We are living on the traditions of this period, but already there
is felt a growing need of a careful selection from ancient literature,
so as to represent antiquity to young scholars as precisely the
cradle of our ideas.

Quite recently Wilamowitz in Germany has sought to meet this
need by compiling a *Greek Reading-Book*, and his experiment has
deeply interested all the teaching profession in his own country.
No doubt this movement will in time reach us in Russia as well;
very probably it would have made its presence felt already, were
it not for the recent unrest in our schools. However this may be,
I have shown you the series of changing points of view from which
the study of antiquity has been regarded during the different
periods of our civilization. This, too, may serve as an answer to the
ignorant reproach that we have nothing now to learn from antiquity, as we have outstripped it; and likewise to the equally ignorant
reproach that classical studies have come to a standstill, and are
not keeping up with the times. But all these aims were, as I have
stated, transitory. They were aims towards which society consciously strove in each of the periods mentioned, and society has
rendered an account for them alike to itself and to us. The true
aim, however, of which men were not conscious, was the all-impor-
tant goal to which all selection tends—namely, the improvement of

humanity; in this case man's cultural, that is to say, his intellectual and moral, improvement.

But, it may be asked, in what way does the path of classical education tend to improve mankind intellectually and morally? This very question suggests another: Wherein lies the educational value of antiquity? We have already raised this latter question, and before answering it I proved to you that, whether our answer may seem satisfactory or not, the fact remains indisputable that the study of antiquity is an extremely important element in education. This has been unmistakably shown, quite independently of that answer, by considerations adduced from the history of culture. I beg you to bear in mind this fact; I attach the greatest importance to it. Precisely in the same way the value of bread as an article of diet was well established long before it had been proved by physiology and organic chemistry. What is physiology in this instance? The analysis of the consuming organism. And chemistry? The analysis of the substance consumed. Now substitute mind for body, education for diet, and antiquity for bread. Do there, then, exist sciences in this connection analogous to physiology and organic chemistry? that is to say, sciences which teach us how to analyze the organism of the consumer and the matter consumed? Let us see.

The consuming element is in this case the human intellect. Its analysis is the business of psychology, and that science is at present still in a state of infancy. Psychology is as yet unable to reply to all the questions addressed to her. This is, indeed, true of physiology as well; but still, the latter science has been vastly more developed, and is older alike in years and in experience. Now, as to the analysis of the diet for consumption, that is to say, antiquity. This analysis is not intrinsically very difficult, but in this case a study of the effects of its elements upon man's psychological nature is indispensable; in fact, a kind of psychological science of knowledges. And no such science is yet in existence, as the mere combination of the words shows you. So, gentlemen, you must not ask too much from me. I have promised you to answer the question proposed, and will do so as far as possible with the present state of psychological sciences. As I have remarked, these are sciences of the future; yet they have already established certain principles upon a fairly sure basis, and their methods are becoming ever more and more accurate, so that we are at least able to apprehend in what manner and in what direction a satisfactory answer to the questions which beset us is to be looked for. Yes, I can affirm so much; but I beg you to remember that this is merely a temporary answer, and that a much fuller and more convincing answer can be given only by our posterity. But before fulfilling my promise I must beg you to bear with me while I make a few remarks on the real meaning of the term 'educational value.' I am particularly anxious that you should accept nothing from me without a severe custom-house scrutiny, so to speak. This may detain us for a few minutes, but in return I shall hope to gain later on somewhat more of your confidence.

And so I put the question: In what sense are we to understand the expression 'educational value'?

Let us begin with the most concrete example possible. A carpenter has a son. He wishes to teach him a carpenter's trade. In this instance the problem is simple and intelligible to all. The carpenter's schooling prepares the boy directly for real life; every knack of the trade which the boy learns will be eminently useful to him in his future work, and in precisely the same way. We can easily picture to ourselves a carpenter's school; it will be, in fact, what we call a professional or technical school. Is there any justification for its existence? Undoubtedly there is, if you admit that it is possible or desirable to settle the trade or profession of a boy at such an early age. But is the principle of 'professional utilitarianism' applicable to intellectual as well as to manual training? To some extent this may be so, as theological schools, military and naval academies, and other secondary schools of the kind may serve to show; but it is only partially applicable.

For most intellectual professions there are no such schools in existence; and even those which I have just mentioned are trying more and more to free themselves from their narrow professional character, and to look with favor on a general education at the expense of any special branch. And, generally speaking, it is recognized that we need schools which do not insist upon determining a priori the future profession of their scholars.

What, then, should be the nature of such schools, assuming always that they are intended to prepare their scholars for real life, that is to say, for their future trade or profession? This is the problem of squaring the circle as applied to educational questions; and the efforts made to-day to solve it are as successful as those directed in former days at the solution of that famous mathematical puzzle itself. I will indicate certain methods of solving the problem which recommend themselves to the man in the street. The first of these is as follows.

There is a demand for a school to train the future lawyers, doctors, professors of natural history, engineers, mathematicians, scholars, and so on; so far, so good. Its program will embrace all the subjects of study which are common to all these departments of science. The shortcomings of this system are plain enough; the fact is that there are no such common courses of study, or, at least, extremely few. You have only to compare the lists of lectures provided for the faculty of law with those for the faculty of natural science, or the program of courses in history and classics with that of any technical institute, and you will be convinced of this. Now consider the second possible way. Select, if you please, in equal proportions courses of law, medicine, physics, mathematics, history, classics, and other subjects, and out of these try and concoct a program fit for a secondary school! Now, there are people simple enough to believe that this is feasible; it is, however, an utter impossibility. In the first place we are confronted with a confusing and deadening multiplicity of subjects, and in the second place the principle of utilitarianism is not even now maintained, for such a school cannot offer any of its scholars more than a tenth part of what he requires. Thus we may ask: What sort of a school is that which combines a bare tenth of useful material with nine-tenths of ballast?

There is a third way. Admitting the untenability of the first two solutions, one may propose to disregard entirely in our secondary schools the future career of our scholars, and demand merely that they leave the schools as educated persons. In other words, professional and utilitarian considerations are deliberately eschewed and the principle merely of education introduced. So far, so good. But what do we mean by an educated person? The answer cannot be far to seek; for we know that there are educated persons. What, then, must one know to be an educated person? An author of great reputation in educational matters has proposed a radical measure for the solution of this problem. His idea was to subject educated persons to a catechism, in other words, to an examination, and so establish a standard of departments of knowledge without which a man would not be 'educated,' and then to make these departments of knowledge the subjects of school-instruction. It would be amusing to carry out this plan and watch the results. You understand, of course, that under this system those departments of knowledge which one educated man possesses still do not fall into the general program, if there be a second educated man who does not possess them; for that shows that one can be educated even without their possession. Indeed, we might imagine a prodigy who could tell us the names of thirty Patagonian villages—that is his specialty; but we could incorporate into our program only what all educated society, or at least the greater part of it, knows about Patagonia; that is to say, nothing at all. And so it would be with all the other courses. And the net result would be: in arithmetic the four rules concerning whole numbers, with a general knowledge of fractions; in geometry, a few ordinary ideas about figures and solid bodies; in algebra, nothing; in trigonometry, nothing; and so on in its entirety; a program which one or two gymnasium classes would fully exhaust. It is easy to see that this way, too, fails to lead us to our goal. What, then, is the mistake? It lies in this, that we consider education to be the mere acquirement of knowledge. But whereas knowledge is forgotten, education is never lost; an educated person, even though he have forgotten all that he has learnt, remains an educated person. In making this statement I am very far from wishing to underestimate the importance of knowledge; on the contrary, I maintain that a man's utility is in proportion to his knowledge. But, gentlemen, different persons require different branches of knowledge. That is the case even at present, and will in the future be more the case than ever; for knowledge is ever becoming more and more specialized. The number of branches of knowledge indispensable to all, or indeed to all educated persons, is even at present far from large, and must diminish in every generation as knowledge itself continues to increase and consequently to be specialized. And thus to draw up the courses of learning for our secondary schools on these principles is an impossibility. And still it is the duty of such schools to give all those who are afterwards to be educated persons precisely what is likely to benefit them all alike; that is their whole object. And how shall they best fulfil this duty? Obviously by preparing a scholar's mind to embrace any branch of knowledge which he may need afterwards with the least possible expenditure of time and strength, and with the greatest possible advantage to himself. This is a truism, stale if you will, but a truism that defies contradiction, and is, in fact, irrefutable.

If it were my task to draw up a program for our secondary schools, I would endeavor to convince you, on the grounds of what I have said, that it must contain the following: first, courses providing a general knowledge, and secondly, courses providing a general education; the latter class would naturally rank as the more important. And to this latter class would naturally belong the courses on mathematics, physics, and classics, corresponding to the three methods of human thought—the deductive, the inductive-experimental, and the inductive-observant.

XVIII

AMERICANISM AND HELLENISM [1]

By Basil L. Gildersleeve

Hesperia, the Western land, was to the Greek of old the Land of Hope, and our Western land is the Land of Hope to the Greek of to-day. The island of Pelops is almost depopulated by the stream of emigration to the modern Atlantis, and the Greek of to-day recognizes in the Americanism of to-day the traits of an ideal Hellenism. And so, though I am not a Greek of to-day, but only a Grecian, I cannot help thinking that the recognition of the affinities of ancient Greek and modern American life, which I have dared to call the American element in Greek life, may serve to quicken the interest of the student of the Greek language and literature, and even if it abide alone, may wake the sense of kindred, after the forms of the Greek alphabet become misty.

This general theme has always been a favorite of mine. Creon tells his son Haemon that Antigone is 'a frigid hugging-piece,' and however frigid my hugging-piece may seem to others, I have pursued it as a phantom of delight ever since I knew what love is, now through the crowds of the Agora, now round the steps of the Bema, now over the meadows of the Muses where Aristophanes disports himself, now over battlefields illuminated by stark figures in blue and gray. I cannot help thinking that this pursuit has made for life, but like everything that makes for life, it has brought with it trouble, and my indiscreet urging of the theme has cost me more than one rebuke. So, for instance, in one of my essays I said: 'It is not in vain that the American student has been endowed with "that singular buoyancy and elasticity" which, accord-

[1 This is the third lecture (pp. 87-130) in Professor Gildersleeve's *Hellas and Hesperia, or the Vitality of Greek Studies in America, Three Lectures,* delivered at the University of Virginia under the conditions of the Barbour-Page Foundation, and published (New York) in 1909. It is reprinted with the consent of the Rector and Visitors of the University of Virginia; slight changes have been introduced at the request of Professor Gildersleeve.— EDITOR.]

ing to Dean Stanley, is the marked peculiarity of our people, nor in vain our unequaled adaptability, our quick perception, our straightforwardness of intellectual vision. We Americans, said Matthew Arnold, think straight and see clear.' And again: 'Ancient history has to be interpreted into terms of American experience, and it would not be saying too much to maintain that many of the aspects of American life enable us to understand the ancients better than some of our European contemporaries do. An audacious, inventive, ready-witted people, Americans often comprehend the audacious, inventive, ready-witted Greek *à demi-mot,* while the German professor phrases and the English "don" rubs his eyes, and the French savant appreciates the wrong half.' Whereupon a British reviewer charged me with 'vainglorious patriotism.' Sometimes, it is true, I stop and ask myself in an access of disillusionment, What right have I to speak of America? and I hear snub-nosed Socrates asking, 'What is American?' 'Tis a harder question perhaps for a man of my antecedents than 'What is Greek?' In the first place, a native is too native to give the right answer, and I dare not invoke the aid of such apostles of Americanism as Professor Brander Matthews, Dr. Henry van Dyke, or President Butler, the most recent American authorities on the subject; and in order to be truly scientific, I should have to muster the evidence of others, from Trollope and Basil Hall of the old time, through Dickens of a later date, down to the witnesses of our own day, frivolous Max O'Rell, unsympathetic Matthew Arnold, and sympathetic James Bryce, and on the basis of those documents draw up a table of American characteristics in which they all agree—our keenness and directness, our audacity, our inventiveness, our light-hearted acceptance of the shifts of fortune, a light-heartedness that makes the Greek Theramenes an American statesman, as he has recently been made the hero of an historical novel, a novel by an American Hellenist, Professor Gaines. Time was when we, men of the South, were more bent on asserting diversity than unity, a diversity that was the result of the conflicting interests, the incessant bickerings, the different ideals, the different social conditions. But we are all Americans now, and our Americanism is borne in upon us by foreign critics, who were the first to teach us that Walt Whitman, whom we all derided fifty years ago, is the true American poet and prophet; all the others mere echoes of European voices. I am sorry to say that Walt Whitman would not have heeded the scholar's plea for the classics. You may remember his deliverance in his *Leaves of Grass:*

Dead poets, philosophs, priests,
Martyrs, artists, inventors, governments long since,
Language-shapers, on other shores,
Nations once powerful, now reduced, withdrawn, or desolate,
I dare not proceed till I respectfully credit what you have left,
    wafted hither.
I have perused it, own it is admirable (moving awhile among it),
Think nothing can ever be greater, nothing can ever deserve more
    than it deserves.
Regarding it all intently a long while, then dismissing it,
I stand in my place, with my own day, here.

There is much more to the same effect in our typical American poet whom Tennyson admired and George Eliot quoted, and nothing could be more characteristic than the utterance:

    I stand in my place, with my own day, here.

And as an American, I am fully in accord with him. A detached American is for the most part a pitiful spectacle. But it is precisely because we stand in our place with our own day, here, that we cannot dismiss the past so cavalierly as Whitman has done. To the dead all things are dead. To him that is alive there is no dead poetry, no dead language. 'Only those languages,' said Lowell in a famous discourse, 'only those languages can be called dead in which nothing living was ever written.' There is no need of crediting the past, as Whitman calls it. The past collects its interest by the inevitable process of eternal laws. Classical antiquity is not driftwood, as Whitman intimates, not driftwood out of which to build fires on the shore of life, calling up the figures of Jason and Medea, of Paris and Helen, and listening to Arion in his singing-robes. The classical caravel is still seaworthy. No Captain Courageous of Gloucester, Massachusetts, is more popular than Odysseus of Ithaca. Retell the story of the wanderings of the much-enduring to a popular audience, if you wish to find out whether Homer is dead, and what Kipling calls 'his bloomin' lyre' has ceased to bloom. No happier hours in my long career can I recall than those I spent in repeating the tale of Old Audacious to a sympathetic audience thirty years ago. Tennyson's Ulysses I need not mention. Stephen Phillips' Ulysses I mention merely to protest against his perversion of the only true story of Odysseus in Hades. It is, then, precisely because we stand in our own place, here, precisely because we are Americans and Walt Whitman is our prophet, that we insist on our inheritance of the precious past, on which and by which we live.

But I have already spoken of Greek as an inheritance. To-day we are to consider not so much the inheritance as the kinship. Hellas speaks to us with a kindred voice, and looks into our eyes with kindred eyes. Like the Greeks, we Americans have found out our oneness by conflict with one another, as well as by contrast with others. The members of the same family seldom see the likeness that strangers recognize at once. There is a national handwriting among all the diversities of chirography, and we write American as we are written down Americans. American is as distinctive now as Greek was then, and it was War, the father of all things, that revealed us to ourselves. America is a find to the American as Greece was a find to the Greeks, to adapt the famous passage of Herodotus. It was the Persian war that gave Greece her unity—a war in which the Greeks themselves were arrayed on different sides, and no sooner was the unity brought about than the old enmity asserted itself, and Greece was split in twain—North against South and South against North.

True, these historical parallels are not to be urged. The unity of the Greek state was the city, the *polis,* and recent historians justly lay great stress on the difference between the city-state, the *Stadtstaat,* and the territorial state, the *Flächenstaat.* We are not to be misled by a name. The 'fierce democratie' of Athens was a narrow oligarchy according to modern conceptions, and the city-state was a mere atom in comparison with our empire states. But there are analogies that cannot be lightly thrust aside as mere fancies. Greek history is after all in some respects a pocket edition of American history, and the founders of the Union turned to Greek history rather than to Roman history when they considered the problems of Federal government; just as in the recent development of American life, the Roman Empire is ever in our thoughts and on our lips. A writer famous in his day, Alphonse Karr, in his *Journey round my Garden,* ridicules the botanist because he neglects the element of size. 'The same botanical description,' he says, 'applies to the baobab tree, which looks like a forest in itself, the circumference of its trunk a hundred feet, its age 6,000 years, and to the mallow, a little trailing plant with rose-colored leaves, so small that you can hardly see it in the grass.' And yet the botanist is not so far wrong after all. In America we are apt to overstress the element of size. It is a national reproach that we do not distinguish 'bigness' and 'greatness.' The organic structure is the

same under different manifestations, and so the pocket-handker-
chief domain of Hellas has the same weft as the enormous canvas
of our American continent.

Those who emphasize the influence of physical surroundings in
the character of a nation—and the emphasis is as old as the scribe
that left on record the story of Issachar—are never weary of enlarging on the diversity of Greek climate, Greek soil, Greek productions, as determining the character of the Greek people. It is
an old story. It is told in Homer, it is the keynote of Herodotus.
It is writ large in Polybius, in Strabo. Curtius, the historian of
Alexander the Great, following Greek authorities, doubtless, makes
the climate of India responsible for the character of the Hindus,
and oddly enough, it is a modern Curtius that has penned the fascinating chapters in which he unfolds the influence of land and sea
on the Greek people. Every geographer, every historian, comments
on the great variety of Greek climate—marvelous variety, considering the limited extent of Greek territory proper. The extremes are
perhaps not quite so great as in this country, but racial sensitiveness might restore the parallel in one direction, as facilities of com-
munication would restore the parallel in another. From Maine to
Florida is practically not so far as from Thessaly to Laconia in the
heyday of ancient Greek life. But what of the universal neighborhood of the sea? No part of Greek territory was more than
forty miles from what they called in one mood, Her that troubleth,
thalatta, in other moods, Him that bridgeth, *pontos* (indefensible
etymologies, I fear, but undoubted facts). To the foreigner the
American prairie has become more characteristic than the American coast-line; and the American flag is rarely seen in foreign ports.
The Greeks were a maritime people, and the dwellers on our vast
plains can hardly be called a seafaring people, but their language
is our language, and English, American English, like Greek, is full
of nautical imagery: we 'ship' our goods; we 'board' our cars.
One recognizes the old Norse yearning for the sea in the prairie
schooner, and far in the interior the echoes of the old Viking time
are easily waked. It is not without significance that our battleships
bear the names of the different States, and inland Tennessee is as
vitally interested in her namesake as Virginia, whose capes stretch
out to receive the commerce of the world. A favorite theme of the
ancient sophists was the reflections of an inlander at sight of a
ship. There is no American inlander of whom such a fancy could
be entertained. The new navy draws its recruits from the Western
States as from the Eastern. The great lakes, the great rivers, pro-

vide for the training of the man from Ohio and the man from Missouri, and offer watery paths for the 'whalebacks' of the Michigander and the Chicagese. So even at this point of seeming dissimilarity there is a certain analogy between Greek and American. Despite all the preachments of political economists, and all the frightful waste of naval armaments, Americans like Greeks are all sea-fighters, just as the Lacedaemonians, who were late in learning the lesson, learned it too well for the Athenians, who were born to the sea.

But continental Greece was not all of Greece. The whole Mediterranean was fringed with Greek colonies—to adopt a figure of Cicero's—and it might well be maintained, as has been maintained by Mr. Freeman, that the true analogue of the United States, which we do not hesitate to call America, is the Cocked Hat Island. Sicily lay in the region which was to the Greeks the Land of Promise. Westward Ho! was an old cry in the time of Archilochus. The West was, as I have said, the Land of Hope to the Greeks, and it is America that is still the Hope of this Pandora world. America is the last word of modern history, as Greece was the last word of ancient history. Like the Greeks, we are the heirs of the ages. The Romans were not ancients. The Romans are of us, and we are living their life, so that it is not necessary to hunt up more or less remote analogies. When we read Ferrero, we are reading the history of our own times. Modern research has pushed antiquity far back, and, with our large knowledge of early conditions, much that was considered axiomatic in my youth would be set down as nonsense now. Think of the elaborate discussions as to the antiquity of the art of writing. If any one were to broach such a subject now, we should be tempted to use the *argumentum laterculinum* of our cousins on the other side, and heave a Ninevitish brick at him. No sooner do we reach by the instrumentality of the spade what we consider the bed-rock of ancient culture, than the bed-rock turns out to be no bed-rock at all, but a layer of concrete superimposed on yet other layers. No sooner do we begin to speak of Mycenaean civilization than we have to consider pre-Mycenaean conditions. The Hittites had it all their own way for a while, and we were inclined to bargain with them as did Abraham for a place in which to bury dead theories, other people's dead theories, but the other *-ites* are bound to have their innings. Enough, the Greeks are to us as they were to the Egyptians of old— mere children—and, if children, then heirs as we are of a rich world of achievement and experience. In time, then, as in space, the American is as the Greek.

And the American, like the Greek, has proceeded to realize his inheritance, and that inheritance is the republican, or, if you choose, the democratic, form of government—the commonwealth, to give it its best name. We cannot well think of Greece as anything but a commonwealth. The kings (*basileis*), the lords (*anaktes*), of the early time were poetical shadows. The commonwealth was the normal form of Greek political life. After every convulsion of the State, the Hellenes reverted as a matter of course to the plane which seems to be basic. But it was not basic. It was the conquest of ages of experience, as was ours. It was won from generations of conflict, as was ours. Traces of the old conditions survive in the names and functions of certain officers in Athens. In Sparta the kingship had a more or less unreal life, but the colonies were all republics, and the colonies had the mania for written constitutions—paper constitutions, we are beginning to call them, and more's the pity; for the art of writing belongs to the religious sphere, and while it may not have been the exclusive property of the priestly guild, there was a sacredness about the written law that was universally recognized. The lawgiver couched his law in writing, and the popular appeal to 'the higher law,' the unwritten law, the saying, 'What is the Constitution among friends?'—these are not cheering symptoms of American life. Whether the 'boss' who looms larger and larger in our political life—the 'boss' who is the incorporation of individualism, as opposed to the fundamental principles of the commonwealth— shall ripen into the *tyrannos* of the Greek state, remains to be seen. What is well worth noting is the Greek horror of the function which has been transmitted to us through the ages. The Greeks were not given to assassination as a political measure. Now and then a man was found conveniently dead in the market for willow-wares, now and then there was a judicial murder. But the tyrant was an exception. The tyrannicide was a theme of eulogy from the immortal pair of friends, commemorated in the scolion of Callistratus, down to the latest Greek rhetorician of the imperial time. 'A fine shroud is the tyrannis' is a famous saying addressed to a famous tyrant, and the man who put on the purple robe had good reason to ask himself how the raiment would look as a cerement. And yet the Greek *tyrannos* at the beginning was as harmless a word as the Dutch 'boss.' The same jealousy of the rights of the people is shown by our English use of the word 'usurper.' The danger of the assumption of undelegated powers has its signal in the name, and we Americans as heirs of the Greek republican spirit do well to watch the encroachments of executive office. Our forefathers, as we have seen, studied the structure of Greek federation. Our contemporaries on the other side are watching the steps that seem to be leading us to Caesarism. The benevolent tyrant can never be to us the ideal form of government. A safe slavery (*asphalōs duleuein*) is as abhorrent to us as it was to the Greeks. It is not an uncommon thesis that the human race was never happier than under the Antonines, and yet the suppression of Christianity was one of the conditions of that happiness in the eyes of the philosopher on the throne. But we must accept the dangers and the degeneracies of the republic with its form. In fact, the student of Greek history is reminded at every turn of the tendencies of our day, if dangers and degeneracies are thought to be harsh expressions; and I might have discharged myself of the function I have undertaken in this lecture by a talk on 'Life in the Time of Aristophanes.' How Athenian life answers to ours, I can illustrate by my own experience; as indeed nearly everything I have said in these conferences, I have lived. Once I was commissioned to give a sketch of Aristophanes' plays in half a page, and those who know Aristophanes and America will recognize the meaning of the summary. 'Aristophanes,' I said, 'Aristophanes, an aristocrat by party allegiance, was from the beginning in opposition to democracy and progress, to the elevation of the masses, to the career open to talent, to free thought, to finer art, to art for art's sake, to community of goods, to women's rights, to every form of sophistic phrase-making and humanitarian claptrap.' The slogans and counter-slogans of American life are all to be heard in the poems of the bald-head bard. And Aristophanes' picture of Athenian life is strikingly like our own—with its fads, its fancies, its futilities. French feuilletonistes and French scholars have written whole books on Aristophanes that are essentially commentaries on actualities, and Aristophanes' most audacious woman-play, the *Lysistrata,* has been reproduced amid rapturous applause before a French audience.

But despite the license of the modern novel, English and American, your lecturer is not prepared to compare the seams in our social life with the seams in the social life of Greece. Public life offers analogies enough—I will not say for warning—the admonitions of history, that so-called 'philosophy teaching by examples,' amount to very little—but for amusement. There is hardly a trick in modern politics that cannot be paralleled, if not in the verse of

Aristophanes, in the prose of Greek historians and orators and thinkers. Caucuses and rings and heelers were as familiar to them as to us, and unfortunately the accuracy of the description of the parasites that infest the life of the commonwealth has not helped to extirpate the brood. The plague-bearing mosquito abides, and has taken on a Greek name; and an Apollo is needed to quell the plague-bearing rats that are the successors of the plague-bearing mice of antiquity.

But I must not allow my discourse to assume the pessimistic character so natural to those whose time of life prompts them to extol the past at the expense of the present. The old teacher, once justly detested, appears to the old pupil glorified by the hues of his own iridescent youth, and the better days of the Republic when analyzed by the light of contemporary documents are not the *Saturnia regna* one fancies them to have been, because of the halo of oratory that encircled the heroes of that time, in the days when life was younger. So I am not going to ransack Plato's *Dialogues* for melancholy pictures of our present in order to reinforce my parallels of Greek and American life. Our ship of state—a figure we owe ultimately to a Greek poet, Alcaeus (for all the Greek poets were more or less nautical, the Boeotian Pindar as well as the islander Bacchylides)—our ship of state has a strange way of righting herself, had that way in the time of the chain-box, which may be supposed to symbolize the days of slavery, and will continue to have it in these times of the water-ballast, which may be supposed to represent the wave of prohibition. One danger of which one hears and thinks a great deal is the danger of having said ship swamped by alien passengers, who will in time become crew, become officers. Here in Virginia—in the Southern States generally—the danger does not seem imminent. In fact, we are inviting foreigners to embark on our undermanned enterprises. But to an old-fashioned man one of the charms of a visit to England is the infrequency of alien names on the signs of the shops. In the retail business section of the city where I live, the English name is the exception. Nearly all the signs seem to have been made in Germany. When the linguist scans the roster of our army and navy, he finds representatives of every European land—as good Americans doubtless as the best, though the names bewray the foreign descent. There is no harm in this, nay, much good in it. There is a tingle of adventure in the mingling of blood. Matthew Arnold has held forth on the exceeding preciousness of Celtic blood in quickening the sluggish current of Anglo-Saxon veins, and Du

Maurier has insisted humorously on the importance, if not the necessity, of a dash of Jewish ichor for the highest manifestation of genius. We all feel that we can care for the natives of Western Europe. Other problems are more serious. A dear friend of mine, now numbered with most of my friends, an alumnus of this university, used to insist years and years ago with what was considered humorous exaggeration on the danger of the complete absorption of the original stock of our population in the Mongolian. The Chinese, he maintained, had a mission analogous to that of the Norway rat, and the introduction to Virginius Dabney's chief literary performance, *Don Miff*, is addressed to his almond-eyed descendant. That was many years before statesmen began to discuss gravely the Yellow Peril.

Now it is not my purpose in these desultory talks of an old student who has spent his life apart from politics to enter into the circle of fire, as it ought to be called, rather than the burning question, of our relations to Asiatic immigration. I can only say, so far as the Greek aspect of the matter goes, that the Greek succeeded in unifying and harmonizing a vast number of foreign elements. When we attempt to push our researches into pre-Hellenic times, we encounter a great variety of strains. The names of stream and mountain give up their secrets, and the story of Greek cults reveals many lines of foreign influence and foreign origin. Great as was the assimilative power of the Greek, not less great, it is to be confidently hoped, is the assimilative power of the American. If we scan the annals of Greek literature narrowly, we find that some of the most characteristic figures are foreigners or half-foreigners. When we think of the great historians, Thucydides looms up as one of the peaks of the *biceps Parnassus,* and Thucydides was only a semi-Greek. The Holkham bust presents us with the features of an English gentleman, and I have heard Percy Gardner, who believes in the lessons of Greek iconography, hold forth on the Jewish cast of the countenance of Zeno the Stoic. After Alexander the spread of the Greek language makes it hard to draw the line between Greek and barbarian. The Asiatic translated his name into Greek, at a later time into Graeco-Latin. What did Lucian's mother call the little Samosatan who had to learn Greek in his boyhood, as we have done, but under more advantageous circumstances? We pedants of to-day may criticize his Greek, but we cannot attain to his lightness, his airiness; and only the closest analysis can distinguish the Syrian oil-color from the Greek water-color. The domination of a nationality comes through its language. No truer Frenchmen than the Gallicized Germans of the eighteenth century, and some of the chauvinistes of our times bear un-French names. And English, or, if you choose, the American type of English, is destined to accomplish the same end for the masses of foreigners that come to our shore. A generation, a short time in the history of the race, is not so short in an undulatory world like ours. Things move more slowly in Europe, but even there the enclave has to give way, and the tide of the dominant language overflows the barriers. Even to-day the sacred soil of Attica is occupied mainly by Albanians, but Albanian must yield to Greek—and Italian quarters and Bohemian quarters will not hold their own against the encroachments of the tide of American life.

And this potent organon of language is wielded by a people at whose versatility the European observer stands aghast. The barriers are to be broken down, not only by the tide of affairs, but by the impetuous winds of human will—of American will. Speed, says Henley, and the hug of God's winds. The versatility of the Greek was notorious. The ready shift of the Greekling under the Roman Empire has been made proverbial by Juvenal; and Johnson, whom no Frenchman loves, whose popularity is a mystery even to such a sympathetic soul as Taine, has imitated Juvenal's characteristic and applied it to the French. And yet it is a Frenchman, as we shall see, that has given most emphatic expression to the astonishing versatility of the American genius. The conditions of our colonial life may have had something to do with it, but the same versatility can be found in our oldest communities. Some of us oldsters have seen a bishop become a general. Priest, actor, ballet-dancer, musical composer, poet, general—such a combination does not stagger those who have known preacher, lawyer, schoolmaster, horse-jockey, prize-fighter, politician, rolled into one—I beg pardon, politician means all that. True, in serious matters like art, the Greek did not move so readily from one province to another. In fact, the limitation of the prose writer to prose, of the poet to poetry, and so on along all the lines of literary effort, is one of the most striking characteristics of the Greek. But in the various demands of practical life, the life which they saw so steadily and lived so whole, if I may be allowed to adapt a famous line, your Greek was always equal to the occasion, and this mobility shows itself also in the sphere of morals, and here the American is quite his equal. Max O'Rell attributed to our English blood the rapid passage from poker to prayers, from three-card monte to four-part psalmody. True, M. Blouet says it is our English blood. It is, I suppose, that 'spleen' by which Frenchmen explain everything. But if it is English, it is enhanced by our intense vitality. Not English, but Greek, is the ready receptivity of foreign ideas. In this respect the Channel is broader than the Atlantic. Nay, there is much that crosses the water to us, and then recrosses it to our English cousins. The American scholar is often more German than the German. Yes! we are versatile, and versatile to a purpose. What does a man like Hopkinson Smith care for the old Greek sneer that has its echo in the English saying 'Jack of all trades and master of none'? What your own Professor Humphreys, with his exact command of all the canons of literature and science? It is to be hoped that the advance of specialization will not rob us of the Greek readiness to turn our hands to anything that lies near. It is the curse of modern machinery that it reduces the human being to a mere feeder of a monster of cogs and belts. 'Advance,' did I say? Specialization is as old as Jubal and Tubal-cain. The Egyptians were noted specialists; there were doctors for every part of the body, and Jack the Ripper was a specialist under the name of the *paraschistes,* or side-splitter, a name that we attach to a very different function from that of the man who opened bodies for embalming. There were specialists in Greece, specialists in surgery, manufacturers of hair-nets for women; specialists in Rome, who made it their business to efface the scars of branded slaves that had risen in the world. But the Greek note is universality, and it is to be hoped that we shall never lose that Greek note, which is the admiration of all who come to our shores, and which is so important a factor in our subjugation of this vast continent.

But before leaving this part of my theme—the likeness of Greek to American, of American to Greek—I must not omit one trait that the genuine American and genuine Greek have in common, although I may be behind the times in asserting it, a trait that belongs to the democratic character of both nationalities. It is not freedom of speech, that *parrhesia* of which the Greeks were so proud. A certain bluntness is found under all forms of government, but it is a subtler freedom than that—it is freedom from snobbery. Flatterers and parasites the Greeks had with them always. They were conspicuous in the decline of the nationality, and Plutarch has an entertaining essay on the way to distinguish the flatterer from the friend. But they were scarcely less conspicuous in an earlier period, and Ribbeck's delightful study of the 'Colax' claims for the parasite a semi-religious origin. But a 'snob' the

Greek never was, and the snobbery of the American is an imported snobbery. *The Book of Snobs* could not have been written by an American of the old type. That the imported disease, like the English sparrow, has increased greatly and multiplied in this country the satirist may maintain. But the salt water of the herring-pond seems to have killed the germ in our American progenitors. True, it is associated with high things and high words, but it spoils high things and high words, and the man of old American stock prefers 'faith' to 'loyalty' and 'obedience' to 'homage.' Snobbish commentators cannot understand how Pindar could have called Hiero 'friend'; the Italian student of the poet compares the Theban singer to a Knight of the Order of the Annunziata, who is the peer of his sovereign. True Americans are all Knights of a spiritual Annunziata order.

I have referred to Professor Brander Matthews as the great champion of Americanism in language and literature and life, and I have been reading a discourse of his pronounced some years ago, in which he repelled the charge that we Americans are a people terribly practical, systematically hostile to all idealism. And it is true that, if there is any adjective that fits an American in European eyes, it is 'practical.' To be an American is to be practical. A German grammarian desirous of vindicating his method to his countrymen emphasized the fact that it had been adopted by a practical American, and that practical American is the man who is addressing you, a man who was at that time thought by his own countrymen to be steeped in German idealism. I have therefore been called practical simply because I am an American, just as I have been called a Yankee by a French critic, because I am an American. True, mistakes enough may be made in the application of these sweeping characteristics of a nationality, and I remember that Robert Louis Stevenson records somewhere how he picked out in a New York hotel a cadaverous, omnivorous individual as a typical American, who turned out to be a genuine Briton. Whatever mistakes may be made in applying these characteristics to this man and that, there can be no mistake about the practical feature of our American people. There are those that have denied us energy, and it has been maintained, perhaps by way of paradox, that your typical American spends his time in a rocking-chair on a back porch, whittling sticks and exemplifying his national indolence by the invention of labor-saving machines. Nothing could be more 'practical' than the labor-saving machine, as nothing can be more audacious than the American protest, futile as it is, against the primal doom of toil. But practical we are, and practical was the Greek. The most artistic of races was at the same time the most bent on getting results, and the latest phase of philosophic thought, pragmatism, most effectively preached by an American, is nothing more than the interpretation of a Greek word. The sphere of human work was divided by the Greek into zones of artistic creation and practical efficiency, *poiein* and *prattein*. *Prattein* encroached more and more on *poiein*, but *poiein* held its own in so far as it gave the life of art to *prattein*. When Horace put *utile* before *dulci*, he was following the Greek order—though the Greek way of mixing liquors differed in different ages, first wine on water, then water on wine. We do not like to think that Shakespeare was so practical a man as the record shows him to have been, that he valued so highly the material results of his work as a dramatist and an actor—but that did not render the work itself less idealistic. But the Greek went further than that. The artistic work itself must be practical. Every tool must follow the lines of greatest efficiency. Poetry was valuable for its moral lessons. Philosophy was not mere speculation, it was largely ethics. The Greek found himself in Socrates, and Plato was in the first line a preacher of righteousness. When Grote, the friend of John Stuart Mill, was looking for a motto to be prefixed to his work on Plato, he had no difficulty in finding one to rejoice the heart of the utilitarian. The glorification of money as the ultimate expression of achievement was ancient Greek as it is modern American. It was said of Euripides that he hated women so because he loved them so, and all the teachings of Cynic and Stoic—all the preachments against the love of money, from the answer of the Pythia to Sparta down to the present day with its praise of the simple life—only show that human nature changes not, and the Greek and the American are advanced types of humanity. 'Money talks' is an American saying. The brazen tongue must wag in a golden mouth. 'Money, money is the man,' is an ancient saying quoted by the loftiest of Greek poets; quoted, it is true, in protest against the domination of filthy lucre; but we, who live in a plutocracy, recognize the voice of the people. *Obolus diabolus* is the title of one of the sermons preached by an old Augustin friar, Abraham a Sancta Clara, and Greek and American alike are not averse from this form of devil-worship.

I am not at the end of my analogies. They come up on every side, at the bidding of fancy, at the bidding of experience; but I am nearing the limit of my time, and this talk—alas! we have no equivalent for the French *causerie*—must come to a close in a few minutes. So far as there is any coherence in what I have said, I have tried to illustrate, or at any rate to point out, certain resemblances between Greek and American life and character. I have not even attempted to be systematic. After an inordinately long introduction I dwelt—or rather lighted, for I have not dwelt on anything—I touched on American and Greek surroundings, American and Greek position in time, the common republican basis of the American and Greek state, the assimilative power of both nationalities, the versatility and practicality of Greek and American. But concrete examples would be at once more interesting and convincing than analysis, and analogies are easily made, easily drawn, it may be said, and as easily unmade, as easily wiped out. What one sees in history is often nothing more than the projection of the individuality of the beholder. We peer into the open eye to see our own image. One statesman reads Plato, and gathers from *Republic* and *Laws* lessons of momentous importance for the conduct of the commonwealth. Another reads Plato, and vows that he has carried away nothing except Eryximachus' remedy for hiccups, so dramatically introduced in the *Symposium*. And when analogy ventures into the domain of prophecy—we all know how the wise man becomes the wiseacre; and the example of Mr. Freeman, who foresaw the dissolution of the great American commonwealth prefigured in the fate of the Achaean League, is ever before the student of our history. The end has been far other than was dreamed of by the philosophizing historian. The petty states of Greece were swept into the current of the Roman Empire, a current that came from without. The attitude of the Roman to the Greek was that of contemptuous tolerance, not of half-wondering hatred. Consolidation, fusion, domination, these are the American processes of which Greece knew nothing. Greece was, after all, a spiritual power, and the lessons that we are to learn come from Rome, as I have already hinted—Rome, once etymologized as the Greek *rhomë*, 'strength,' anon as the English 'stream.' And so we come back to the ship of state, which the Greek poet launched so many centuries ago. A mighty stream is this on which you and I are borne as part of a proud fleet. But there were times when the current meant wreckage; and I turn my eyes from the days of danger and distress, too real to me still for indulgence in fanciful historical parallels.

My plea has been for the vitality of the studies to which I have been addicted, and as those studies have been part of my own life—

not simply a *meros* but a *melos*—I have never disentwined the thews and sinews that have kept me going after a fashion until now. My Greek study has not simply been a marginal note on my American life, and vice versa. My life has been written *bustrophedon* fashion, and as I turn the furrow, the Greek line can't be distinguished from the American. A Southerner, I shared the fortunes of my people in the Civil War, but whether on the edge of battle in the field or in the vise of penury at home, my thoughts were with those who registered the experiences of the Peloponnesian war, with Thucydides and Aristophanes. But I am sure it will be a relief to this personal tone if I can turn on the phonograph and introduce a new speaker on the subject I have tried to sketch. This time I will call on a modern Greek to tell you what he thinks of Hellenism and Americanism, of the relation of Hellas to Hesperia.

The modern Greek, whatever may be said about his racial affinities with the ancient Greek, commends himself to our affection and regard by his passionate identification of the Hellenes that now are with the Hellenes that once were. It is all living Greece to him. Hellenism is his watchword, and not un-Greek is the eager appropriation of all that modern civilization offers. One is constantly reminded of agencies that were set to work seventy or eighty years ago, such as the Society for the Diffusion of Useful Knowledge, to which we owe Müller's *History of Greek Literature*—a book that can never become obsolete. A similar society is in active operation in Greece, and one of the prime movers was (I am sorry to say *was*) my friend, that finest type of the modern Greek, Dimitrios Bikélas, the famous author of *Loukis Laras,* a novel that has been translated into almost every European tongue. The name of the series may be roughly rendered Library of Useful Knowledge, and as I was meditating the theme of my present lecture, I came across the number that deals with America. I am rather fond of reading books that depict American life from the point of view of foreigners, and I had just been reading a series of articles in which a modern Greek immigrant expresses his astonishment at the cheapness of American viands and the extravagant charges of American bootblacks. So I turned, not without interest, to what our modern Hellene had to say about the modern Hesperia, and I was still more interested to find that the concluding pages of the booklet were given up to a somewhat elaborate parallelism of Hellenism and Americanism. Americanism, the author maintains, is really a revival of Hellenism, and the Americanization of the world, which he seems to consider inevitable, is really carrying on the good work begun by Alexander. I wish I had space to give in detail his list of analogues, his vindication of American society, as based on the soundest ethical, hygienic, and economic principles. Some of these analogues I am afraid you would consider fanciful, some that are true in principle are hardly borne out by the actual facts. The ancient Spartans, says our author, used to throw into the ravine called Caiadas all defective infants—a proceeding against which the eulogists of Christianity were wont to declaim with intense abhorrence. Analogous to this, he thinks, is the restriction of immigration to those who are physically fit for the work of life. The modern American, he goes on to say, has the Greek passion for physical perfection. The America of to-day, like the Greece of yore, reposes on democratic principles. Each man is master of his own fate, and our modern Greek seems to believe in presidential potentialities as well as presidential possibilities for every American schoolboy. It is indeed very interesting to see how our generous encomiast accepts legislation as realization, how he hails the preachments of divines and lecturers as an assurance of prophecies fulfilled. 'To will perfection,' he seems to think, 'is the norm of man,' and he is not so far wrong. We are as our ideals. Marriage is to be forbidden to those who are physically and mentally unfit for the connubial relation, and the American child is to be the most perfect product of the age. Oddly enough, he does not count the facility of divorce as an evidence of our readiness to multiply experiments in that direction. The crowning glory of Americanism, he declares, is the American woman. The more American women married to Europeans, the better for the European races. The Lacedaemonian women in antiquity were in great demand as nurses. The American woman ought to be in great demand as a wife—quite apart, he takes care to add, from the substantial dowry so many of them bring to the common stock. America makes for life, for progress. The Americanization of Europe is inevitable— we see it in every port, in every capital of Europe—and moving as it does on Hellenic lines, it is a blessing to the world as was the Hellenization of the Orient of old. All this is rather amusing than convincing, and yet there is enough sober truth behind the smiling sophistry to warrant the citation here as an *envoi* to my own analogies, which, I trust, are at least a little less fanciful than those of my Athenian colleague.

And now as I am about to close this lecture, it occurs to me that I have omitted one striking trait of the Greek character, which is also a marked feature of our own nationality. Ready wit, audacity, resourcefulness, practicality, all these we have in common with the Greeks. We are versatile as they were, we moralize as they moralized, Franklin is as Theognis, but these are not necessarily amiable ways, and I am going to take refuge in that delightful tolerance for which Matthew Arnold could find no adequate translation, because he thought that *epieikeia* was a national Greek virtue. He made a shift of rendering it into English by 'sweet reasonableness'; and it is this 'sweet reasonableness'—this readiness to put up with things, this acceptance of the situation, this large allowance for individual failings, this good humor in the crowded mart of life, this *epieikeia* which some consider the bane of our politics—it is this *epieikeia,* to which I make my final appeal.

XIX

PAGANISM [1]

By Ernest Renan

Of all the religions that have been professed by civilized peoples, that of the Greeks is the least precise and the least settled. The Pelasgic cults would seem to have been in general barbarous and uncouth. It is surprising that the people with whom the typical civilization was for the first time completely realized should have long remained, in respect to religion, so far inferior, I do not say merely to the Semitic nations, who were, in antiquity, superior in point of religion to the Indo-European peoples, but to more than one branch of the Indo-Europeans—for example, the Indian, the Persian, and the Phrygian. The very great difficulty encountered in studying Greek mythology arises just from this quality of imperfection in dogma. The ancient Greeks had no well-determined rule of faith, and their religion, charming when taken as poetry, is, when viewed according to our theological ideas, a mere mass of contradictory fables, the true meaning of which it is very hard to unravel. The new school properly refrains from seeking there for anything that resembles profound mysteries and an exalted symbolism. We have to deal with confused memories of an early worship of nature, with traces of primitive sensations which took on bodily form and became personages, these personages being supplied with adventures by means of plays upon words and, if I dare say so, cock-and-bull stories, like those that are hatched in the imagination of a child. A people at once lively, mobile, and forgetful, composed the exquisite framework of these fables, which, embellished by poetry and art, became a sort of mythology for all the peoples of the Graeco-Roman world.

Greece never had a sacred book, nor a symbol, nor councils, nor

[1 Translated from *Nouvelles Études d'Histoire Religieuse* (pp. 14-30). Renan's essay on *Paganisme* (pp. 13-30) is a review of Alfred Maury's *Histoire des Religions de la Grèce Antique*, Vol. 1 (1857). A paragraph at the beginning, a part of the fourth, and a part of the closing paragraph have been omitted in translation.—EDITOR.]

a priesthood organized for the preservation of dogmas. The poets
and artists were her true theologians; what to think of the different
divinities was left pretty much to the individual and his arbitrary
conceptions. Hence came that marvelous freedom which allowed
the Greek spirit to move spontaneously in every direction without
encountering anywhere about it the restraint of a revealed text;
and hence also for art, untrammeled by theological control, and possessing the right to create at its own pleasure the types of the divine
world, there were incomparable advantages; but hence, too, for religion, a vexatious uncertainty which permitted the cult to float at
the mercy of every wind, gave boundless scope to the caprices of
individual devotion, and finally produced an incredible flood of
folly and nonsense. In this chaos of contradictory fables there is
nothing more difficult than to seize upon the true essence of the
Hellenic religion—I mean to say, the nourishment it furnished to
the craving for a belief. This is what M. Maury has tried to discover. The interpretation of particular myths occupies him less
than the questions relative to worship, morals, and the forms under
which the sentiment of piety manifested itself in paganism. . . .

Is there, actually, a more striking phenomenon than the discovery, in the ancient religions of the common race which has
created civilization from the Island of Ceylon to Iceland, of the
same resemblance as in their languages? If any proposition at the
present day has been demonstrated, it is that the most diverse
peoples of that race—Hindus, Persians, Armenians, Phrygians,
Greek, Italiots, the Germanic, Slavonic, and even Celtic peoples—
originally had a single cult consisting in the adoration of the forces
of nature, regarded as free agents. The systems which sought to
explain Greek mythology by borrowings from Egypt, Judea, Phoenicia, by a learned symbolism, by an alteration of the truths of
revelation—all these systems, I affirm, must be abandoned.[2] Greek
mythology is one of the forms in which we find reclothed, in the
course of time, and under the sway of local conditions, that naturalism, the earliest and the purest type of which is presented by the
Vedas. Doubtless the religious heritage common to all the Indo-
European peoples was very inconsiderable, if we regard only the
number and philosophic value of the ideas included; doubtless each
several branch of the race as a whole developed the primitive sub-

[2] Certainly the progress of investigation leads one to regard the mythological
borrowings by Greece from Phoenicia as having been considerable; still, the
primitive Aryan nucleus remains, in Greek religion as a whole, the primary
generating force.

stance in a self-adapting fashion, and Greece in particular transformed it in accordance with her own plastic genius and delicate
taste; yet the basis is everywhere the same; wherever the Indo-
European race has preserved any memory of its ancient religious
condition, one catches the echo, more or less faint, of sensations
revealing to man a divine world concealed behind nature.

How did the human mind derive a vast assemblage of fables from
this naturalism, in appearance so simple? How did it transform
physical elements into persons, and the myths concerning them into
adventures whose connection with the original meaning of the
myths it is often impossible to recognize? Here is the point where
modern criticism has frequently shown sagacity in its glimpses of
the truth. Sometimes the reason for these metamorphoses is perfectly obvious; for example, when the fire on the domestic hearth
(*hestia* or *vesta*) and the subterranean fire (*vulcanus*) become two
divinities—the first, chaste and venerable, the second, mournful and
laborious. At other times, the freaks of popular imagination, and
the impossibility of retaining the significance of a legend through
successive generations, brought about singular deviations. Produced by an early age, when man and nature were hardly separated
and possessed so to speak but a single consciousness, the naïve
dogmas of the primitive religion shortly ceased to be understood,
and sank to the level of anecdote and romance.

I shall cite but one example. The calm and voluptuous feeling
awakened by the first rains of spring inspired the ancestors of the
Indo-European race with an idea which is to be discovered in the
mythologies of virtually all their descendants. The moisture fer-
tilizing the soil was conceived of as the mysterious union of two
divinities, the Sky and the Earth. 'The pure heaven,' says Aeschylus, an excellent interpreter of the old fables, 'desires to penetrate
the earth; the earth, on its part, aspires to the union; the rain falling from the amorous heaven impregnates the earth, and the latter
brings forth for mortals pasturage for the flocks and the gifts of
Ceres.' As the imagination of primitive peoples always confounded
a sensation with the accompanying circumstances, that bird whose
song mingles with the showers of spring, the cuckoo, became
involved in the myth, and its soft and melancholy cry represented
to the simple men of the earliest period the amorous sighs of the
divine couple. Now would you like to know what happened to this
myth, at once so fascinating and impressive, when interpreted by a
less delicate age? It became an equivocal tale, over which Aristophanes made merry, to which the people added ridiculous details,

and which gave occasion to gross practices. It was said that one
cold day while Juno was on Mount Thornax, a benumbed cuckoo
sought refuge in her bosom. The goddess took pity on the bird;
but scarcely had she given it shelter when Jupiter resumed his
natural form. People added that when the goddess resisted, Jupiter was forced to promise to marry her.

It would be difficult to imagine how very frequent such transformations of stories were in antiquity. From one end to the other,
Greek mythology is simply a vast misinterpretation, by virtue of
which the divinities that had proceeded from the rapture of the man
of the early ages, face to face with nature, became human. The
same thing occurred in India, and has continued down to our own
day. Smallpox and cholera are there personified. The legends of
the major divinities constantly undergo, if not additions, at all
events notable alterations in form. And yet nowhere else is the
impress of the primitive nature-worship so clearly marked as in
the religion of the Brahmins. It is to the fire, under its name as an
element (*agni, ignis*), that the hymns of the Veda are addressed.
The *dévas* themselves (*divi, dii*) were not born of a process of metaphysical reasoning, analogous to that by which monotheism deduces
the necessity of a supreme cause. They are one of those classes of
aerial beings with which the primitive Aryan peopled all nature,
beings conceived of as in many respects inferior to man.

It was in the worship of heroes especially that the variations of
religious sentiment found opportunity for development, and led
to singular results. The heroes are not, as was long believed, human
beings deified; they are of the same origin as the gods. In nearly
every case one finds a god and a hero answering to the same allegory, and representing, under two distinct figures, a single phenomenon, a single star, a single meteor. The hero is thus the double
of a divinity, the pale reflection, a sort of parhelion, of the efful-
gence of a major deity. True it is, that in comparing the legend of
the god with that of the hero, one commonly finds the latter to be
far more copious. But the cause of this difference is quite simple.
The hero, being regarded as a man, and, in accordance with popular
opinion, having left traces of his existence here below, necessarily
obtained a greater vogue, and made more of an appeal to the sentiments of the crowd; just as the saints, in the less enlightened parts
of Christendom, occupy a much more important place than God
himself, precisely because, being inferior, they are not separated
from mortals by so insuperable a distance.

It was above all at the time when people affected to derive moral instruction from the pagan religion that the heroes gained in importance and popularity. It cannot be denied that they actually lent themselves far better than the gods to that kind of teaching. The adventures in which their valor, subjected to severe tests, was seen at times to yield, only to reassert itself, were set forth by the poets as models of resignation and courage. Hercules in particular was made use of in this way by those whom one might call the preachers of paganism. Hercules, according to a very probable hypothesis which the demonstrations of M. Maury raise to the level of certitude, was an ancient divinity of the air (*Hera-clès*) whose cult, in the hands of the warlike race of the Dorians, took on an altogether heroic character which was transformed, under the influence of the poets and philosophers, into a moral allegory pure and simple. This demi-god, arising like all the other Hellenic types of divinity from a personification of the elements, but rendered singularly uncouth through confusion with the Tyrian Melkarth, finally became the ideal of human perfection—a kind of saint who was furnished with an edifying biography, in connection with whom an attempt was made to awaken in men's souls a sense of duty. This may appear incredible; but India supplies us with more than one example of analogous transformations. Vishnu, who plays in Hindu mythology a part similar to that of Hercules, was in the beginning only a personification of the air, an image of the celestial vault illuminated by the sun. Subsequently there were attributed to him labors for the most part derived from the benefits conferred by the sun, and he became a sort of redeemer, devoting himself to the salvation of the human race.

How could intuitions so simple, corresponding in their origin to nothing philosophical or ethical, satisfy during so many centuries, and even in an epoch of splendid civilization, the religious needs of the most refined races? And at the present day, how does it come that a country like India, smitten, it is true, with an age-long decadence, but one where human thought nevertheless has bestirred itself with much force and originality, remains obstinately attached, in spite of preaching by Christian and Moslem, to a religious system which, it would seem, should not have survived beyond the earliest days of the human race? It is custom alone, the influence of which is above all decisive in matters of religion, that will serve to explain so extraordinary a phenomenon. Handed down by tradition, these fables, in spite of their absurdity, appealed to the imagination and the heart because they were old. Religious sentiment is prone to attach itself to an ancient dogma even when it sees this dogma

vanquished and left behind. Not far from a little village of Brit-
tany where I spent my childhood, there was a chapel sacred to the
Virgin, containing a Madonna that was held in great reverence.
One night the chapel took fire, and there was nothing left of the
statue but a charred and formless trunk. The alms of the faithful
had soon repaired the poor little sanctuary; on the altar a new
statue replaced the old one, which, not to destroy it, they relegated
to an out of the way corner; whereupon the simple faith of the
peasants in that neighborhood was greatly troubled. The new
Virgin, in spite of her costly veil and brilliant apparel, could not
command any prayers; they all took their vows to the charred
fragment which had been deprived of its honors. This old, mutilated statue had formerly heard their prayers, and received the
confidences of their troubles; to have gone to another Virgin, because she was new and more beautifully attired, would in their
eyes have been an act of disloyalty.

Accordingly, the first duty of criticism, in order to comprehend
the beliefs of the past, is to place itself in the position of the past.
Physical science, on the one hand, by excluding from nature everything that resembles free agency, and monotheism, on the other, by
making us conceive of the world as a sort of machine without other
form of life than that conferred upon it by the Supreme Artificer,
have made it very difficult for us to understand a religion whose
point of departure was nature conceived as animate. But how
many other manifestations have there been in the history of religion, the causes of which elude ordinary good sense, which nevertheless have beguiled whole sections of humanity! When people
who have but a slight acquaintance with matters outside of Europe
are told that Buddhism is a religion devoid of God, or at least one
in which the gods (*dévas*) are beings of so little consequence that,
in order to attain to the ultimate perfection, they are obliged to
become men, and to owe their salvation to a man, the thing seems
inconceivable; nevertheless the statement is true to the letter, and
the religion in question is the one which at the present time numbers the largest following in the world. In general, we do not form
broad enough notions of the diversity of the products of the human
spirit. It is only the comparative study of languages, literatures,
and religions, which, by enlarging the circle of accepted ideas,
makes one realize under how many different aspects the world has
been and can be considered.

One thing is certain. To our way of judging, antiquity, apart
from the schools of philosophy, lacked one of the elements which

we regard as essential to sound thinking; I mean, a clear conception of nature and its inexorable laws. During brilliant epochs, no disadvantage arose from that. On the contrary, the scientific spirit, which it is the eternal glory of Greece to have introduced into the world, in a sense owes its origin to polytheism. It is quite remarkable, indeed, that the nomad Semitic peoples, who from the beginning seem more or less to have tended toward monotheism, never had an indigenous science or philosophy. Islam, which is the purest product of the Semitic genius, and may be regarded as the ideal form of monotheism, has stifled all curiosity, all investigation into causes, among the peoples who are under its sway. 'God is great!' 'God knows!'—such is the response of the Arab to the narratives best calculated to astonish him. The Jews, so superior in point of religion to all the other peoples of antiquity, do not present one single trace of a scientific movement before their contact with the Greeks. 'From the earliest times,' as M. Ravaisson well says, 'the Hebrew religion, in order to account for man and nature, had invoked the holy and omnipotent God, the Eternal One, anterior and superior to the world, sole author of all things, and supreme legislator over all. On the contrary, the innumerable divinities of other religions, and notably of the Hellenic, were only particular powers, mutually limited, comparable to natural objects, and subject in much the same way to imperfection and change. As a result, seeing in the universe—in its successive phenomena and in its different parts—a unity, an order, a harmony, which neither the discordant wills of the gods nor their chance adventures in any way served to explain, the need was very early felt of trying to discover, by means of the reason, that universal reason in things, concerning which mythology was silent. Such was, it would seem, the origin of philosophy amongst the Greeks.'[3]

Accordingly, the absence of a rule of religion proved only an advantage so long as the Greek spirit preserved its vigor and originality. But when intellectual culture lost ground, superstition, to which polytheism offered too little obstruction, spread over the world, and damaged even the best minds. I know of nothing sadder in this regard than the spectacle presented by philosophy from the third century of our era on. What men they were—Ammonius, Plotinus, Proclus, Isidore! What nobility of mind and heart! Where is the martyr to compare for her austere beauty with Hypatia? More than all, what a man was Porphyry, perhaps the

[3] Ravaisson, *Mémoires de l'Académie des Inscriptions et Belles-Lettres* 21. 1. 1 ff.

only scholar in antiquity (as Niebuhr and M. Letronne have well
shown) who was critical and exact! And yet what an indelible blot
appeared in the life of these great persons! What aberrations in
all matters concerning demons, familiar spirits, and white magic!
Porphyry, an excellent critic in all other respects, in the field of
metempsychosis and apparitions accepts things that are hardly less
extravagant than table-turning and spirit-rapping. Some time ago
I set about reading the lives of these great men, in so many ways
admirable, with a view to presenting them as the saints of philosophy; and assuredly for their beauty of character, their moral
grandeur, their elevation of spirit, and often, too, for the legends
attaching to their names, they are worthy to be set side by side with
the most revered Christian ascetics. But their credulity on the
head of spirits grieved me, and prevented my taking any pleasure
in the beautiful aspects of their lives. There, too, is the poison
which taints the otherwise highly attractive character of Julian. If
the restoration of paganism was to serve no other purpose than to
revive the crude superstitions with which one sees that emperor
so constantly occupied, it is hard to understand that a man of so
much intelligence should have acquired the evil name of 'apostate'
for the sake of such trivial nonsense.

XX

PAGANISM AND MR. LOWES DICKINSON [1]

By Gilbert K. Chesterton

Of the New Paganism (or neo-Paganism), as it was preached flamboyantly by Mr. Swinburne or delicately by Walter Pater, there is no necessity to take any very grave account, except as a thing which left behind it incomparable exercises in the English language. The New Paganism is no longer new, and it never at any time bore the smallest resemblance to Paganism. The ideas about the ancient civilization which it has left loose in the public mind are certainly extraordinary enough. The term 'pagan' is continually used in fiction and light literature as meaning a man without any religion, whereas a pagan was generally a man with about half a dozen. The pagans, according to this notion, were continually crowning themselves with flowers and dancing about in an irresponsible state, whereas, if there were two things that the best pagan civilization did honestly believe in, they were a rather too rigid dignity and a much too rigid responsibility. Pagans are depicted as above all things inebriate and lawless, whereas they were above all things reasonable and respectable. They are praised as disobedient when they had only one great virtue—civic obedience. They are envied and admired as shamelessly happy when they had only one great sin—despair.

Mr. Lowes Dickinson, the most pregnant and provocative of recent writers on this and similar subjects, is far too solid a man to have fallen into this old error of the mere anarchy of Paganism. In order to make hay of that Hellenic enthusiasm which has as its ideal mere appetite and egotism, it is not necessary to know much philosophy, but merely to know a little Greek. Mr. Lowes Dickinson knows a great deal of philosophy, and also a great deal of Greek, and his error, if error he has, is not that of the crude

[1 *Paganism and Mr. Lowes Dickinson*, No. XII in Mr. Chesterton's *Heretics* (pp. 153-170), is here reprinted through the courtesy of the publishers, John Lane Company.—Editor.]

hedonist. But the contrast which he offers between Christianity and Paganism in the matter of moral ideals—a contrast which he states very ably in a paper called *How long halt ye?* which appeared in the *Independent Review*—does, I think, contain an error of a deeper kind. According to him, the ideal of Paganism was not, indeed, a mere frenzy of lust and liberty and caprice, but was an ideal of full and satisfied humanity. According to him, the ideal of Christianity was the ideal of asceticism. When I say that I think this idea wholly wrong as a matter of philosophy and history, I am not talking for the moment about any ideal Christianity of my own, or even of any primitive Christianity undefiled by after events. I am not, like so many modern Christian idealists, basing my case upon certain things which Christ said. Neither am I, like so many other Christian idealists, basing my case upon certain things that Christ forgot to say. I take historic Christianity with all its sins upon its head; I take it, as I would take Jacobinism, or Mormonism, or any other mixed or unpleasing human product, and I say that the meaning of its action was not to be found in asceticism. I say that its point of departure from Paganism was not asceticism. I say that its point of difference with the modern world was not asceticism. I say that St. Simeon Stylites had not his main inspiration in asceticism. I say that the main Christian impulse cannot be described as asceticism, even in the ascetics.

Let me set about making the matter clear. There is one broad fact about the relations of Christianity and Paganism which is so simple that many will smile at it, but which is so important that all moderns forget it. The primary fact about Christianity and Paganism is that one came after the other. Mr. Lowes Dickinson speaks of them as if they were parallel ideals—even speaks as if Paganism were the newer of the two, and the more fitted for a new age. He suggests that the pagan ideal will be the ultimate good of man; but if that is so, we must at least ask with more curiosity than he allows for, why it was that man actually found his ultimate good on earth under the stars, and threw it away again. It is this extraordinary enigma to which I propose to attempt an answer.

There is only one thing in the modern world that has been face to face with Paganism; there is only one thing in the modern world which in that sense knows anything about Paganism; and that is Christianity. That fact is really the weak point in the whole of that hedonistic neo-Paganism of which I have spoken. All that genuinely remains of the ancient hymns or the ancient dances of Europe, all that has honestly come to us from the festivals of

Phoebus or Pan, is to be found in the festivals of the Christian Church. If any one wants to hold the end of a chain which really goes back to the heathen mysteries, he had better take hold of a festoon of flowers at Easter or a string of sausages at Christmas. Everything else in the modern world is of Christian origin, even everything that seems most anti-Christian. The French Revolution is of Christian origin. The newspaper is of Christian origin. The anarchists are of Christian origin. Physical science is of Christian origin. The attack on Christianity is of Christian origin. There is one thing, and one thing only, in existence at the present day, which can in any sense accurately be said to be of pagan origin, and that is Christianity.

The real difference between Paganism and Christianity is perfectly summed up in the difference between the pagan, or natural, virtues, and those three virtues of Christianity which the Church of Rome calls virtues of grace. The pagan, or rational, virtues are such things as justice and temperance, and Christianity has adopted them. The three mystical virtues which Christianity has not adopted, but invented, are faith, hope, and charity. Now much easy and foolish Christian rhetoric could easily be poured out upon those three words, but I desire to confine myself to the two facts which are evident about them. The first evident fact (in marked contrast to the delusion of the dancing pagan)—the first evident fact, I say, is that the pagan virtues, such as justice and temperance, are the sad virtues, and that the mystical virtues of faith, hope, and charity are the gay and exuberant virtues. And the second evident fact, which is even more evident, is the fact that the pagan virtues are the reasonable virtues, and that the Christian virtues of faith, hope, and charity are in their essence as unreasonable as they can be.

As the word 'unreasonable' is open to misunderstanding, the matter may be more accurately put by saying that each one of these Christian or mystical virtues involves a paradox in its own nature, and that this is not true of any of the typically pagan or rationalist virtues. Justice consists in finding out a certain thing due to a certain man and giving it to him. Temperance consists in finding out the proper limit of a particular indulgence and adhering to that. But charity means pardoning what is unpardonable, or it is no virtue at all. Hope means hoping when things are hopeless, or it is no virtue at all. And faith means believing the incredible, or it is no virtue at all.

It is somewhat amusing, indeed, to notice the difference between the fate of these three paradoxes in the fashion of the modern mind. Charity is a fashionable virtue in our time; it is lit up by the gigantic firelight of Dickens. Hope is a fashionable virtue to-day; our attention has been arrested for it by the sudden and silver trumpet of Stevenson. But faith is unfashionable, and it is customary on every side to cast against it the fact that it is a paradox. Everybody mockingly repeats the famous childish definition that faith is 'the power of believing that which we know to be untrue.' Yet it is not one atom more paradoxical than hope or charity. Charity is the power of defending that which we know to be indefensible. Hope is the power of being cheerful in circumstances which we know to be desperate. It is true that there is a state of hope which belongs to bright prospects and the morning; but that is not the virtue of hope. The virtue of hope exists only in earthquake and eclipse. It is true that there is a thing crudely called charity, which means charity to the deserving poor; but charity to the deserving is not charity at all, but justice. It is the undeserving who require it, and the ideal either does not exist at all, or exists wholly for them. For practical purposes it is at the hopeless moment that we require the hopeful man, and the virtue either does not exist at all, or begins to exist at that moment. Exactly at the instant when hope ceases to be reasonable it begins to be useful.

Now the old pagan world went perfectly straightforward until it discovered that going straightforward is an enormous mistake. It was nobly and beautifully reasonable, and discovered in its death-pang this lasting and valuable truth, a heritage for the ages, that reasonableness will not do. The pagan age was truly an Eden or golden age, in this essential sense, that it is not to be recovered. And it is not to be recovered in this sense again that, while we are certainly jollier than the pagans, and much more right than the pagans, there is not one of us who can, by the utmost stretch of energy, be so sensible as the pagans. That naked innocence of the intellect cannot be recovered by any man after Christianity; and for this excellent reason, that every man after Christianity knows it to be misleading. Let me take an example, the first that occurs to the mind, of this impossible plainness in the pagan point of view. The greatest tribute to Christianity in the modern world is Tennyson's *Ulysses*. The poet reads into the story of Ulysses the conception of an incurable desire to wander. But the real Ulysses does not desire to wander at all. He desires to get home. He displays his heroic and unconquerable qualities in resisting the

misfortunes which balk him; but that is all. There is no love of
adventure for its own sake; that is a Christian product. There is
no love of Penelope for her own sake; that is a Christian product.
Everything in that old world would appear to have been clean and
obvious. A good man was a good man; a bad man was a bad man.
For this reason they had no charity; for charity is a reverent
agnosticism towards the complexity of the soul. For this reason
they had no such thing as the art of fiction, the novel; for the novel
is a creation of the mystical idea of charity. For them a pleasant
landscape was pleasant, and an unpleasant landscape unpleasant.
Hence they had no idea of romance; for romance consists in thinking a thing more delightful because it is dangerous; it is a Christian idea. In a word, we cannot reconstruct or even imagine the
beautiful and astonishing pagan world. It was a world in which
common sense was really common.

My general meaning touching the three virtues of which I have
spoken will now, I hope, be sufficiently clear. They are all three
paradoxical, they are all three practical, and they are all three paradoxical because they are practical. It is the stress of ultimate need,
and a terrible knowledge of things as they are, which led men to set
up these riddles, and to die for them. Whatever may be the meaning of the contradiction, it is the fact that the only kind of hope
that is of any use in a battle is a hope that denies arithmetic.
Whatever may be the meaning of the contradiction, it is the fact
that the only kind of charity which any weak spirit wants, or which
any generous spirit feels, is the charity which forgives the sins
that are like scarlet. Whatever may be the meaning of faith, it
must always mean a certainty about something we cannot prove.
Thus, for instance, we believe by faith in the existence of other
people.

But there is another Christian virtue, a virtue far more obviously
and historically connected with Christianity, which will illustrate
even better the connection between paradox and practical necessity. This virtue cannot be questioned in its capacity as a historical
symbol; certainly Mr. Lowes Dickinson will not question it. It has
been the boast of hundreds of the champions of Christianity. It has
been the taunt of hundreds of the opponents of Christianity. It is,
in essence, the basis of Mr. Lowes Dickinson's whole distinction
between Christianity and Paganism. I mean, of course, the virtue
of humility. I admit, of course, most readily, that a great deal of
false Eastern humility (that is, of strictly ascetic humility) mixed
itself with the main stream of European Christianity. We must

not forget that when we speak of Christianity we are speaking of a whole continent for about a thousand years. But of this virtue even more than of the other three, I would maintain the general proposition adopted above. Civilization discovered Christian humility for the same urgent reason that it discovered faith and charity— that is, because Christian civilization had to discover it or die.

The great psychological discovery of Paganism, which turned it into Christianity, can be expressed with some accuracy in one phrase. The pagan set out, with admirable sense, to enjoy himself. By the end of his civilization he had discovered that a man cannot enjoy himself and continue to enjoy anything else. Mr. Lowes Dickinson has pointed out, in words too excellent to need any further elucidation, the absurd shallowness of those who imagine that the pagan enjoyed himself only in a materialistic sense. Of course, he enjoyed himself, not only intellectually even, he enjoyed himself morally, he enjoyed himself spiritually. But it was himself that he was enjoying; on the face of it, a very natural thing to do. Now, the psychological discovery is merely this, that whereas it had been supposed that the fullest possible enjoyment is to be found by extending our ego to infinity, the truth is that the fullest possible enjoyment is to be found by reducing our ego to zero.

Humility is the thing which is for ever renewing the earth and the stars. It is humility, and not duty, which preserves the stars from wrong, from the unpardonable wrong of casual resignation; it is through humility that the most ancient heavens for us are fresh and strong. The curse that came before history has laid on us all a tendency to be weary of wonders. If we saw the sun for the first time it would be the most fearful and beautiful of meteors. Now that we see it for the hundredth time we call it, in the hideous and blasphemous phrase of Wordsworth, 'the light of common day.' We are inclined to increase our claims. We are inclined to demand six suns, to demand a blue sun, to demand a green sun. Humility is perpetually putting us back in the primal darkness. There all light is lightning, startling and instantaneous. Until we understand that original dark, in which we have neither sight nor expectation, we can give no hearty and childlike praise to the splendid sensationalism of things. The terms 'pessimism' and 'optimism,' like most modern terms, are unmeaning. But if they can be used in any vague sense as meaning something, we may say that in this great fact pessimism is the very basis of optimism. The man who destroys himself creates the universe. To the humble man, and to the humble man alone, the sun is really a sun; to the humble man, and to the humble man alone, the sea is really a sea. When he looks at all the faces in the street, he does not only realize that men are alive, he realizes with a dramatic pleasure that they are not dead.

I have not spoken of another aspect of the discovery of humility as a psychological necessity, because it is more commonly insisted on, and is in itself more obvious. But it is equally clear that humility is a permanent necessity as a condition of effort and self-examination. It is one of the deadly fallacies of Jingo politics that a nation is stronger for despising other nations. As a matter of fact, the strongest nations are those, like Prussia or Japan, which began from very mean beginnings, but have not been too proud to sit at the feet of the foreigner and learn everything from him. Almost every obvious and direct victory has been the victory of the plagiarist. This is, indeed, only a very paltry by-product of humility, but it is a product of humility, and, therefore, it is successful. Prussia had no Christian humility in its internal arrangements; hence its internal arrangements were miserable. But it had enough Christian humility slavishly to copy France (even down to Frederick the Great's poetry), and that which it had the humility to copy it had ultimately the honor to conquer. The case of the Japanese is even more obvious; their only Christian and their only beautiful quality is that they have humbled themselves to be exalted. All this aspect of humility, however, as connected with the matter of effort and striving for a standard set above us, I dismiss as having been sufficiently pointed out by almost all idealistic writers.

It may be worth while, however, to point out the interesting disparity in the matter of humility between the modern notion of the strong man and the actual records of strong men. Carlyle objected to the statement that no man could be a hero to his valet. Every sympathy can be extended towards him in the matter if he merely or mainly meant that the phrase was a disparagement of hero-worship. Hero-worship is certainly a generous and human impulse; the hero may be faulty, but the worship can hardly be. It may be that no man would be a hero to his valet. But any man would be a valet to his hero. But in truth both the proverb itself and Carlyle's stricture upon it ignore the most essential matter at issue. The ultimate psychological truth is not that no man is a hero to his valet. The ultimate psychological truth, the foundation of Christianity, is that no man is a hero to himself. Cromwell, according to Carlyle, was a strong man. According to Cromwell, he was a weak one.

The weak point in the whole of Carlyle's case for aristocracy lies, indeed, in his most celebrated phrase. Carlyle said that men were mostly fools. Christianity, with a surer and more reverent realism, says that they are all fools. This doctrine is sometimes called the doctrine of original sin. It may also be described as the doctrine of the equality of men. But the essential point of it is merely this, that whatever primary and far-reaching moral dangers affect any man, affect all men. All men can be criminals, if tempted; all men can be heroes, if inspired. And this doctrine does away altogether with Carlyle's pathetic belief (or any one else's pathetic belief) in 'the wise few.' There are no wise few. Every aristocracy that has ever existed has behaved, in all essential points, exactly like a small mob. Every oligarchy is merely a knot of men in the street—that is to say, it is very jolly, but not infallible. And no oligarchies in the world's history have ever come off so badly in practical affairs as the very proud oligarchies—the oligarchy of Poland, the oligarchy of Venice. And the armies that have most swiftly and suddenly broken their enemies in pieces have been the religious armies—the Moslem armies, for instance, or the Puritan armies. And a religious army may, by its nature, be defined as an army in which every man is taught, not to exalt, but to abase himself. Many modern Englishmen talk of themselves as the sturdy descendants of their sturdy Puritan fathers. As a fact, they would run away from a cow. If you asked one of their Puritan fathers, if you asked Bunyan, for instance, whether he was sturdy, he would have answered, with tears, that he was as weak as water. And because of this he would have borne tortures. And this virtue of humility, while being practical enough to win battles, will always be paradoxical enough to puzzle pedants. It is at one with the virtue of charity in this respect. Every generous person will admit that the one kind of sin which charity should cover is the sin which is inexcusable. And every generous person will equally agree that the one kind of pride which is wholly damnable is the pride of the man who has something to be proud of. The pride which, proportionally speaking, does not hurt the character, is the pride in things which reflect no credit on the person at all. Thus it does a man no harm to be proud of his country, and comparatively little harm to be proud of his remote ancestors. It does him more harm to be proud of having made money, because in that he has a little more reason for pride. It does him more harm still to be proud of what is nobler than money—intellect. And it does him most harm of all to value himself for the most valuable thing on earth—goodness. The man who is proud of what is really creditable to him is the Pharisee, the man whom Christ himself could not forbear to strike.

My objection to Mr. Lowes Dickinson and the reassertors of the pagan ideal is, then, this. I accuse them of ignoring definite human discoveries in the moral world, discoveries as definite, though not as material, as the discovery of the circulation of the blood. We cannot go back to an ideal of reason and sanity; for mankind has discovered that reason does not lead to sanity. We cannot go back to an ideal of pride and enjoyment; for mankind has discovered that pride does not lead to enjoyment. I do not know by what extraordinary mental accident modern writers so constantly connect the idea of progress with the idea of independent thinking. Progress is obviously the antithesis of independent thinking; for under independent or individualistic thinking, every man starts at the beginning, and goes, in all probability, just as far as his father before him. But if there really be anything of the nature of progress, it must mean, above all things, the careful study and assumption of the whole of the past. I accuse Mr. Lowes Dickinson and his school of reaction in the only real sense. If he likes, let him ignore these great historic mysteries—the mystery of charity, the mystery of chivalry, the mystery of faith. If he likes, let him ignore the plough or the printing-press. But if we do revive and pursue the pagan ideal of a simple and rational self-completion we shall end—where Paganism ended. I do not mean that we shall end in destruction. I mean that we shall end in Christianity.

XXI

FROM *OLD PICTURES IN FLORENCE* [1]

By Robert Browning

'If you knew their work, you would deal your dole.'
　　May I take upon me to instruct you?
When Greek art ran, and reached the goal,
　　Thus much had the world to boast *in fructu*:
The truth of man, as by God first spoken,
　　Which the actual generations garble,
Was re-uttered, and soul (which limbs betoken)
　　And limbs (soul informs) made new in marble.

So, you saw yourself as you wished you were,
　　As you might have been, as you cannot be—
Earth here, rebuked by Olympus there;
　　And grew content in your poor degree
With your little power, by those statues' godhead,
　　And your little scope, by their eyes' full sway,
And your little grace, by their grace embodied,
　　And your little date, by their forms that stay.

You would fain be kinglier, say, than I am?
　　Even so, you will not sit like Theseus.
You would prove a model? The son of Priam
　　Has yet the advantage in arms' and knees' use.
You're wroth—can you slay your snake like Apollo?
　　You're grieved—still Niobe's the grander!
You live—there's the Racers' frieze to follow.
　　You die—there's the dying Alexander.

[1] Stanzas 11-20.

So, testing your weakness by their strength,
  Your meagre charms by their rounded beauty,
Measured by art in your breadth and length,
  You learned—to submit is a mortal's duty.
When I say 'you,' 'tis the common soul,
  The collective, I mean: the race of man
That receives life in parts to live in a whole,
  And grow here according to God's clear plan.

Growth came when, looking your last on them all,
  You turned your eyes inwardly one fine day,
And cried with a start: What if we so small
  Be greater and grander the while than they?
Are they perfect of lineament, perfect of stature?
  In both, of such lower types are we
Precisely because of our wider nature;
  For time, theirs—ours, for eternity.

To-day's brief passion limits their range;
  It seethes with the morrow for us, and more.
They are perfect—how else? they shall never change.
  We are faulty—why not? we have time in store.
The Artificer's hand is not arrested
  With us; we are rough-hewn, nowise polished.
They stand for our copy, and, once invested
  With all they can teach, we shall see them abolished.

'Tis a lifelong toil till our lump be leaven—
  The better! What's come to perfection perishes.
Things learned on earth we shall practise in heaven.
  Works done least rapidly art most cherishes.
Thyself shalt afford the example, Giotto!
  Thy one work, not to decrease or diminish,
Done at a stroke, was just (was it not?) 'O'!
  Thy great Campanile is still to finish.

Is it true that we are now, and shall be hereafter,
  But what and where depend on life's minute?
Hails heavenly cheer or infernal laughter
  Our first step out of the gulf or in it?
Shall man, such step within his endeavor,
  Man's face, have no more play and action
Than joy which is crystallized for ever,
  Or grief, an eternal petrifaction?

On which I conclude that the early painters
    To cries of 'Greek art, and what more wish you?'
Replied: 'To become now self-acquainters,
    And paint man man, whatever the issue!
Make new hopes shine through the flesh they fray,
    New fears aggrandize the rags and tatters;
To bring the invisible full into play!
    Let the visible go to the dogs—what matters?'

Give these, I exhort you, their guerdon and glory
    For daring so much, before they well did it.
The first of the new, in our race's story,
    Beats the last of the old; 'tis no idle quiddit.
The worthies began a revolution,
    Which if on earth you intend to acknowledge,
Why, honor them now! (ends my allocution)
    Nor confer your degree when the folk leave college.

BIBLIOGRAPHY

[The list is meant to be suggestive rather than full. Moreover it does not include books from which selections have been taken for the present volume, unless these books contain other important matter of a similar kind; accordingly the Bibliography is supplemented by the Table of Contents. On the whole it has seemed better to divide the titles into classes than to give all in one alphabetical series; but it should be understood that the divisions are not everywhere mutually exclusive. The slightly varying use of parentheses corresponds in general to a varying emphasis, sometimes upon part of a book, sometimes upon the whole.]

I. THE GREEK RACE AND ITS GENIUS

ARNOLD, MATTHEW. Hebraism and Hellenism. (In *Culture and Anarchy* [etc.]. New York, 1883.)

DICKINSON, G. LOWES. *The Greek View of Life.* London, 1896.

HEGEL, G. W. F. *Lectures on the History of Philosophy*, tr. E. S. Haldane. (Vol. 1, pp. 149-155.) London, 1892.

MOORE, CLIFFORD H. *The Religious Thought of the Greeks from Homer to the Triumph of Christianity.* Cambridge, Mass., 1916.

MURRAY, GILBERT. Greece and the Progress of Man. (In *The Rise of the Greek Epic*, Lecture 1, pp. 21-49. Second edition. Oxford, 1911.)

RUSKIN, JOHN. *Works*, ed. Cook and Wedderburn. (See Vol. 39, Index *s. v.* 'Greece,' 'Greeks.') London and New York, 1903-1912.

STAUFFER, ALBRECHT. *Zwölf Gestalten der Glanzzeit Athens.* Munich and Leipzig, 1896.

STOBART, J. C. *The Glory that was Greece, a Survey of Hellenic Culture and Civilization.* London and Philadelphia, 1911.

SYMONDS, JOHN ADDINGTON. *The Greek Poets.* First Series. (Chapter 12, The Genius of Greek Art, pp. 412-438.) London, 1877.

——. *The Greek Poets.* Second Series. (Chapter 12, Conclusion, pp. 373-399.) London, 1876.

THOMSON, J. A. K. *The Greek Tradition.* London, 1915.

WILAMOWITZ-MOELLENDORFF, ULRICH VON. Von des Attischen Reiches Herrlichkeit. (In *Reden und Vorträge*, pp. 27-64. Berlin, 1901.)

WINCKELMANN, JOHANN JOACHIM. *Edle Einfalt und Stille Grösse. Eine mit Goetheschen und Herderschen Worten eingeleitete Auswahl aus Johann Joachim Winckelmanns Werke.* Ed. Walter Winckelmann. Berlin, 1909.

——. *Werke*, herausgegeben von C. L. Fernow, Heinrich Meyer, Johann Schulze. (See Vol. 8, Allgemeines Sachregister, by Siebelis, *s. v.* 'Alten,' 'Griechen,' 'Griechenland.') 8 vols. Dresden, 1808-1820.

II. The Later Influence of Individual Ancient Authors

ADAM, JAMES. *The Vitality of Platonism, and Other Essays.* Cambridge, England, 1911.

COMPARETTI, DOMENICO. *Vergil in the Middle Ages.* London, 1908.

CUNLIFFE, JOHN W. *The Influence of Seneca on Elizabethan Tragedy.* (Anastatic reprint.) New York, 1907.

KERLIN, ROBERT T. *Theocritus in English Literature.* Lynchburg, Virginia, 1910.

MENÉNDEZ Y PELAYO, MARCELINO. *Horacio en España.* Second edition. 2 vols. Madrid, 1885.

REINHARDSTOETTNER, KARL VON. *Plautus: Spätere Bearbeitungen Plautinischer Lustspiele.* Leipzig, 1886.

THAYER, MARY REBECCA. *The Influence of Horace on the Chief English Poets of the Nineteenth Century.* (*Cornell Studies in English*, No. II.) New Haven, 1916.

ZIELINSKI, THADDAEUS. *Cicero im Wandel der Jahrhunderte.* Third edition. Leipzig, 1912.

III. Antiquity and the Middle Ages

ARNOLD, MATTHEW. Pagan and Mediaeval Religious Sentiment. (In *Essays in Criticism.* First Series. New York, 1883.)

DÖLLINGER, JOHANN JOSEPH IGNAZ VON. Einfluss der Griechischen Literatur und Kultur auf die Abendländische Welt im Mittelalter. (In *Akademische Vorträge*, Vol. 1, pp. 162-186. Munich, 1890.)

LOOMIS, LOUISE ROPES. *Mediaeval Hellenism.* (Columbia University Dissertation. Contains a valuable bibliography, pp. 111-115.) Lancaster, Pa., 1906.

MULLINGER, JAMES BASS. *The Schools of Charles the Great and the Restoration of Education in the Ninth Century.* London, 1877.

PRANTL, CARL. *Geschichte der Logik im Abendlande.* 4 vols. Leipzig, 1855-1870.

TAYLOR, HENRY OSBORN. *The Classical Heritage of the Middle Ages.* New York, 1901.

WERNER, JAKOB. *Lateinische Sprichwörter und Sinnsprüche des Mittelalters, aus Handschriften gesammelt.* Heidelberg, 1912.

IV. Antiquity and the Renaissance

BURCKHARDT, JACOB. *The Civilization of the Renaissance in Italy.* (Part 3, The Revival of Antiquity, pp. 171-280.) London, 1898.

LOOMIS, LOUISE R. *The Greek Renaissance in Italy.* (In *The American Historical Review*, January, 1908. Vol. 13, pp. 246-258.)

NOLHAC, PIERRE DE. *Pétrarque et l'Humanisme.* 2 vols. New edition. Paris, 1907.

VOIGT, LUDWIG GEORG. *Die Wiederbelebung des Classischen Alterthums, oder Das Erste Jahrhundert des Humanismus.* Third edition. Berlin, 1893.

V. The Ancients and the Moderns in General

Arnold, Matthew. On the Modern Element in Literature. (In *Essays in Criticism*. Third Series. Boston, 1910.)

Butcher, S. H. *Some Aspects of the Greek Genius*. (Chapter 1, What We Owe to Greece.) Second edition. London and New York, 1893.

Cooper, Lane. *Ancient and Modern Letters*. (In *The South Atlantic Quarterly*, July, 1912.)

Egger, Auguste Émile. *L'Hellénisme en France*. 2 vols. Paris, 1869.

Gildersleeve, Basil L. *Hellas and Hesperia, or the Vitality of Greek Studies in America*. New York, 1909.

Jebb, Sir Richard. *Essays and Addresses*. Cambridge, England, 1907.

Kelsey, Francis W. [Editor]. *Latin and Greek in American Education, with Symposia on the Value of Humanistic Studies*. New York, 1911.

Livingstone, R. W. *The Greek Genius and its Meaning to Us*. Oxford, 1912.

Mahaffy, John Pentland. *What Have the Greeks Done for Modern Civilization?*. New York and London, 1909.

Perrault, Charles. *Parallèle des Anciens et des Modernes en ce qui Concerne les Arts et les Sciences*. Paris, 1688.

Rigault, H. *Histoire de la Querelle des Anciens et des Modernes*. (*Oeuvres Complètes* de H. Rigault, Vol. 1.) Paris, 1859.

Schneider, Gustav. *Hellenische Welt- und Lebensanschauungen in ihrer Bedeutung für den Gymnasialen Unterricht*. Gera, 1893, (Part 2) 1896.

Théry, Augustin François. *De l'Esprit et de la Critique Littéraires chez les Peuples Anciens et Modernes*. 2 vols. Paris, 1832.

Zielinski, Thaddaeus. *Our Debt to Antiquity*. London and New York, 1909.

VI. The Classics and English Literature

Collins, John Churton. *Greek Influence on English Poetry*. London, 1910.

Gayley, Charles M. *The Classic Myths in English Literature*. Boston, 1911.

Gordon, G. S. [and others]. *English Literature and the Classics*. Oxford, 1912.

Murray, Gilbert. What English Poetry may still Learn from Greek. In *Essays and Studies by Members of the English Association*. Vol. III, collected by W. P. Ker. Oxford, 1912.

Quiller-Couch, Arthur. On the Lineage of English Literature (II). (In *On the Art of Writing*, pp. 166-190. Cambridge, 1916.)

Tucker, T. G. *The Foreign Debt of English Literature*. London, 1907.

VII. The Classics and Particular Modern Authors

Anders, H. R. D. *Shakespeare's Books, a Dissertation on Shakespeare's Reading and the Immediate Sources of his Works*. Berlin, 1904.

Dorrinck, Alfred. *Die Lateinischen Zitate in den Dramen der Wichtigsten Vorgänger Shakespeares*. (Strassburg dissertation.) Strassburg i. E., 1907.

Droop, Adolph. *Die Belesenheit Percy Bysshe Shelley's*. Weimar, 1906.

Fuhrmann, Ludwig. *Die Belesenheit des Jungen Byron*. (Berlin dissertation.) Friedenau bei Berlin, 1903.

HOFFMAN, WILLY. *William Cowper's Belesenheit.* (Berlin dissertation.) Berlin, 1908.

JONSON, BEN. *Discoveries.* A Critical Edition . . . [by] Maurice Castelain. Paris, n. d. [? 1896].

KELLER, WILLIAM JACOB. *Goethe's Estimate of the Greek and Latin Writers.* Madison, Wisconsin, 1916.

KETTLER, FRANZ. *Lateinische Zitate in den Dramen namhafter Zeitgenossen Shakespeares.* (Strassburg dissertation.) Bremen, 1909.

LIENEMANN, KURT. *Die Belesenheit von William Wordsworth.* (Berlin dissertation.) Berlin, 1908.

MOORE, EDWARD. *Studies in Dante.* First Series. (Scripture and Classical Authors in Dante.) Oxford, 1896.

MUSTARD, WILFRED P. *Classical Echoes in Tennyson.* New York and London, 1904.

NOLHAC, PIERRE DE. *Petrarch and the Ancient World.* Boston, 1907.

OSGOOD, CHARLES G. *The Classical Mythology of Milton's English Poems.* (*Yale Studies in English*, No. VIII.) New York, 1900.

ROOT, ROBERT K. *Classical Mythology in Shakespeare.* (*Yale Studies in English*, No. XIX.) New York, 1903.

SAWTELLE, ALICE ELIZABETH. *The Sources of Spenser's Classical Mythology.* New York, 1896.

STARICK, PAUL. *Die Belesenheit von John Keats und die Grundzüge seiner Literarischen Kritik.* Berlin, 1910.

SYMONDS, JOHN ADDINGTON. [Review of] *Petrarch.* By Henry Reeve. In the *Quarterly Review*, Vol. 146, pp. 384-413 (esp. pp. 390-404). London, 1878.

VIII. MISCELLANEOUS

BOISSIER, GASTON. *La Fin du Paganisme.* Third Edition. Paris, 1898.

BOTSFORD, GEORGE W., AND SIHLER, ERNEST G. *Hellenic Civilization.* New York, 1915.

BUTCHER, S. H. *Harvard Lectures on Greek Subjects.* London and New York, 1904.

COOPER, LANE. *Aristotle on the Art of Poetry. An Amplified Version. with Supplementary Illustrations, for Students of English.* Ithaca, 1947.

HARDIE, WILLIAM ROSS. *Lectures on Classical Subjects.* London, 1903.

HATCH, EDWIN. *The Influence of Greek Ideas and Usages upon the Christian Church.* (The Hibbert Lectures, 1888.) Eighth edition. London, 1901.

JARDÉ, A. *La Grèce Antique et la Vie Grecque.* Paris, 1914.

JHERING, RUDOLF VON. *Geist des Römischen Rechts.* (Bedeuting des Römischen Rechts für die Moderne Welt, Vol. 1, pp. 1-16; Das Wesen des Römischen Geistes, Vol. 1, pp. 318-340.) Fourth edition. Leipzig, 1878.

SMYTH, HERBERT WEIR [Editor]. *Harvard Lectures on Classical Subjects.* Boston and New York, 1912.

STOBART, J. C. *The Grandeur that was Rome, a Survey of Roman Culture and Civilization.* London and Philadelphia, 1913.

SYMONDS, JOHN ADDINGTON. Athens. (In *Sketches and Studies in Italy and Greece.* Third Series, pp. 339-364. London and New York, 1898.)

WILAMOWITZ-MOELLENDORFF, ULRICH VON [and others]. *Die Griechische und Lateinische Literatur und Sprache.* Berlin and Leipzig, 1905. (*Die Kultur der Gegenwart*, herausgegeben von Paul Hinneberg. Teil I, Abteilung VIII.)

IX. BIBLIOGRAPHICAL

BETZ, LOUIS-P. *La Littérature Comparée. Essai Bibliographique.* (L'Antiquité Grecque et Romaine . . . dans les Littératures Modernes, pp. 281-338.) Second edition, Strassburg, 1904.

HARRIS, WILLIAM J. *The First Printed Translations into English of the Great Foreign Classics.* London and New York, [1909].

PALMER, HENRIETTA R. *List of English Editions and Translations of Greek and Latin Classics Printed before* 1641. London, 1911.

INDEX

INDEX OF PROPER NAMES

[The titles listed in the Bibliography (pp. 281-285) are not included in this Index. References to a few proper adjectives are included, but those to 'Greek' and 'the Greeks' are omitted.]